Food Safety and Technology Governance

Recent advances in agri-food technology have brought increasing complexity and emerging challenges to food safety regulation and governance, with many countries greatly divided in their regulatory approaches. As more advanced CRISPR-based gene-editing technologies and novel foods such as cloned animal products, non-traditional plants, nanofood, and plant-based meat are rapidly being developed, debates arise as to whether the existing models of governance require revision to ensure consumer safety. Of equal importance is the extensive use of pesticides, additives, and animal drugs, which raise concerns over the methods and approaches of government approval and phasing out of potentially risk-causing chemicals. Heightened public criticism of food safety and technology poses a significant challenge to governments around the world, which struggle to strike a proper balance between technocracy- and democracy-oriented risk governance models.

Drawing on expertise from the United States, European Union, Japan, China, Korea, Association of South East Asian Nations, Malaysia, and Taiwan, this book explores existing and emerging issues of food law and policy in the context of technology governance to offer an overarching framework for the interaction between food regulation and technology.

It will be essential reading for academics, students, and practitioners with an interest in food law and policy, agricultural law and policy, and food safety and nutrition studies.

Kuei-Jung Ni is Professor of Law and Director of the Center for Trans-Pacific Partnership and Transnational Trade Laws at School of Law, National Yang Ming Chiao Tung University (NYCU), Taiwan.

Ching-Fu Lin is Professor of Law at National Tsing Hua University (NTHU), Taiwan.

Food Safety and Technology Governance

Edited by Kuei-Jung Ni and Ching-Fu Lin

Routledge
Taylor & Francis Group
LONDON AND NEW YORK

First published 2023
by Routledge
4 Park Square, Milton Park, Abingdon, Oxon OX14 4RN

and by Routledge
605 Third Avenue, New York, NY 10158

Routledge is an imprint of the Taylor & Francis Group, an informa business

British Library Cataloguing-in-Publication Data
A catalogue record for this book is available from the British Library

Library of Congress Cataloging-in-Publication Data
A catalog record for this book has been requested

ISBN: 978-1-032-22280-6 (hbk)
ISBN: 978-1-032-22282-0 (pbk)
ISBN: 978-1-003-27191-8 (ebk)

DOI: 10.4324/9781003271918

Typeset in Bembo
by Apex CoVantage, LLC

Contents

Contributors

Muhammad Nizam Awang is a faculty member of the Faculty of Syariah and Law and Institute of Halal Research and Management at the Universiti Sains Islam Malaysia (USIM). Muhammad's research, teaching, and expert advice focus broadly within the law and policy of environmental and health protection, particularly the ways in which law, actors, and institutions respond to the governance of new and enabling technologies and the market (i.e. nanotechnology, synthetic biology, Halal). His current main project sits broadly within the theme of digital health governance. He is enthusiastic about how law, policy, and ethics shape medical data privacy and security of data in light of emerging trends of data analytics (machine learning) and algorithmic decision-making systems. Past projects include legal and policy challenges of governing nanotechnologies in food and genetically modified foods and the ecosystem approach to regulating the Halal industry, with a special focus on governance of experts and expertise.

Kai-Chih Chang is an assistant professor at Soochow University (Taiwan) School of Law. He previously served as an Advisory Expert at the Institute of Diplomacy and International Affairs, Ministry of Foreign Affairs (Taiwan), and taught at National Yang Ming Chiao Tung University and Tunghai University. His research focuses on public international law, international trade law, and international dispute settlement. Professor Chang received his S.J.D. from Indiana University Maurer School of Law. He also held an LL.M. in international legal studies from New York University, a Master of Laws from National Chiao Tung University, and his LL.B. from National Chengchi University. He is currently the Associate Editor of the Chinese (Taiwan) Yearbook of International Law and Affairs.

Wen-Shen Chu is a senior researcher and former Director of the Bioresource Collection and Research Center (BCRC) under the Food Industry Research and Development Institute (FIRDI), Taiwan. He earned his Ph.D. in genetics, cell biology, and development (GCD) from the University of Minnesota. His research areas include regulation and safety assessment of genetically modified foods and feeds, biological technology, and microbial genetics. Dr. Wen-Shen Chu received the Mr. Tong Zeng Memorial Patent

Invention Award from the Taiwan Association for Food Science and Technology, the Mr. Cheng-Yuan Hsieh Outstanding Contribution Award from the FIRDI, and the Research Award from the Agricultural Chemical Society of Taiwan. His five-year project on "Culture Collection, Identification, Strain Improvement and Application" has been nominated for the Excellence Award by Taiwan's Ministry of Economic Affairs.

Alie De Boer How can you scientifically prove that foods are legally safe and healthy? As Assistant Professor in the field of nutrition and food law at Campus Venlo of Maastricht University (the Netherlands), Dr. Alie de Boer studies the interplay between nutritional sciences and (European) food law to analyze the position of scientific evidence in food authorization procedures as well as the effects of these policies. This results in both new scientific findings and practical knowledge for food business operators, consumer organizations, and policymakers. After obtaining her Ph.D. at Maastricht University in 2015 on the interactions between nutrition and medicine in effect and law, Dr. de Boer founded the Food Claims Centre Venlo, the first research centre to conduct multi- and interdisciplinary research into nutrition and (EU) food law. She is a popular speaker on the topics of nutrition and health claims and contributes to different socially relevant activities to increase awareness on health and safety of nutrition and how this is regulated.

Neal Fortin is a professor in the Food Science and Human Nutrition Department and Director of the Institute for Food Laws & Regulations at Michigan State University (www.IFLR.msu.edu). He teaches classes in United States food regulation, international food law, Codex Alimentarius, and food and drug law. Mr. Fortin is also an attorney concentrating in food law. His book, *Food Regulation: Law, Science, Policy, and Practice*, is the most widely used textbook on U.S. food law. The views expressed are those of the author.

Ching-Fu Lin is Professor of Law at National Tsing Hua University (NTHU), where he teaches global health law, food law and policy, artificial intelligence law and policy, introduction to law and technology, and international law and global governance. Professor Lin received his LL.M. and S.J.D. from Harvard Law School, with the honor of the John Gallup Laylin Memorial Prize (best paper in public international law) and Yong K. Kim Memorial Prize (best paper in East Asian legal studies). He also holds a double degree in law (LL.B.) and chemical engineering (B.S.) from National Taiwan University. Professor Lin has served as Visiting Researcher at the Berkman Klein Center for Internet and Society at Harvard University in the United States as well as Visiting Fellow at Graduate Institute of International and Development Studies in Geneva, Switzerland. He has also been Peter Barton Hutt Student Fellow at Petrie-Flom Center for Health Law Policy, Biotechnology, and Bioethics, as well as Visiting Scholar Coordinator at the East Asian Legal Studies Program, Harvard Law School. More recently,

Professor Lin received the Junior Research Award from NTHU in 2017 and the Young Scholar Fellowship (2018–2023) from Taiwan's Ministry of Science and Technology in 2018. Active in legal academia, Professor Lin has been invited to lecture in many academic/practical settings, such as the World Trade Organization, Summer Academy in Global Food Law and Policy in Spain, Brescia University School of Law in Italy, and World Food Law Program and the United Nations Food and Agriculture Organization in the United States. His legal scholarship has appeared in numerous journals and edited collections, including *Harvard International Law Journal*, *Virginia Journal of International Law*, *University of Pennsylvania Journal of International Law*, *Cornell International Law Journal*, *Columbia Science and Technology Law Review*, *Food and Drug Law Journal*, *Journal of World Trade*, and *International Journal of Law and Information Technology*.

Eunjeong Ma is a collegiate associate professor in the Department of Creative IT Engineering at Pohang University of Science and Technology (POSTECH). Having been trained in science and technology studies, she works on socio-cultural dimensions of pharmaceuticals and medical technologies. Currently, her research is centered on questions about senior citizens and technological interventions, and she also does research on collaborative research methods and platforms between engineering and the humanities/social sciences.

Kuei-Jung Ni is Professor of Law and Director of the Center for Trans-Pacific Partnership and Transnational Trade Laws at School of Law, National Yang Ming Chiao Tung University, Taiwan. He specializes in international economic law, environment law, and bio-technology law, especially covering the cross-cutting issues of trade, environment, and public health. His present study focuses on exploring transnational regulations on food safety and risk analysis, including normative works of competent international regimes, such as WTO, RTA, Codex, the Biodiversity Convention, and so on, and national implementations as well. He has written dozens of articles appearing in trade, environment, and health law journals. Recent publications include *Food Safety and International Trade* (Angle, 2022); "Science and Risk Analysis in CPTPP/SPS-Plus: Role Model or Unbearable Burden" (Journal of Food Law and Policy, Vol. 15(2), pp. 22–47, 2019); *Science and Technology in International Economic Law*, co-edited with Bryan Mercurio (Routledge, 2014). He was visiting Melbourne Law School, Harvard Law School, UC at Berkeley, School of Law. Professor Ni received his Ph.D. in law from the University of Edinburgh, an LL.M from the University of California at Berkeley, and an LL.B from the National Taiwan University.

Sharifudin Md Shaarani is a professor and research director of the Faculty of Science and Technology at the Universiti Sains Islam Malaysia (USIM). Professor Dr. Shaarani received his Ph.D. in food technology from the University of Cambridge, masters in food technology from the University of

Reading, and B.Sc. in food science with business management from University Kebangsaan Malaysia. His areas of expertise include food science and technology, food innovation, food standards—auditing & consultation, and food labeling legislation. Professor Dr. Sharifudin has won the Gold Medal twice at the Research and Innovation Competition (PEREKA).

Juanjuan Sun is Associate Law Professor at Heibei Agricultural University and Research Fellow of Center for Coordination and Innovation of Food Safety Governance at Renmin University of China Law School. Research interests include regulatory theory, food law and agricultural law. Personal achievements include editing books such as *Comparative Study among the USA, EU and China on Food Safety Regulation* and *Building Food Safety Governance in China* and translating books such as *European Food Law Handbook, Private Food Law and Food Safety=Behavior.*

Steph Tai's scholarly research examines the interactions between environmental and health sciences and administrative law. These include the consideration of scientific expertise and environmental justice concerns by administrative and judicial systems, and as well as the role of scientific dialogue in food systems regulation and the ways in which private governance incorporates scientific research. Professor Tai was an adjunct law professor at Georgetown from 2002–2005 and a visiting professor at Washington and Lee University School of Law during the 2005–2006 academic year. Professor Tai's teaching interests include administrative law, environmental law, food systems law, environmental justice, risk regulation, contracts (especially private governance and supply chains!), and comparative Asian environmental law. Raised in the South by two chemists, Professor Tai decided to combine their chemistry background with a legal education to improve the use of science in environmental protection. At Georgetown, Professor Tai was the Editor-in-Chief of the *Georgetown International Environmental Law Review* and was a member of the Georgetown Manfred Lachs Space Law Moot Court Team. After graduating from Georgetown, Professor Tai worked as the editor-in-chief of the *International Review for Environmental Strategies*, a publication by the Institute for Global Environmental Strategies in Japan. Professor Tai has also served as a judicial law clerk to the Honorable Ronald Lee Gilman on the U.S. Court of Appeals for the Sixth Circuit. Professor Tai then worked as an appellate attorney in the Environment and Natural Resources Division of the U.S. Department of Justice, briefing and arguing cases involving a range of issues, from the protection of endangered cave species in Texas to the issuance of dredge and fill permits under the Clean Water Act. From 2013–2014, Professor Tai served as a U.S. Supreme Court Fellow as a researcher in the Federal Judicial Center. Professor Tai actively represents amici in federal circuit court and Supreme Court cases. During the summer before joining the Wisconsin Law School faculty, Professor Tai teamed up with several other law professors to work on two Supreme Court amicus briefs: one for a group of legislators in *Environmental Defense* *v. Duke Energy Corp.*, No. 05-0848, and another for a group of scientists in *Massachusetts v. Environmental Protection Agency*, No. 05-1120. Professor Tai still continues this work, representing commercial fishers in *Entergy Corp. v. Environmental Protection Agency*, Nos. 07-588, 07-589, 07-597; organic farmers in *Monsanto v. Geertson Seed Farms*, No. 09-475; former senior environmental agency officials in *Decker v. Northwest Environmental Defense Center*, Nos. 11-338, 11-347; and prominent climate scientists in *West Virginia v. Environmental Protection Agency*, D.C. Cir. Nos. 15-1363 et al. Professor Tai's leisure time is spent lifting weights, boxing, reading fiction, listening to terrible pop punk, scouring farmers' markets, and annoying a rescue iguana named Megyn Kelly.

Yuan Hung Tseng earned his Ph.D. in medicine from Chung Shan Medical University, Taiwan. He also holds two master's degrees. He earned an LL.M. from the National Yunlin University of Science and Technology, Taiwan, as well as a master's of sociology of law from Lund University, Lund, Sweden.

Yeh-Han Wang got both his medical and master's degrees in science, technology, and society (STS) from National Yang-Ming University (NYMU) in 2009 and 2018, respectively. Now he is a doctoral student in the Division of Health Policy and Law, Institute of Public Health, NYMU. Furthermore, he is also an attending physician working in the Department of Anatomic Pathology, Taipei Institute of Pathology. He contributes his research work in two major fields. One is surgical pathology and cytology; the other is STS and public health. His primary academic interests focus on the topics of (1) international guidelines and local practice and (2) new drug innovation and companion tests. His master thesis investigates the development and use of Iressa, the first targeted drug treating lung cancer. The argument captures a crucial moment in biomedicine where the new paradigm for medical knowledge and clinical practice revolves around pharmaceuticals. He plans to investigate the challenges that cervical smear screening policy faces nowadays due to the progression of technology and implementation of HPV vaccination and surveillance as a Ph.D. research project.

Tomiko Yamaguchi specializes in the sociology of knowledge and science and technology studies. She has worked on a range of research projects examining the ways in which social reality is constructed in situations involving conflict and controversy in the agrifood sector; her primary focus has been the ways in which knowledge about agrifood is interpreted, reaffirmed, and altered in day-to-day interactions between stakeholders attempting to exert influence in a situation and how and why dominant interpretations give power to some stakeholders and not others. She has examined social conflicts concerning GMOs in the context of Japan and India, BSE, nanotechnology in food, and functional foods. She is currently working on social dimensions of plant gene editing technologies. Publications include "Performativity of Expectations: The Emergence of Plant Gene Editing Technologies in Japan" in *Elementa: Science of the Anthropocene* in 2020, an edited book entitled *Social Shaping of the Science of Forecasting* (in Japanese) in 2019, and "Social Imaginary and Policy Practice: The Food Safety Arena in Japan" that appeared in *Food Policy* in 2014.

Pei-kan Yang is Professor of Law at Department of International Business, National Chengchi University (NCCU), in Taiwan since 2013. Previously he was Assistant Professor at Feng-Chia University (2006~2011) and Taipei Medical University (2011~2013) and also taught at Soochow University. He offers courses on international trade law, commercial law, legal methods, and the WTO dispute settlement system. He specializes in international economic law and international health law and has published many articles on trade- and health-related issues in accredited academic journals. He is also a researcher of the Research Center for International Organization and Trade Law under the Commerce College of NCCU and a member of the Asian Center for WTO & International Health Law and Policy under National Taiwan University. Professor Yang received his LL.B. and LL.M. from National Taiwan University, College of Law, in 1996 and 2002 and his J.D. and from Duke University, School of Law, in 2006. He serves as a member of the editorial committee of the *Contemporary Asia Arbitration Journal* (CAA) and the *Asian Journal of WTO & International Health Law and Policy* (AJWH). He also serves as a board member to the Society of Law and Medicine in Taiwan and a commissioner of the Advisory Council for GMO Food under Ministry of Health and Welfare (MOHW). Professor Yang has been recommended on the roster of legal experts on Framework Convention on Tobacco Control (FCTC) by MOHW to the World Health Organization (WHO) and commissioned to assist MOHW in participating in many sessions of Conference of Parties to the WHO/FCTC or engaging in various international exchange activities.

1 Introduction

Kuei-Jung Ni and Ching-Fu Lin

> If people let government decide what foods they eat, their bodies will soon be in as sorry a state as are the souls of those who live under tyranny.
>
> Thomas Jefferson (1743–1826)

Food is not only produced from traditional agricultural practices for consumption but also from complex industrial processes. Increasingly, new processes and production methods involving technologies and medicines have changed the perception of food. Modern food processes and production methods have brought about a variety of benefits,[1] making food growth faster, more affordable, and in some cases healthier. In particular, food produced with the help of emerging technologies such as genetic engineering may relieve food insecurity and hunger in developing countries, as climate change has made these problems worse.[2]

To be sure, these beneficial results should be appreciated, and national policies to promote agri-technologies and industry are largely desirable. However, their uncertain risks and unknown hazards may also come into play in the future, and thus, they cannot be ignored. The demand to balance food production with increasing health concerns is also essential, especially from the perspective of the right to health and the right to safe food.

Pesticides, additives, and animal drugs, including hormones, ractopamine, and antibiotics, have been commonly used, but they continue to concern consumers and have garnered conflicting views over their safety across the globe. Food-borne hazards carrying both potential risks and benefits have also raised controversies over the methods and approaches of government approval and phase-out of the uses. For example, the European Union (EU), relying on studies conducted by the European Food Safety Authority (EFSA) on the residuals

1 "The United States Department of Agriculture (USDA): Biotechnology Frequently Asked Questions—What are the benefits of Agricultural Biotechnology?" *available at* www.usda.gov/topics/biotechnology/biotechnology-frequently-asked-questions-faqs.

2 Kaiser Jamil, "Biotechnology—A Solution to Hunger? The United Nations Chronicle", *available at* www.un.org/en/chronicle/article/biotechnology-solution-hunger.

DOI: 10.4324/9781003271918-1

of hormones[3] and ractopamine, still prohibits the importation of animal foods containing these drugs.[4] Although antibiotics have been banned for feeding animals in the EU, the United States (U.S.) has yet to phase out the practice officially. Instead, it applies a voluntary policy in discouraging the industry from the practice.[5]

Further, rapid advances in agri-food technologies have brought increasing complexity and emerging challenges to food safety regulation and governance along the global supply chain.[6] One strong example can be found in the long-debated issue of genetically modified (GM) crops. Despite their potential economic benefits, GM crops have encountered public fears and controversies over scientific evidence and risk assessment.

Such controversies have greatly divided countries like the U.S. and the EU in terms of their regulatory approaches and have further led to various trade disputes within the World Trade Organization (WTO)[7] and beyond. Through rapid technological development, a growing number of various GM foods continue to enter the market, such as GM salmon farming and sales in North America that have attracted both scholarly and practical concerns over food safety, biodiversity, and regulatory adequacy. Because there is no solid evidence demonstrating the health risk of using such technologies, many GM foods have remained marketable, but they are subject to mandatory labels that have been widely applied both in the EU[8] and the U.S.[9]

3 *See* European Food Safety Authority's "Opinion of the Scientific Panel on Contaminants in the Food Chain on a Request from the European Commission Related to Hormones Residuals in Bovine Meat and Meat Products" (June 12, 2007) 510 The EFSA Journal.

4 *See* European Food Safety Authority's "Safety Evaluation of Ractopamine: Scientific Opinion of the Panel on Additives and Products or Substances Used in Animal Feed" (Apr. 2, 2009) 1041 The EFSA Journal.

5 The U.S. Food and Drug Administration (FDA) Guidance for Industry (GFI) #213: "New Animal Drugs and New Animal Drug Combination Products Administered in or on Medicated Feed or Drinking Water of Food-Producing Animals: Recommendations for Drug Sponsors for Voluntarily Aligning Product Use Conditions with GFI #209."

6 *See generally* Ching-Fu Lin, "Global Food Safety: Exploring Key Elements for an International Regulatory Strategy" (2011) 51(3) Virginia Journal of International Law 637–96; Ching-Fu Lin, "Public-Private Interactions in Global Food Safety Governance" (2014) 69(2) Food and Drug Law Journal 143–60.

7 Regarding animal drugs, *see* Appellate Body Report, *EC—Measures Concerning Meat and Meat Products (Hormones)*, WTO Doc. WT/DS26/AB/R, WT/DS48/AB/R (Jan. 16, 1998); Appellate Body Report, *United States—Continued Suspension of Obligations in the EC—Hormones Dispute*, WTO Doc. WT/DS320/AB/R (Oct. 16, 2008). On GMOs, *see* Panel Report, *European Communities—Measures Affecting the Approval and Marketing of Biotech Products*, WTO Doc. WT/DS291/R, WT/DS292/R, & WT/DS293/R (Sept. 29, 2006).

8 Regulation (EC) No 1830/2003 of the European Parliament and of the Council of 22 September 2003 concerning the traceability and labelling of genetically modified organisms and the traceability of food and feed products produced from genetically modified organisms and amending Directive 2001/18/EC.

9 An Amendment to the Agricultural Marketing Act of 1946, 114 Cong. (7 U.S.C. § 1621 et seq.): Subtitle E—National Bioengineered Food Disclosure Standard, sec. 293(a)(1).

Additionally, innovative and complex gene-editing technologies that involve CRISPR technology on various crops have also triggered a debate regarding whether the existing models of governance should be revised. There now seems no coherent approach for governing CRISPR technology's marketing approval. The recent EU ruling[10] favoring the regulation of CRISPR consistently with that of GMOs highlights the cautious stance toward the new technologies, whose benefits and risks are far more unidentified.

Beyond GM or CRISPR-edited food products, more and more "novel foods" (*e.g.* cloned animal products, non-traditional plants, nanofood, and plant-based meat) and "functional foods" merit a review of existing regulatory frameworks and innovative institutional design to ensure better governance. Further, heightened public criticism in the areas of food safety and technology poses significant challenges to governments around the world, which are struggling to strike a proper balance between technocracy- and democracy-oriented risk governance models. Similarly, legitimacy, transparency, and accountability issues are of paramount importance in shaping and reshaping local, national, regional, international, and even transnational frameworks for food safety regulation and technology governance.

On the other hand, new technology may also serve as a governance tool that enables regulators and businesses to better protect consumers from problems such as contamination or food fraud. The application of blockchain technology to food tracing and tracking appears to be a crucial example. While blockchain is often linked to cryptocurrencies such as Bitcoin, it may also empower governance mechanisms to address food safety problems by facilitating transparency and traceability. Many technology-based regulatory models have been recently adopted by giant transnational retailers along the global supply chain.

Ensuring food safety has become a local and global mandate and constitutes a benchmark by which governmental performance can be evaluated. We are living in a globalized world, where few countries may survive on their own. Trade in food and agricultural products continues to increase and amounted to USD 1.5 trillion in 2018.[11] Harmonization of national food safety measures without compromising the appropriate national levels of protection is an unavoidable challenge facing the international community.

Concerning the global arena, the Codex Alimentarius Commission (CAC) was established to adopt international standards for food safety. The standards have been recognized as a benchmark by which to safeguard food safety, but it

10 Case C-528/16 Confederation Paysanne and Others, the Court of Justice of the European Union, July 25, 2018.

11 *The Food and Agriculture Organization (FAO): The State of Agricultural Commodity Markets* (2020 edition), at 3, *available at* www.fao.org/3/cb0665en/cb0665en.pdf.

is still not binding *per se*,[12] and the legitimacy of the adoption procedure continues to be controversial.[13]

The WTO has governed the application of sanitary and phytosanitary measures affecting trade, including those for preserving food safety.[14] WTO members are required to ensure observance of basic principles based upon science, transparency, proportion, non-discrimination, and so on.[15] It nonetheless falls into nations' regulatory space to pursue different levels of protection, methods, and approaches to reach their policy goals. Observing trade disciplines alone cannot guarantee eventual local food safety.[16] The Food and Agriculture Organization (FAO) and the World Health Organization (WHO) are two organs of the United Nations responsible for food safety management from a global perspective. The FAO and the WHO co-authored the document "Food Safety Risk Analysis," which has been instrumental in guiding national authorities in establishing their food risk analysis regimes.[17] Likewise, this blueprint, though useful, is not enforceable, as it is not intended to provide "prescriptive instructions on how to implement risk analysis."[18] An international framework may indeed contribute to the harmonization of regulations and standards and may also ease frictions.[19] Proper food safety nonetheless still rests on responsive and effective national preparation and associated mechanisms.

All in all, the ever-changing landscape in the interaction between food safety and technology development raises a myriad of research questions from various analytical angles. What is the prospect for food safety governance at the

12 Codex Procedure Manual, 27th ed., 2019, at 21, *available at* www.fao.org/3/ca2329en/CA2329EN.pdf (last accessed Feb. 10, 2021) [hereinafter Codex Procedure Manual].

13 *See generally* Kuei-Jung Ni, "Does Science Speak Clearly and Fairly in Trade and Food Safety Disputes? The Search for an Optimal Response of WTO Adjudication to Problematic International Standard-Making" (2013) 68 Food and Drug Law Journal 97, 100–105; Ching-Fu Lin, "Scientification of Politics and Politicization of Science: Reassessing the Limits of International Food Safety Lawmaking" (2013) 15 Columbia Science & Technology Law Review 1–40.

14 The Agreement on the Application of Sanitary and Phytosanitary Measures, Apr. 15, 1994, Marrakesh Agreement Establishing the World Trade Organization, Annex 1A, 1867 U.N.T.S. 493 [hereinafter the SPS Agreement].

15 Ibid, arts. 2, 5.

16 *See generally*, Ching-Fu Lin & Yoshiko Naiki, "An SPS Dispute without Science? The Fukushima Case and the Dichotomy of Science/Non-Science Obligations under the SPS Agreement" (forthcoming 2022) European Journal of International Law.

17 Food and Agric. Org. & World Health Org., *Food Safety Risk Analysis: A Guide for National Safety Authorities* (2007), *available at* https://www.fao.org/3/a0822e/a0822e00.htm?msclkid=9538f928a69f11eca4c09c9bc58521b2

18 Ibid, at xii.

19 *See generally* Ching-Fu Lin, "Mapping a Meta-Framework for Global Food Safety Governance: National, International and Transnational Dimensions" in Vera Parisio (ed), *Food Safety and Quality Law: A Transnational Perspective* (Turin, Giappichelli Editore 2016); Ching-Fu Lin, "Mega-Regional Transformation of Global Food Safety Governance: Normative Roots and Ramifications" in Shin-yi Peng et al. (eds), *Governing Science and Technology under the International Economic Order: Regulatory Divergence and Convergence in the Age of Megaregionals* (Northampton, Edward Elgar Publishing 2018).

local, national, regional, international, and transnational levels in the context of rapid technological development? Is the time ripe for us to review and rethink the existing regulatory framework for GM and/or CRISPR-edited food? How will disruptive technologies reconfigure the manner in which we formerly perceived and designed food safety regulations? Should we revisit the prevailing scholarly discourse on risk regulation in an era of disruptive technology? How should we evaluate regulatory effectiveness and efficiency in different governance phases, such as risk communication, risk assessments, and risk communication? What roles might private actors play in building new models of governance in collaboration with governments and civil societies? From a comparative law perspective, what do policy experiences and experiments in different jurisdictions tell us about shaping and reshaping contemporary food law and policy?

Good food safety systems must deal with a continually changing world, especially accommodating the challenges of sophisticated agriculture and food technologies. Technology-related food safety governance also involves various layers, including laws, regulations, policies, standards, institutional arrangements, scientific capacity, training, and public education and communication, among other elements.[20]

This collected volume primarily reflects concerns surrounding how food and agri-technologies can be managed and regulated to ensure food safety. It is centered on reviewing and analyzing relevant regulatory regimes, of which relevant approaches, policies, principles, procedures, and mechanisms sustaining operations will be covered.

This book is largely based on a collection of papers presented at the Conference on Food Law and Policy focusing on the theme "Food Safety and Technology Governance," which took place in Taipei, Taiwan, on May 10–11, 2019. The collection benefited from debates and discussions among participants, including academicians, practitioners, and policy makers across the globe, who shared their interests in existing and emerging issues concerning food law and policy in the context of technology governance.

Under the analytical framework of the dynamic, normative interactions between food safety and technology governance, a number of prominent scholars and practitioners have come together from the U.S., EU, Japan, China, Korea, Association of Southeast Asian Nations (ASEAN), Malaysia, and Taiwan to offer their valuable expertise and insight. With great vision, this edited volume establishes an overarching framework for the interaction between food regulation and technology development, under which lie a series of dynamic and interactive scholarly examinations.

This collection is composed of four components and features a total of 14 chapters covering timely and crucial issues—from comparative approaches and regulations, the nanoscale substance in food, and CRISPR-edited crops to

20 Ibid, at 2.

e-commerce and small and medium enterprises along the global food supply chain, blockchain-based food traceability mechanisms, and functional/healthy food management—this manuscript will be of significant academic and practical value to the existing scholarship and policy landscape.

Risk governance systems in major jurisdictions such as the U.S. and the EU, which are premised upon a contemporary set of risk analysis principles and approaches, have increasingly been under stress due to the advent of various merging agri-food technologies. How such risk governance systems, which reflect the respective jurisdictions' legal, scientific, social, economic, and political underpinnings, may be able to configure and reconfigure in the context of changing technology landscape merits scholarly examination. Part I includes three chapters that probe into the risk governance systems, principles, and approaches in the U.S. and the EU by way of specific case studies—antibiotics in food animals, nutrition and food assessments, and gene technology in food—and provides a new perspective for readers to rethink and reconceptualize the multifaceted roles risk governance plays in the area of food safety.

In Chapter 2, Kuei-Jung Ni of National Yang Ming Chiao Tung University reveals how the Food and Drug Administration (FDA) in the U.S. managed to solve the rampant use of antibiotics by, *inter alia*, voluntarily phasing out certain antibiotics used in animal feeding operations instead of engaging in the withdrawal of antibiotic permission. The chapter suggests that the precaution and cost-benefit analysis literally serve as principles and policy tools sustaining the FDA policy, as the inconclusiveness of relevant scientific findings remains and formal enforcement may not be cost effective. Apart from analyzing relevant judicial rulings on the voluntary approach, the author explores the implications of these principles underpinning the FDA's policy for phasing out antibiotics, despite the absence of an explicit invocation by the FDA.

Chapter 3, authored by Alie de Boer of Maastricht University, unravels the role of EFSA as laid down in law and reviews the practical reality of scientific advice provided under the mandate of European food law, highlighting that health claims and benefit assessments make up a large portion of the work undertaken by the EFSA, although the exact methodologies to conduct such assessments are under-developed. The research questions asked in the chapter highlight the fundamental inquiries of contemporary food safety governance, particularly because risks regulation and scientific evidence are being treated as the basis of law and policy developments in Europe and beyond.

In Chapter 4, Neal Fortin of Michigan State University examines government oversight and jurisdictional overlaps in the U.S. in terms of regulating gene technology with food. At least nine different statutes that regulate different aspects of gene technology with food are governed and enforced by three agencies, the U.S. Department of Agriculture (USDA), the FDA, and the Environmental Protection Agency (EPA). The chapter reveals that this fragmented structure lends the appearance of disorganization, and the nomenclature in these statutes for various actions is occasionally inconsistent, but the deficiency does not indicate a lack of thoroughness in the oversights. Fortin also provides a hypothetical case study illustrating the navigation of a developer of a GM plant, through research and development to regulatory steps before commercialization.

Emerging technologies pose a diverse range of challenges and opportunities for the shaping and reshaping of food safety governance across borders. Part II assesses the ever-changing landscape in the interaction between food safety and technology development by way of in-depth case studies on e-commerce and the global food supply chain, the production of cell-cultured food products derived from livestock and poultry, and distributed ledger technology-enabled food traceability governance—and sheds new light on existing research questions, with innovative analytical angles.

In Chapter 5, Kai-Chih Chang of Soochow University positions his analysis on the tensions and balances between health protection and the promotion of international trade along cross-border supply chains of food products. By way of an analysis of the WTP's SPS Agreement and recent free trade agreements, such as the Comprehensive and Progressive Agreement for Trans-Pacific Partnership (CPTPP), the author discusses the regulatory challenges posed by scattered, small-scale, and potentially poorly declared shipments of food products to customs to conduct efficient and effective inspections and also explores how new e-commerce technologies and platforms may affect SME exports, SPS risk, and food safety regulation.

In Chapter 6, Ching-Fu Lin of National Tsing Hua University explores blockchain's potential to revolutionize the global food supply chain, which seems particularly salient. This involves transforming paper-based documents into a blockchain-enabled identity to generate a high level of transparency and data integrity, enabling smaller farmers to bypass middlemen in crop trading and cash transfers and providing an efficient and cost-effective way to manage the production system. At the same time, as Lin points out, "blockchainizing" the governance of food safety, traceability, and sustainability may also pose a new layer of regulatory questions about technical capacity and infrastructure gaps, scalability and implementation costs, global standardization politics, cybersecurity and data protection, and the technologically inherent limits of blockchain, calling for a more technologically informed policy-making process before rushing into the hype of blockchainizing food law.

Chapter 7, authored by Steph Tai of the University of Wisconsin, raises crucial questions surrounding how to regulate the labeling of artificial meat, with a recent statute defining meat as something "derived from harvested production livestock or poultry." While the USDA and FDA also propose that "both the USDA and the FDA should jointly oversee the production of cell-cultured food products derived from livestock and poultry," this chapter examines these legal actions in a broader food studies context and assesses how definitions have shaped and continue to shape consumer expectations of what constitutes various categories of food.

Regulators in different jurisdictions have been exploring optimal approaches to governing new food products derived from genome-edited technologies and/or novel materials. Part III discusses governance options and institutional design models for regulating gene-edited food products, as well as novel foods in Argentina, Japan, Australia, the U.S., the EU, ASEAN, South Korea, Taiwan, and Canada, offering a solid comparative research analysis.

Gene-editing technology can modify and improve crop characteristics without inserting foreign genes, which has become an emerging and booming technologies in recent years. In Chapter 8, Wen-Shen Chu of the Food Industry Research and Development Institute (FIRDI) and Pei-kan Yang of National Chengchi University engage in a comparative survey of the current regulatory status of gene-edited products among selected countries. They emphasize that excessive over-strict regulation will stifle the development of innovative biotechnology and the potential to realize the power of gene-editing technology. Innovative technologies need to be accompanied by effective management, the formulation of laws and regulations, and substantial application to maximize the innovation and transformation of the bio-industry.

In Chapter 9, Juanjuan Sun of Heibei Agricultural University examines the issues surrounding the regulation of novel food that have been raised in the EU in reaction to safety concerns regarding foods that are either made using newly developed technology or imported from a foreign country that do not have a history of consumption in a given place. The chapter analyzes how China has established a comparable system to regulate novel foods, considering the specific situation in China, where novel food material and health food are closely linked, given that certain traditional materials can be used for both food and medicine. Sun presents the general evolution of novel food regulation in China, focusing on specific aspects related to the development of the food industry and the longstanding food culture.

In Chapter 10, Yuan Hung Tseng, who is a medical doctor with law degrees, examines various aspects of controversies in the EU's novel food regulation (NFR) since its first proposal by the European Executive in 1992, through the first version promulgated in 1997, to the latest version that went into effect in 2018. Many scholars have engaged in extensive discussions, which are primarily focused on the content of the statutes and on the legitimacy and applicability of the NFR in regulating the food traded into the EU under international trade agreements. The chapter, by contrast, revisits regulations from the perspective of the sociology of law and sociology; draws on three aspects of food neophobia as the framework to explore the problems of the law; and points out inherent tensions between the EU administrative tools, consumer protection, and scientific assessments.

Chapter 11, authored by Muhammad Nizam Awang and Sharifudin Md Shaarani of Islamic Science University of Malaysia, analyzes the regulatory responses to nanofood being included as part of novel food regulations in ASEAN countries by deliberating on the regulatory definitions of novel foods and market authorization procedures, including the conditions of use, labeling requirements, and pre-market authorization requirements. Nanotechnologies have been valorized as one of the platform technologies of the twentieth century, where their resulting applications and products span electronic and electric products, energy and environment, the automotive sector, and food and agriculture. Concerns over safety of nanomaterials have progressively grown with the volume of commercialized nanofood products in the market. This has brought food safety authorities around the world to review the adequacy of existing regulatory frameworks to manage the risk and safety concerns posed by food cultivated, produced, processed, and packaged using nanotechnology and nanomaterials. The chapter argues that the normative legal yardstick established by food regulations in ASEAN is enough to capture nanofood and nanoscale substances in food based on the wide product categories under food laws, which must be based on the outcome of appropriate risk assessment and not be discriminatory against free trade with other countries.

Due to recent advances in emerging agri-food technologies, novel entities that have entered the category of "food" blur the boundaries between food and drugs and present new challenges to legal and regulatory agencies. The emergence of novel entities has not only provided new business opportunities and consumer choices but has also disrupted existing businesses and raised renewed concerns over safety. At the level of law and public policy, the safety of such products is determined within the framework of existing legal and regulatory categories, which might not be adequate to regulate novel entities. Further, because both goods and services increasingly travel across national borders, it is important to explore how classification systems for such goods and services are governed and the conflicts and contradictions that arise as a result.

In Chapter 12, Tomiko Yamaguchi of International Christian University sheds light on discourses surrounding the use of health foods, in particular where societal concerns over safety and expectations about the use of science and technology in making novel foods intersect with expectations of market expansion in Japan. In the past decades, food safety concerns have become central issues in Japanese society. The rapid transformation of the food and agricultural sector through the use of science and technology for food production and processing is of particular importance, and one arena in which societal tensions surface is the use of health foods. Health foods are met with high expectations from people in industry, both domestic and abroad, who are trying to enter the Japanese market or expand their market share, yet at the same time, such foods also raise safety concerns. It is important to understand the concerns that arise over the safety and quality of food in the wake of expectations of future market growth. This chapter conducts two important case studies and offers insight on how health foods are regulated in Japan.

In Chapter 13, Yeh-Han Wang of National Yang Ming Chiao Tung University examines the blurred boundaries between effective health foods and ineffective drugs in food safety governance by way of a case study on how glucosamine products are marketed and regulated in Taiwan. As pointed out by the chapter, food and drugs have long been established categories, but their relationship is not necessarily a dichotomy. As the case of glucosamine products demonstrates, the development and marketing of health food effectively redefine the boundary of food and drugs, leading to challenges in regulation. This chapter describes how the Health Food Control Act of Taiwan failed to regulate glucosamine products and highlights the coproduction of scientific knowledge from the classification and regulation of foods and drugs in and across countries and regions.

Last but not least, Chapter 14, authored by Eunjeong Ma of Pohang University of Science and Technology, addresses how the line between food and drugs is drawn in South Korea and the mechanism of classification as a technology of governance. The chapter uses the *baek shu oh* case to provide for an entry point for examining the technology of food governance in South Korea and argues that the explosive expansion of the health foods market can be best understood as an asymmetric assemblage of post-colonial relations linking domestic and international regulatory authorities, consumer market agencies, techno-scientific research institutions, the academy, and medicinal plants.

Combined, the last three chapters compare country case studies in Taiwan, Japan, and Korea by probing governance challenges caused by blurring boundaries between food and drugs, as well as the actions and/or interactions of concerned parties in trying to make use of opportunities or resolving tensions. As these chapters' comparative studies demonstrate, emerging technologies place virtually any classification system under a stress test, because such a system is inevitably interlinked with cultural, historical, social, economic, and political circumstances, and the blurred boundaries between food and drugs have far-reaching consequences in many areas of public life, such as public policies, health food markets, and consumer perceptions.

This collaborative project received generous financial and technical support from Taiwan's Ministry of Science and Technology, National Yang Ming Chiao Tung University, and National Tsing Hua University. We are indebted to our research assistant, I-Ching Chen, for her excellent work. Last but not least, we are indebted to Siobhán Poole and the rest of the team at Routledge for the editorial assistance and support, as well as the anonymous reviewers for their invaluable comments and guidance. It is our hope that this book will contribute to the legal and policy discourse on the dynamic interactions between food safety and technology governance and beyond.

Part I

Rethinking Risk Governance and Food Safety

Principles and Approaches

2 Phasing Out Certain Antibiotics in Food Animals

The U.S. Approach in Light of Precautions and Cost-Benefit Analysis

*Kuei-Jung Ni**

I. Introduction

The antibiotic penicillin was first discovered in 1928,[1] and it represented a significant medical breakthrough. These drugs have proven very effective in containing and eliminating germs, such as *E. coli*. However, their rampant use has led to the occurrence of drug resistance, which in turn creates alleged superbugs. The problem first raised attention in the 1960s. The World Health Organization (WHO) has studied the issue for decades using data from 114 countries. In April 2014, the WHO published the first official global report on antibiotic resistance, highlighting that it has become a common and serious public health crisis.[2] A WHO official emphasized, "[u]nless we take significant actions to improve efforts to prevent infections and also change how we produce, prescribe and use antibiotics, the world will lose more and more of these global health goods and the implications will be devastating."[3]

The European Union (EU) has swiftly responded to the health risks caused by antibiotic resistance. In the 1990s, a strong scientific finding on the link between the use of antibiotics in food animals and antibiotic resistance in

* Preliminary research on this topic was partially published in Chinese in *Taiwan Law Review*, No. 246, pp. 172–185 (2015). An earlier version was presented at theInternational Conference on Food Law and Policy: Food Safety and Technology Governance, Taipei, Taiwan, May 10–11, 2019. This chapter has been modified and updated in accordance with new developments. The study was supported by a research grant from the Ministry of Science and Technology (MOST), Taiwan, the Republic of China (108–2410-H-009–028-MY3).

1 http://en.wikipedia.org/wiki/Antibiotics.

2 WHO, "Antimicrobial Resistance: Global Report on Surveillance 2014," *available at* http://apps.who.int/iris/bitstream/10665/112642/1/9789241564748_eng.pdf (last accessed Jan. 30, 2020). The recent survey on the issue *see* "Global Antimicrobial Resistance Surveillance System (GLASS) Report: Early Implementation 2016–2017", *available at* https://apps.who.int/iris/bitstream/handle/10665/259744/9789241513449-eng.pdf?sequence=1 (last accessed Feb. 3, 2020).

3 The remarks of Dr. Keiji Fukuda, "WHO's Assistant Director-General for Health Security", *at* www.who.int/mediacentre/news/releases/2014/amr-report/en/#.U3El598DvKc.facebook (last accessed Feb. 15, 2020).

DOI: 10.4324/9781003271918-3

humans had yet to be confirmed. Based on a precautionary consideration, the EU began to ban the use of antibiotics for growth promotion. The European Court of Justice had confirmed the legality of applying the precautionary principle as a basis in outlawing antibiotics for such an application.[4] As more data emerges, several competent European health authorities have jointly found that antimicrobial resistance can be transmitted to humans from animals and food.[5]

In the United States (U.S.), the production and use of antibiotics used to be relatively popular in treating illness and promoting the growth of food animals. It has been more than 50 years since the U.S. began to approve the marketing of antibiotics.[6] Past regulatory regimes[7] were also friendly toward the pharmaceutical industry. Consequently, more than 80% of antibiotics are used in livestock.[8] Most food animals consumed by human beings contain residual antibiotics. Drug resistance in humans caused by the overuse of antibiotics in promoting animal growth alerted the U.S. Food and Drug Administration (FDA). In the 1970s, the FDA initiated a withdrawal process for certain animal drugs authorized by the Food, Drug, and Cosmetic Act (FDCA),[9] but it suspended the procedure shortly thereafter. After 30 years, the FDA decided to change its course of action. Instead of reinstating the original withdrawal process, the FDA considered a voluntary phasing out of the use of antibiotics by the pharmaceutical industry, which it contended would be more effective and less costly. Thus, the FDA issued "Guidance for Industry" documents to implement the voluntary policy.[10] Yet the decision to terminate the withdrawal process was challenged by the National Resources Defense Council (NRDC), which argued the decision violated the FDCA. The federal court eventually sided with the FDA's decision.[11]

Since the adoption of the voluntary policy, most drug manufacturers have been willing to follow the FDA's guidance. According to the FDA's survey,

4 Case T-13/99, Pfizer Animal Health SA v. Council of the European Union [2002] ECR II-3305, at 130, 140 [hereinafter *Pfizer*].

5 *See* the joint scientific opinion of the EFSA, ECDC, EMA, and the European Commission's Scientific Committee on Emerging and Newly Identified Health Risks (SCENIHR), Nov. 2009, *at* www.efsa.europa.eu/en/topics/topic/antimicrobial-resistance (last accessed Mar. 10, 2020).

6 The U.S. FDA website, *available at* www.fda.gov/newsevents/publichealthfocus/ucm235649.htm; www.fda.gov/forconsumers/consumerupdates/ucm378100.htm.

7 *See* the following discussions on "FDA Regulatory Regimes in Facilitating the Approval of Animal Drugs" of this chapter.

8 *See* David A. Kessler, "Antibiotics and the Meat We Eat," *The New York Times*, Mar. 27, 2013, Sec. A.

9 The Food, Drug, and Cosmetic Act (FDCA), 21 USC § 360b(c).

10 FDA Guidance for Industry (GFI) #213: "New Animal Drugs and New Animal Drug Combination Products Administered in or on Medicated Feed or Drinking Water of Food-Producing Animals: Recommendations for Drug Sponsors for Voluntarily Aligning Product Use Conditions with GFI #209," *available at* www.fda.gov/downloads/AnimalVeterinary/GuidanceComplianceEnforcement/GuidanceforIndustry/UCM299624.pdf [hereinafter GFI#213].

11 *National Resources Defense Council (NRDC) v. Food and Drug Administration (FDA)* (2nd Cir., July 24, 2014) [hereinafter NDPR Appeal].

the sale of antibiotics for food animals has dropped significantly since 2013.[12] The effectiveness of the policy seems quite clear. However, critics remain concerned about whether public health crises can be thoroughly solved, partly because the guidance documents have no binding force. Because the antibiotic restriction only applies to growth promotion and disease, preventive uses are still permitted, and it was alarming that the new policy may create a loophole with no guarantee for decreasing the use of antibiotics by farmers.[13]

In addition to briefly analyzing the judicial reviews of the courts that sided with the FDA's position, this chapter specifically aims to reveal the regulatory approaches underlying the U.S. FDA's policy on combating antibiotic resistance. The chapter will discuss how precautionary principles and cost-benefit analysis (CBA) affect the policy and disclose their implications, regardless the lack of an explicit invocation of the approaches by the FDA.

II. FDA Regulatory Regimes in Facilitating the Approval of Animal Drugs

In the wake of modern pharmaceutical developments, drugs used to promote animal growth, including some antibiotics, gained political support several decades ago. From an economic and industrial point of view, drugs can save production costs and enhance production by shortening feed cycles. Fulfilling the policy to develop the food-producing animal industry, two federal laws tended to facilitate the marketing of these drugs.

In 1968, Congress passed the Animal Drug Amendment to the FDCA,[14] which provides a simplified procedure for new animal drug approvals. Seeking to streamline the approval process and soften the burden on drug companies, the 1996 Animal Drug Availability Act[15] emphasizes collaboration between the FDA and the industry in building a common understanding of data submissions, and, in particular, field tests for animal drugs are no longer required.[16] In short, the FDA policy on animal drugs has maintained a pro-industry orientation.

12 Statement from FDA Commissioner Scott Gottlieb, M.D. on the FDA's 2017 Report on Declining Sales/Distribution of Antimicrobial Drugs for Food Animals, a Reflection of Improved Antimicrobial Stewardship, Dec. 18, 2018, *at* www.fda.gov/news-events/press-announcements/statement-fda-commissioner-scott-gottlieb-md-fdas-2017-report-declining-salesdistribution?utm_campaign=121818_Statement_FDA%20Commissioner%20statement%3A%202017%20Antimicrobial%20Animal%20Drug%20Report&utm_medium=email&utm_source=Eloqua.

13 *See* Sabrina Tavernise, "F.D.A. Restricts Antibiotics Use for Livestock", *The New York Times*, Dec. 12, 2013, A1.

14 21 U.S.C. § 306b.

15 21 U.S.C. § 301.

16 Ibid. Sec. 505(d).

III. The Response of the FDA to Antibiotic Resistance Due to Overuse in Food Animals

The FDA has been watching the problem of antibiotic resistance due to the rampant use of antibiotics on farm animals for many decades. Nonetheless, the agency had yet to take any formal action until very recent years.

The FDA approved the use of antibiotics for growth promotion and feed efficiency–subtherapeutic uses in the 1950s by issuing New Animal Drug Applications (NADAs) for penicillin and tetracyclines. Since then, animal drugs have been widely used in feeding food-producing animals, such as cattle, swine, and chickens. In the 1960s, the FDA sensed the risks to human and animal health posed by the subtherapeutic use of antibiotics on farm animals. In 1970, the agency began a study on the risks linked to the use of antibiotics. The Bureau of Veterinary Medicine (BVM) of the FDA, with assistance from the National Advisory Food and Drug Committee (NAFDC), was responsible for data review and research for several years. Through the recommendations of the NAFDC, the director of the BVM concluded the following:

> on the basis of new information before him with respect to these drug products, evaluated together with the evidence available to him when they were originally approved, that the drug products are not shown to be safe under the conditions of use prescribed, recommended, or suggested in their labeling. The evidence, in fact, indicate[d] that such penicillin use may be unsafe, particularly if the higher or therapeutic levels of penicillin should be used as substitutes for the levels currently used subtherapeutically.[17]

The director thus decided to engage in the process of withdrawing approval of growth-promoting uses of certain antibiotics by issuing notices of an opportunity for hearing (NOOHs) in 1977. In the notices, the FDA confirmed the finding that the use of antibiotics in livestock promotes the development of antibiotic-resistant bacteria, which was transferred "from animals to humans as a result of direct human-animal contact, the consumption of contaminated food, and the widespread presence of resistant bacteria in the environment."[18]

Yet, from the 1970s to the late 1980s, other medical institutions failed to fully endorse the finding of the FDA. Both the National Academy of Sciences (NAS) and the Institute of Medicine, a unit of the NAS, held a relatively conservative position toward the transmissibility of antibiotic resistance between food-producing animals and humans.[19]

17 Penicillin-Containing Premixes: Opportunity for Hearing, 42 Fed. Reg. 43772 (Aug. 30, 1977). ("Penicillin NOOH"); Tetracycline NOOH, 42 Fed. Reg. 56264 (Oct. 21, 1977).

18 Ibid.

19 The IOM stated that it was "unable to find data directly implicating the subtherapeutic use of feed antimicrobials in human illness and that much of the available evidence was primarily circumstantial,

Despite the confirmation and release of the notices, the FDA has yet to hold any hearings on the proposed withdrawals. The suspension was partly attributable to the interventions of Congress, which requested more research and solid scientific evidence to uphold the FDA decision.[20]

After an almost 35-year delay in the withdrawal process, on June 28, 2010, the FDA finally announced a novel approach to address the problem in draft Guidance No. 209.[21] The agency demonstrated its efforts to phase out certain antibiotics used in farm animals not by a method of coercion but by persuasion, which encouraged drug manufacturers to voluntarily phase out their use. Consequently, shortly after the release of the draft, on December 16, 2011, the FDA rescinded the 1977 NOOHs.[22]

In December 2013, the FDA provided more concrete recommendations for drug manufacturers to remove the labeling of antibiotics for growth promotion.[23] FDA officials believe that voluntary participation "is the fastest, most efficient way to make these changes."[24]

To facilitate surveillance and monitoring of antimicrobial use and resistance, the FDA has required antimicrobial drug sponsors to annually report the amounts of antimicrobial drugs sold or distributed for use in food-producing species during the prior year.[25] According to a recent survey, it appears that the FDA policy has been working. The data released by the FDA shows that the amount of medically important antibiotics sold for use in food-producing animals in the U.S. has declined, although its use still increased during a certain period.[26]

---

often ambiguous, and sometimes conflicting," Human Risks with the Subtherapeutic Use of Penicillin or Tetracyclines in Animal Feed, IOM (1989).

20 Peter Hutt et al., *Food and Drug Law: Cases and Materials* (4th ed., Westbury, NY, Foundation Press 2014), at 1087.

21 FDA Guidance for Industry (GFI) #209, The Judicious Use of Medically Important Antimicrobial Drugs in Food-Producing Animals, U.S. Department of Health and Human Services, Food and Drug Administration, Center for Veterinary Medicine, Apr. 13, 2012, *available at* www.fda.gov/downloads/AnimalVeterinary/GuidanceComplianceEnforcement/GuidanceforIndustry/UCM216936.pdf [hereinafter GFI #209].

22 Withdrawal of Notices of Opportunity for a Hearing; Penicillin and Tetracycline Used in Animal Feed, a Notice by the Health and Human Services Department, in which FDA explained the reason for the decision that the "FDA is engaging in other ongoing regulatory strategies . . .", *available at* www.federalregister.gov/documents/2011/12/22/2011-32775/withdrawal-of-notices-of-opportunity-for-a-hearing-penicillin-and-tetracycline-used-in-animal-feed (last accessed Mar. 15, 2020).

23 *See* GFI#213, *supra* note 10.

24 *See* FDA website at www.fda.gov/forconsumers/consumerupdates/ucm378100.htm.

25 Section 105 of the Animal Drug User Fee Amendments of 2008 (ADUFA) amended Section 512 of the FDCA. *See* also Antimicrobial Resistance Information of FDA, *available at* www.fda.gov/emergency-preparedness-and-response/mcm-issues/antimicrobial-resistance-information-fda (last accessed May 8, 2020).

26 The recent report indicated that "domestic sales and distribution of medically important antimicrobials for use in food-producing animals increased nine% between 2017 and 2018. Despite this increase, 2018 is the second-lowest year on record and the overall trend continues to indicate that

IV. FDA'S Regulatory Principles and Approaches Underpinning the Phasing Out of Antibiotics in Food-Producing Animals

The food risk analysis regime developed by the WHO/FAO suggests several policy principles and approaches that may assist risk managers in deciding on an appropriate policy option.[27] Overall, two approaches reflect the regulatory philosophy surrounding the governance of antibiotic problems, namely the precautionary and cost-benefit analysis approaches. The following explains how these approaches may implicitly sustain current FDA policies on the one hand and dissuade the agency from engaging in enforceable actions on the other.

A. Rebirth of Precaution or Hidden Precaution?

The precautionary principle or approach has become a regulatory discipline to avoid irreversible damage when scientific uncertainty for a given risk exists. The principle is recognized as a general principle of international law, which may guide states in protecting environmental and health interests.[28] The principle has also been clearly written in the EU legal systems that address public health and environmental concerns. The Treaty on European Union specifies the principle as the basis of public policy.[29] In terms of food regulations, precaution is also incorporated as one of the governing principles in the European General Food Law[30] and genetically modified food regulations.[31]

The term of "precautionary principle" does not plainly appear in the U.S. statutes. However, the idea influenced U.S. regulatory regimes in dealing with potential health and environmental risks during the 1970s. The legislative approach in the pursuit of qualitative goals for controlling health and environmental risks[32] leaves much space for competent authorities, including

---

ongoing efforts to support antimicrobial stewardship are having an impact: sales in 2018 are down 21% since 2009, the first year of reporting, and down 38% since 2015, the peak year of sales and distribution"; *see* "FDA Releases Annual Summary Report on Antimicrobials Sold or Distributed in 2018 for Use in Food-Producing Animals," Dec. 10, 2019, *available at* www.fda.gov/animal-veterinary/cvm-updates/fda-releases-annual-summary-report-antimicrobials-sold-or-distributed-2018-use-food-producing. The report is *available at* www.fda.gov/media/133411/download.

27 FAO and WHO, *Food Safety Risk Analysis: A Guide for National Safety Authorities* (2006), at 31, *available at* www.fao.org/docrep/012/a0822e/a0822e00.htm [hereinafter FAO and WHO Guide].

28 Patricia Birnie et al., *International Law & the Environment* (3rd ed., Oxford, Oxford University Press 2009), at 159–64.

29 Article 130r of the EU Treaty reads: "Community Policy . . . shall be based on the precautionary principle."

30 European Parliament & Council Regulation 178/2002, O.J.L 031 (Feb. 1, 2002), *available at* http://eur-lex.europa.eu/LexUriServ/LexUriServ.do? uri=CELEX:2002R0178: EN:NOT.

31 European Parliament & Council Directive 2001/18/EC, O.J.L 106 (Mar. 12, 2001), *available at* https://eur-lex.europa.eu/legal-content/EN/TXT/PDF/?uri=OJ:L:2001:106:FULL&from=EN.

32 Gail Charnley & Michael D. Rogers, "Frameworks for Risk Assessment, Uncertainty, and Precaution" in Jonathan Wiener et al. (eds), *The Reality of Precaution: Comparing Risk Regulation in the United States and Europe* (Oxfordshire, Routledge 2011), at 371.

Occupational Safety and Health Administration (OSHA), the Environmental Protection Agency (EPA), FDA, and so on, to take precautionary actions on a case-by-case basis. Hence, it may be inaccurate to state that the principle has never been applied by U.S. regulators.

Since the use of precaution is subject to agency discretion, their actions would be scrutinized by the court. In reviewing the EPA's decision to ban lead in gasoline, the Supreme Court in *Ethyl*[33] favored the EPA action, although no rigid scientific evidence supports the linkage between lead in gas and damage to public health. By contrast, in the Benzene ruling,[34] the Court rebutted OSHA's standard-setting for benzene exposure on the ground that the agency failed to demonstrate a "significant risk" to justify the proposed standard.[35] Therefore, as the qualitative orientation of federal statutes remains, the latitude and justification of applying precautionary measures will depend on the will of competent administrative agencies and the position of the judicial branches. If the agencies tend to be more cautious about public interests at the expense of the industry, they will be more willing to take precautionary measures. In this case, the court can uphold the actions by deferring to the decisions of agencies. Alternatively, the courts may denounce such overreaching actions because they lack solid scientific evidence.

Certain precautionary approaches have also affected U.S. food regulations. The Delaney Clause is a vivid statute requiring the FDA to ban the use of additives if they may induce cancer without necessarily engaging in quantitative risk assessment.[36] Shifting the burden of proof of safety to the industry also reflects the spirit of precaution.[37] For instance, the FDA normally will require the industry to demonstrate the safety of food additives, food-borne pathogens, or chemical contamination.[38] The industry's implementation of the FDA's Hazard Analysis and Critical Control Points (HACCP) is another example of applying risk-based precaution to prevent food-borne diseases.[39] Charnley and Rogers observe that the U.S. Department of Agriculture (USDA) responded to the bovine spongiform encephalopathy outbreak by taking precautionary measures to ban the importation of Canadian livestock.[40]

The procedure of the withdrawal of NADA to some extent reflects the precautionary approach. The governing law does not demand the FDA engage in a rigid evaluation of the level of safety. The application of the withdrawal process

33 *Ethyl v. EPA*, 426 U.S. 941 (1976).

34 *Industrial Union Department v. American Petroleum Institute*, 448 U.S. 607 (1980).

35 Ibid.

36 FDCA, 21 U.S.C. §§ 409(c)(3)(A), 706(b)(5)(B).

37 Pfizer, *supra* note 4, para. 392. *See* Ian Forrester & Jaap C. Hanekamp, "Precaution, Science and Jurisprudence: A Test Case" (2006) 9 Journal of Risk Research 297, 308. But some observe that the effect of applying the precautionary principle does not necessarily shift all the burden of proof of showing safety to producers for every instance. However, it does alleviate the burden of regulators to present solid evidence to justify their actions. *See* Birnie et al., *supra* note 28, at 157–58.

38 Charnley & Rogers, *supra* note 32, at 370.

39 Ibid at 370–71.

40 Ibid at 371.

normally reduces the burden of agencies in showing the risks, either in qualitative or quantitative form, and then shifts the burden to drug companies to prove safety. In effect, the FDCA requires regulators to demonstrate the *prima facie* unsafe evidence of the targeted animal drugs according to the result of a risk assessment.[41] The drug sponsors need to prove their safety in order to nullify the initial unsafe finding.[42] Otherwise, approval for marketing the drug will be terminated.

The FDA's failure to finalize the withdrawal process does not prevent it from engaging in the persuasive approach, even voluntarily, which was indicative of applying precautionary measures. As previously noted, it remains questionable if solid scientific evidence is available so as to justify the withdrawal of such permission. No definitive scientific consensus on the relationship between the consumption of food animals and human antibiotic resistance has been fully established. However, the FDA still continues on the path to phase out the use of drugs for growth promotion.

B. *The Hurdle Raised by Cost-Benefit Analysis*

Toward risk governance on the environment, health, and safety, states are expected to avoid unjust and unnecessary interference in the market. To realize better decision-making quality, risk managers normally need to conduct a regulatory impact assessment (RIA), in which the CBA has become one of its core mandates.[43] In effect, to justify the intervention, the benefits of a proposed regulation must outweigh the costs arising from its implementation.[44]

The Regan administration, in signing Executive Order 12291, began to require all agencies to fulfill CBA in producing regulations, which will be subject to the review of the Office of Information and Regulatory Affairs (OIRA) under the Office of Budget and Management (OBM).[45] Subsequently, both President Clinton and President Obama continued to honor the requirement,

41 FDCA, 21 U.S.C. §360b(e)(1).

42 FDCA, 21 U.S.C. §360b(e)(4). *See* Withdrawal of Approval of the New Animal Drug Application for Enrofoxacin in Poultry: Final Decision of the Commissioner (July 27, 2005) (The Commissioner concluded that "CVM has met its initial burden of coming forward with evidence to show there are serious questions about enrofoxacin's safety, the burden then shifts to Bayer to show that the use of enrofloxacin in chickens and turkeys is safe and that FDA should continue to approve such use.") [hereinafter Enrofoxacin Withdrawal].

43 OECD, Regulatory Impact Assessment: OECD Best Practice Principles for Regulatory Policy 6, 11, 27(2020), *available at* www.oecd-ilibrary.org/docserver/7a9638cb-en.pdf?expires=1595825164&id=id&accname=guest&checksum=BBE5D2BB06AA85C074909B73A4CCF791 (last accessed May 1, 2020).

44 *See generally* Richard A. Posner, *Economic Analysis of Law* (9th ed., Blue Springs, Aspen Publishing 2014), at 514; Cass R. Sunstein, *The Cost-Benefit Revolution* (Cambridge, The MIT Press 2018).

45 EO No. 12291, 3 C.F.R. 127 (1981), *available at* www.archives.gov/federal-register/codification/executive-order/1229.html.

with some elaboration.[46] The Clinton administration, noting the limit of quantifiable methods, especially recognized qualitative evaluation.[47] Obama's era was the first time allowing the value of human dignity, which is difficult to quantify, to be considered in CBA.[48] Currently, there is no sign that the status of the CBA will be modified.[49]

The U.S. law had yet to mandate a CBA for enacting regulations until Congress passed the Unfunded Mandates Reform Act in 1995,[50] which requires agencies to engage in CBA for any regulations whose financial impact would reach the threshold of US$100 million or more unless the task is prohibited by law.[51] The requirement on CBA is primarily procedural and does not constitute a substantive criterion to negate or justify the regulations in question.[52] In terms of federal health, safety, and environmental statutes, there remains no universal and coherent legislative philosophy for approving or rejecting the approach.[53] Thus, in these regulatory sectors, the realization of the CBA practice and its effect will largely hinge on how seriously the OMB executes the president's orders and to what extent competent agencies respond to such a mandate.

In practice, governmental compliance with CBA could be burdensome and costly. The FDA usually has to face the challenges of the OMB/OIRA for failing the CBA requirement in drafting regulations. For instance, the issuance of the rules implementing the Food Safety Modernization Act was delayed due to the OMB's lengthy review process.[54] The CBA burden combined with the unbearable costs arising from the notice-and-comment procedures have discouraged the agency from engaging in a formal rulemaking process.[55] Such bureaucratic constraints, in conjunction with other concerns of time-consuming and resource limitations in rulemaking, now entail the FDA to increasingly

46 EO No. 12866, 3 C.F.R. 638 (1993), *available at* www.archives.gov/files/federal-register/executive-order/pdf/12866.html; EO No. 13563, 3 C.F.R. 215 (2012), *available at* www.archives.gov/files/federal-register/executive-order/pdf/13563.html

47 Ibid. *See also* Giandomenico Majone, "Political Institutions and the Principle of Precaution" in Jonathan B. Wiener et al. (eds), *The Reality of Precaution: Comparing Risk Regulation in the United States and Europe* (2011), at 428.

48 EO No. 13563, *supra* note 46; *see also* Sunstein, *supra* note 44, at 20.

49 Sunstein, *supra* note 44, at 20–21 (specifying the Trump administration has largely followed the approach).

50 2 U.S.C. §§551–559, 701–706.

51 2 U.S.C. §1532.

52 Nicholas Ashford, "The Legacy of the Precautionary Principle in US Law: The Rise of Cost-Benefit Analysis and Risk Assessment as Undermining Factors in Health, Safety and Environmental Protection" in Nicolas de Sadeleer (eds), *Implementing the Precautionary Principle: Approaches from the Nordic Countries, the EU and the United States* (2006), at 357.

53 *See* Lawrence O. Gostin & Lindsay F. Wiley, *Public Health Law: Power, Duty, Restraint* (3rd ed. 2016), at 209.

54 Hutt et al., *supra* note 20, at 48–49.

55 Ibid at 55–56.

favor the issuance of "guidance" documents as a tool to affect the industry rather than resorting to binding regulations.[56]

The industry's rebuttal to the FDA's withdrawal of NADA on the ground that the agency's failure to adequately fulfill a CBA may raise another hurdle for the agency in resorting to drafting regulations. Unless certain federal laws explicitly prohibit or require CBA, it may be up to the court to decide whether the analysis has been lawfully undertaken. In practice, some rulings did not mandate the weighing of costs and benefits in addressing the safety of drugs in question,[57] while other decisions required the task.[58] The litigation costs and the unpredictability of the rulings may dissuade the FDA from proceeding with a withdrawal process.

V. Judicial Review of the Legality of FDA's Decision to Withhold the Withdrawal Process

A. The District Court's Ruling on the Permissibility of FDA's Delay of Engaging in Withdrawal of Antibiotic Drugs

The FDA's decision not to pursue regulatory actions against antibiotic drug manufacturers has met some legal challenges. As the FDA pursued an alternative approach to phasing out antibiotics, the Natural Resources Defense Association (NRDA) filed suit to request the agency to reinstate and continue its original withdrawal procedure, which should have proceeded many years ago.[59] The FDA responded that "it was not legally required to do so, and the issue is now moot because the 1977 NOOHs have been withdrawn."[60]

The main contentious issue faced by the court is to decide whether the FDA remains bound by the law to continue the withdrawal proceedings, including holding hearings and making final withdrawal orders accordingly, even though the initial NOOHs were rescinded.

Both parties disputed the legal and procedural mandates of the FDCA in § 360b(e)(1), which governs the withdrawal of approval of NADAs. The statute underlines four steps to finalize the withdrawal procedure: (1) the release of an unsafe finding, (2) the issuance of notice for hearings, (3) the holding of public

56 *See* Todd D. Rakoff, "The Choice between Formal and Informal Modes of Administrative Regulation" (2000) 52 Administrative Law Review 159, 168 (pointing out the cost of complying with notice-and-comments is relatively high, which constitutes one of the reasons for the FDA not to favor a formal rulemaking). *Cf* Executive Order 13422 (2007) (mandating CBA review for all significant guidance documents).

57 *See* Enrofoxacin Withdrawal, *supra* note 42 (the commissioner relied on the Supreme Court's *Donovan* ruling that denied the requirement of CBA for assessing occupational safety).

58 *For example, Hess & Clark, Inc. v. FDA*, 495 F.2d 975 (D.C. Cir. 1974); *Rhone-Poulenc, Inc. v. FDA*, 636 F.2d 750 (D.C. Cir. 1980).

59 Natural Resources Defense Council v. Food and Drug Administration, 884 F. Supp. 2d 127 (S.D.N.Y. 2012).

60 Ibid at 137.

hearings for affected sponsors, and (4) the ordering of the withdrawal of application if the sponsors fail to demonstrate the safety of the drugs.

The FDA took a narrow view of the procedure and contended that the law requires the withdrawal only after hearings are held. Since it never held hearings and has already withdrawn the 1977 NOOHs, the FDA argued that no further action was required. By contrast, the plaintiffs claimed that the original findings that the use of antibiotics on farm animals was not safe shall sufficiently oblige the FDA to engage in a withdrawal procedure.[61]

The court agreed with the position of the plaintiffs, whose interpretation was "based on its text and grammatical structure"[62] of the law. The court's inclination to favor the plaintiffs can be verified by examining "the structure of § 360b as a whole and the overriding purpose of the FDA."[63] In effect, an unsafe finding of the drug in question by the FDA will trigger the withdrawal process. It found that the director of the BVM did make findings in its original notices about the unsafety of the subtherapeutic use of penicillin and tetracycline. Thus, such findings mandate the FDA to continue the subsequent withdrawal procedure.[64]

Indeed, the FDA has rescinded the 1977 NOOHs. The move, the court considered, would not affect the obligation of the FDA to complete the withdrawal proceedings as long as the unsafe findings remain.[65] The court, in reviewing the FDA's recent announcement in rescinding the notice, found that the FDA remains concerned about the health problem of using antibiotics in animal feed, and the agency has not yet rescinded its original findings.[66]

Finally, although the FDA opted for other regulatory strategies—namely the voluntary approach of phasing out certain antibiotics—the court ruled that the new approach "does not relieve it of its statutory obligation to complete withdrawal proceedings."[67] The court found that "[t]he statute does not empower the agency to choose a *different course of action* in lieu of withdrawal proceedings, such as that embodied in the 2010 Draft Guidance."[68]

B. The Appellate Decision Deferring to FDA's Interpretation

In contrast to the opinions of the district court, the appellate court considered that the FDCA does not explicitly mention when the alleged "finding" happens. The court found that the interpretations by the two parties seem feasible, as the sequence of the withdrawal process is unclear by a reading of the text.

61 Ibid.
62 Ibid at 141.
63 Ibid at 143.
64 Ibid at 148–49.
65 Ibid at 149.
66 Ibid at 150.
67 Ibid at 151.
68 Ibid.

By examining the text, context, and regulations for implementing the law, the court decided to sustain the interpretation of the FDA, which argued that a finding can only be made after a hearing about the safety of the drugs has been concluded.

Apart from using the previous interpretation techniques, the court's favoring of the position of the FDA follows on its analysis of background legal concepts.[69] Unless Congress has a clear mandate, the court maintained that its interpretation should not depart from conventions regarding administrative procedure. It held that the FDA interpretation is consistent with conventional wisdom.

First, the FDA's position is in accordance with the general understanding of the administrative decision, which normally reflects the result of the final deliberations and would not be made until the conclusion of the process. The practice aligns with other legislation, such as the Social Security Act and the Federal Rule of Evidence.[70]

Second, the court recognized the significant impact of withdrawing a marketing approval. Thus, it agreed with Congress that the withdrawal should hinge on a relatively cautious hearing that allows evidence from both sides to be presented. A contrary view was considered unorthodox by the court.[71]

Third, referring to civil and criminal procedures, the court found that the preliminary conclusion should not constitute and dictate the final decision, which is subject to the court's final confirmation. By the same token, any charge against the affected party during an administrative procedure cannot lead to a final finding until the hearing process has been concluded.[72]

Fourth, the court questioned the interpretation of the plaintiff, considering there was no indication of a formal unsafe reference, given that the original NOOH had been withdrawn.[73]

Fifth, probably the most important factor sustaining the FDA's stance is the traditional recognition of the discretion enjoyed by agencies. The court noticed that agencies have a variety of duties and limited resources. This is a very important and difficult decision in terms of deciding how and when resources will be used. The agency should enjoy the discretion of setting the priority for implementing the law.[74]

VI. A Critical Review on FDA Voluntary Policy

According to the FDA's strategic plan, pharmaceutical companies may respond to their intention of voluntary compliance within three months after the

69 NRDC Appeal, *supra* note 11, at 40.
70 Ibid at 41–42.
71 Ibid at 44.
72 Ibid at 45, 46.
73 Ibid at 49, 50.
74 Ibid at 51.

notice. As previously mentioned, most drug companies deferred to the policy. In effect, food animal producers can only use pharmaceutical companies' drugs sold in the market for therapeutic purposes. Indeed, the predominant support by the industry signals an encouraging and strong starting point for implementing the FDA policy. However, it leaves some legal questions unresolved, which may trigger additional disputes in the future.

First, the legality of using antibiotics to promote animal growth in the real world remains a dubious proposition. Because no law prohibits such a use *per se*, uncooperative companies can still legally sell the drugs approved by the FDA for that purpose. No law in force forbids farmers from buying such drugs from companies.

Second, as the FDA guidance for the judicious use of antibiotic drugs is on a voluntary basis, there is no guarantee that the affected drug companies cannot reinstate the label for growth use. There has not yet been any consequential punishment or coercive measures exercised for violations of such a "gentlemen's agreement."

The FDA's choice of a voluntary policy to some extent was understandable. According to its "Guidance for Industry (GFI) #209,"[75] released in April 2012, the FDA admitted the legal hurdles facing the agency if it opts to initiate an official withdrawal action of NADA. The FDA needs to initially bear the burden in providing evidence about the safety concerns.[76] Yet the affected companies can rebut the finding.[77] The withdrawal process can be lengthy, and the ultimate ruling appears unpredictable and may not necessarily be in favor of the FDA position.

Unless it is engaged in the withdrawal of the NADA process, the FDA has no other legal power or tools by which drug companies are forced to phase out the sale of antibiotics for growth-promotion purposes. This legal impediment reveals the insufficiency of the current regulatory framework, which cannot effectively and legitimately address the challenges posed by antimicrobial resistance that obviously constitutes serious public health crises. The lack of an appropriate authority accorded the FDA to tackle such emergencies demonstrates an urgent need for Congress to do the right thing.

VII. Concluding Remarks

This chapter has explained that the overall policy of the FDA in addressing antibiotic resistance reflects the idea of precaution. Although the precautionary principle or approach has yet to be explicitly written into statute, the precaution remains influential over competent agencies in responding to health risks, which is particularly revealed in the shifting of the burden of proof on safety.

75 GFI #209, *supra* note 21, at 18.
76 FDCA, U.S.C. § 512(e)(1)(B).
77 Ibid.

The chapter also found that the FDA's voluntary approach is to some extent a result of evading the burdensome CBA.

On the other hand, it appears that the FDA's approach has won the legal battle at the current stage, given the court's inclination to defer to the FDA's discretion not to continue the original withdrawal procedure. While the voluntary policy has successfully reduced the use of antibiotics for growth promotion, critical questions remain unresolved.

First, in interpreting the FDCA, the appellate court held that the finding of safety will not occur until the conclusion of a hearing process. Yet the restrictive view may cast the original scientific finding that triggers the hearing process in a vague and embarrassing position. Consequently, there would be no room for such a "finding" in the FDCA *per se*.

Second, applying a voluntary policy may save legal costs and avoid lengthy proceedings. It is also a reflection of the FDA's tendency to avoid the possible hurdles raised by the implementation of CBA. The bypass of the withdrawal procedure embodied in the FDCA reveals the insufficiency of legal tools. Apart from withdrawing the NADA, there are no other laws in effect controlling the use of antibiotics in the growth promotion of animals. If the policy eventually proves below expectations, it will slow the process of phasing out such use and worsen the health crisis.

Many drafts regulating antibiotics for growth purposes on a comprehensive scale have been introduced in the U.S. Congress.[78] However, none of them have been adopted. An optimal solution depends on the empowerment of the FDA with adequate legal authorities and tools to control antibiotic resistance.

78 *For example,* The Preservation of Antibiotics for Medical Treatment Act of 2013 (PAMTA) in the House; The Preventing Antibiotics Resistance Act of 2017 (PARA) in the Senate; The Delivering Antimicrobial Transparency in Animals Act (DATA) in 2015, and the Antimicrobial Data Collection Act (ADCA) in 2013, both in the House and Senate.

3 The Role of Scientific Evidence in European Food Assessments

Alie de Boer

I. Introduction

The importance of scientific evidence as the basis of policy is highly emphasized within Europe, especially concerning the regulation of risks.[1] One of the sectors in which science is key in policy development is the field of food and food safety. Following various food scares in the 1990s (including the bovine spongiform encephalopathy (BSE) crisis and the dioxin crisis), EU food law was completely reformed and the requirement to use independent scientific evidence was emphasized more in the newly developed framework regulation for food and food safety within the EU: Regulation (EC) No 178/2002 laying down the general principles and requirements of food law, establishing the European Food Safety Authority (EFSA), and laying down procedures in matters of food safety.[2] Scientific evidence should contribute to the main aim of EU food law: achieving the highest level of consumer protection.[3]

Nutritional sciences, however, are developing at high speed, and new insights regarding new, innovative products and technologies, but also health effects of food and food ingredients, are evolving rapidly. And while nutritional sciences thrive with ongoing critical appraisal of their concepts and ideas, food laws and subsequent guidelines require definite statements concerning food safety and health. This results in the issue that legislation is often based on dated or even outdated scientific concepts and cannot make use of the most recent

1 European Commission, *Strengthening Evidence Based Policy Making Through Scientific Advice Reviewing Existing Practice and Setting Up a European Science Advice* (Luxembourg, Publications Office of the European Union 2015); B. Stibernitz, "A Brief Comment on Science-based Risk Regulation Within the European Union", (2012) 3(1) European Journal of Risk Regulation 86, 86–91.

2 Regulation (EC) No 178/2002 of the European Parliament and of the Council of 28 January 2002 laying down the general principles and requirements of food law, establishing the European Food Safety Authority and laying down procedures in matters of food safety. OJ L 31, p. 1–24. *Consolidated version 26 May 2021.*

3 E. Vos, "EU Food Safety Regulation in the Aftermath of the BSE Crisis" (2000) 23:3 Journal of Consumer Policy, 227, 227–55.

DOI: 10.4324/9781003271918-4

advancements.[4] Especially in subsequently developed sectoral legislation, that, for example, deals with the authorization of health claims[5] or with the authorization of new food products,[6] scientific evidence is key: when health effects or safety of the products requesting market access is not established within a scientific dossier, the risk assessor will not advise the risk manager to allow such a claim or product on the European market.[7] The tension between nutritional sciences and law becomes evident in the use of scientific findings under these specific food laws: consensus must be reached upon the established effects and the causal relationships identified between ingredients and these effects, but it is highly uncertain when new and innovative methods are sufficiently developed to be accepted under these regulatory procedures.

The process of analyzing scientific evidence related to food authorizations is often referred to as risk assessment.[8] In the General Food Law, the concepts of risk assessment, risk management, and risk communication are used to describe the systematic risk analysis approach upon which food policy and decisions should be based. EU food legislation, however, does not only deal with risks: while the authorization procedure for novel foods requires scientific evidence for proving that a product is not unsafe, also, for health claims, scientific findings are required that establish the health effect or the efficacy of the product bearing the claim. The authority that conducts risk assessments in the EU, EFSA, describes its efforts as scientific assessments.[9] It could therefore be questioned whether EU food law provides a mandate for only *risk assessment*, while in nutritional sciences, risks and benefits of foods are often studied concurrently, or whether there is a legal basis for conducting such *scientific assessments*. This chapter aims to unravel the role of the EFSA as laid down in law and to

4 A. Bast & J. C. Hanekamp, *Toxicology: What Everyone Should Know* (London: Elsevier Academic Press 2017), at 71–8; A. de Boer, "Scientific Assessments in European Food Law: Making It Future-Proof" (2019) 108 Regulatory Toxicology and Pharmacology 104437; V. Silano, "Science, Risk Assessment and Decision-Making to Ensure Food and Feed Safety in the European Union" (2009) 4 European Food and Feed Law Review 400, 400–05; M. H. Zwietering, "Risk assessment and risk management for safe foods: Assessment needs inclusion of variability and uncertainty, management needs discrete decisions" (2015) 213 International Journal of Food Microbiology 118–23.

5 Regulation (EC) No 1924/2006 of the European Parliament and of the Council of 20 December 2006 on nutrition and health claims made on foods. OJ L 404, p. 9–25. *Consolidated version 13 December 2014.*

6 Regulation (EU) No 2015/2283 of the European Parliament and of the Council of 25 November 2015 on novel foods. OJ L 327, p. 1–22. *Consolidated version 27 March 2021.*

7 A. de. Boer, "Fifteen Years of Regulating Nutrition and Health Claims in Europe: The Past, the Present and the Future" (2021) 13(5) Nutrients 1725.

8 A.de Boer, *supra* note 4.

9 EFSA Scientific Committee, A. Hardy, D. Benford, T. Halldorsson, M. J. Jeger, K. H. Knutsen, S. More, A. Mortensen, H. Naegeli, H. Noteborn, C. Ockleford, A. Ricci, G. Rychen, J. R Schlatter, V. Silano, R. Solecki, D. Turck, T. Brock, A. Chesson, S. Karenlampi, C. Lambre, Y. Sanz, T. Goumperis, J. Kleiner & D. Maurici. "Scientific Motivations and Criteria to Consider Updating EFSA Scientific Assessments" (2017) 15(3) EFSA Journal e04737.

analyze the practical reality of scientific advice provided under the mandate of European food law.

II. The Development of EU Food Law

Subsequent to the collaboration that was started between different West European nations in an attempt to protect peace which was set up in 1949, six nations established the European Economic Community in 1958 to support closer collaboration.[10] This supra-national organization evolved to become the European Union (EU), currently comprising 28 Member States which cooperate closely on a political, economic, and monetary level.[11] In 1957, by signing the Treaty of Rome, a single market was established throughout the different Member States in which goods, services, people, and money can move freely.[12] To ensure that within this single market, a level playing field is established throughout the different Member States, various pieces of legislation have been developed within the EU that deal with economic, monetary, and political issues.[13] Today, the EU's executive body (the European Commission) can propose to regulate certain areas, after which the Council of the European Union and the European Parliament are empowered to further develop and adopt such legislation.[14] The Commission and the Member States themselves implement the developed legislation. By becoming a member of the EU, the Member States subscribe to all benefits as well as commitments of the partnership but remain autonomous states[15]: legislation developed at Union level is enforced by national authorities.

The free movement of foodstuffs throughout the European Community was one of the key areas for which the free movement of goods in the internal market was essential, as established by the Treaty of Rome signed in 1957.[16]

10 A. de Boer, *Interactions Between Nutrition and Medicine in Effect and Law* (Maastricht, Maastricht University, 2015); European Union, "A Peaceful Europe – The Beginnings of Cooperation" (2015), *available at* https://european-union.europa.eu/principles-countries-history/history-eu/1945-59_en.

11 European Union, "History" (2015), *available at* https://europa.eu/citizens-initiative/how-it-works/history_en.

12 Directorate-General for Human Resources and Security, Directorate 'Coordination and Preparation of Publications', European Commission, *Europe Without Frontiers: Completing the Internal Market* (Luxembourg, Publications Office of the European Union 1990).

13 European Commission, Directorate-General for Communication, *How the European Union Works* (Luxembourg, Publications Office of the European Union 2015).

14 B. van der Meulen & M. van der Velde, *The Institutions of the European Community. In European Food Law Handbook* (Wageningen, Wageningen Academic Publishers 2008), at 161–216.

15 European Union, "EU institutions and other bodies" (2015), *available at* https://european-union.europa.eu/institutions-law-budget/institutions-and-bodies/institutions-and-bodies-profiles_en; B. van der Meulen & M. van der Velde, *The Institutions of the European Community. In European Food Law Handbook* (Wageningen, Wageningen Academic Publishers 2008), at 161–216.

16 E. H. Leibovitch, "Food Safety Regulation in the European Union: Toward an Unavoidable Centralization of Regulatory Powers" (2007) 43 Texas International Law Journal 429–52; B. van der Meulen, "The Structure of European Food Law" (2013) 2(2) Laws 69–98.

In 1964, the first specific European legal act dealing with foods was developed, which aimed to harmonize hygiene requirements for meat production.[17] Scientific and technological developments in the production of, among other things, food additives and flavorings resulted in the 1970s in the development of legislation to deal with these specific substances, as well as in rules upon other ingredients that became specifically prohibited or permitted.[18] The 1974 case ruling of the Court of Justice in the Cassis de Dijon Case[19] introduced an essential principle in European food law: the principle of mutual recognition. Due to this principle, Member States were no longer allowed to prohibit the sale of food products that were lawfully produced and marketed in another Member State, because these products should be able to move freely through the internal market.[20] In 1985, a new approach to dealing with food on a European level was decided upon, because Member States were shown to be unable to unanimously develop specific legislation for foods. Therefore, from 1987, newly adopted legislation on foods would mainly result in ensuring that food products would be labeled into more detail to guarantee consumers would be able to make a well-informed choice.[21] The 1992 Maastricht Treaty, which adjusted the EU treaties again, introduced a new general objective of food law: food legislation should require a "high level of health protection".[22] Different EU-wide food scares in the 1990s, including the BSE crisis and the dioxin crisis, however, led to the call to radically reform food law.[23] Where EU food law mainly focused on the harmonization of national legislation to reduce barriers to trade before these crises, the scandals identified that reducing trade barriers could not be the prevailing objective of food law anymore: protecting consumers from food hazards and from being misled should be the main aim of European food legislation.[24]

17 Council Directive 64/433/EEC of 26 June 1964 on health problems affecting intra-Community trade in fresh meat. Repealed by Directive 2004/41/EC of the European Parliament and of the Council of 21 April 2004 repealing certain directives concerning food hygiene and health conditions for the production and placing on the market of certain products of animal origin intended for human consumption and amending Council Directives 89/662/EEC and 92/118/EEC and Council Decision 95/408/EC; European Commission DG Sanco, *50 Years of Food Safety in the European Union* (Luxembourg, Office for Official Publications of the European Communities 2007).

18 European Commission DG, *supra* note 17; Leibovitch, *supra* note 16.

19 Rewe-Zentral AG v Bundesmonopolverwaltung für Branntwein, Judgement of the Court of 20 February 1979. Case 120/788. European Court Reports 1979–00649.

20 European Commission DG, *supra* note 17; Leibovitch, *supra* note 16; B. van der Meulen, "The Structure of European Food Law" (2013) 2(2) Laws 69, 69–98.

21 Leibovitch, *supra* note 16.

22 B. v an der Meulen, *EU Food Law Handbook* (Wageningen, Wageningen Academic Publishers 2014).

23 van der Meulen, *supra* note 20; Vos, *supra* note 3.

24 C. Ansell & D. Vogel, *What's the Beef? The Contested Governance of European Food Safety* (Cambridge, MA: The MIT Press 2006); A. Szajkowska, "From Mutual Recognition to Mutual Scientific

As a first step in response to these major food scares, the EC presented their Green Paper on the general principles of food law in the European Union[25] in 1997. Following from this advisory paper, the Commission's White Paper on Food Safety of 2000[26] described 84 action points to develop and modernize appropriate food and feed (safety) legislation. This resulted in the development of a new framework regulation for foods, known as the General Food Law (GFL, Regulation (EC) No 178/2002) that was published in 2002 and last updated in 2019 by Regulation 2019/1381, the Transparency Regulation.[27] The GFL is considered the cornerstone of European food law today by providing a framework for national and European legislation on food and all related issues.[28] Next to describing the general principles, requirements, and definitions of food, the GFL also establishes the EFSA. EFSA is the independent European scientific agency that provides scientific advice as well as scientific and technical support on all aspects concerning food and feed safety. [29] Advice from EFSA can be found in opinions and guidance documents that are requested and used by the different EU institutions and Member States.

III. Scientific Evidence in Food Law

Already in their 1997 Green Paper, the European Commission stressed the importance of independent scientific advice as the basis for all regulatory activities of the Community.[30] Together with the instruments of control and risk analysis, scientific evidence was described as a third essential instrument to ensure the development of effective consumer health policies.[31] Within the GFL, the importance of scientific evidence is also highlighted: Article 6 emphasizes the need for scientific evidence to analyze the risk that a food poses, to ensure a high level of consumer protection. In Article 3 of this framework regulation, the concepts of risk analysis and its underlying three components of risk assessment, risk management, and risk communication are defined. In

Opinion? Constitutional Framework for Risk Analysis in EU Food Safety Law" (2009) 34(6) Food Policy 529, 529–38.

25 European Commission (1997). The general principles of food law in the European Union—Commission Green Paper. COM176.

26 European Commission (2000). White paper on Food Safety. COM719.

27 A.de Boer, *supra* note 4.

28 European Parliament and the Council. (2002). Regulation (EC) No 178/2002 laying down the general principles and requirements of food law, establishing the European Food Safety Authority and laying down procedures in matters of food safety. *OJ L 31*, 1–24; Szajkowska, *supra* note 24.

29 European Parliament and the Council. (2002). Regulation (EC) No 178/2002 laying down the general principles and requirements of food law, establishing the European Food Safety Authority and laying down procedures in matters of food safety. *OJ L 31*, 1–24.

30 Vos, *supra* note 3.

31 Vos, *supra* note 3.

risk analysis, the scientific assessment of a risk is separated from the political (risk management) decision, in which also other considerations are taken into account next to the scientific evidence.

A. Risk Analysis

As previously described in the literature, risk assessment has become one of the key principles of food law in general, as well as in the operations of international organizations working on standards, including Codex Alimentarius and the Sanitary and Phytosanitary Measures Agreement of the World Trade Organization (WTO).[32] Risk analysis (risk assessment, together with risk management and risk communication) has formed a structured approach to analyze risk and identify measures that can be taken to deal with this risk.[33] As highlighted already in the recitals of the GFL (specifically in recital 17), this systematic method should provide European policies a solid base upon which effective, proportionate, and targeted actions can be taken. Although this structured approach is expected to result in a more consistent approach to food safety regulations, even over various domains and in dealing with differing risks, it is essential that the full approach be based on scientific information.[34] In the rapid development of technologies and innovative products, however, sometimes insufficient information is available to fully analyze the risk. In such cases of so-called "scientific uncertainty," the GFL allows for risk managers to base a provisional management measure upon the precautionary principle (Art 7): only when a first risk assessment has identified the possibility of harmful effects may a provisional measure be taken while further scientific information should be gathered to conduct a comprehensive risk assessment. Herewith, the risk manager is allowed to ensure a high level of consumer protection, even when the scientific evidence is incomplete. As described in Article 6 of the GFL on risk analysis, however, a risk manager should take the precautionary principle into account *next to* the results of risk assessment and not *instead of* such a risk assessment.

32 A. de Boer, "Risk analysis for foods", in B. M. J. van der Meulen & B. Wernaart (eds.), *Applied Food Science* (Wageningen, Wageningen Academic Publishers, forthcoming); S. Henson & J. Caswell, "Food safety regulation: an overview of contemporary issues" (1999) 24(6) Food Policy 589, 589–603; M. J. Nauta, R. Andersen, K. Pilegaard, S. M. Pires, G. Ravn-Haren, I, Tetens & M. Poulsen, "Meeting the Challenges in the Development of Risk-Benefit Assessment of Foods" (2018) 76 Trends in Food Science & Technology 90, 90–100.

33 Henson & Caswell, *supra* note 32; A. H. Meyer, "Risk Analysis in Accordance with Article 6, Regulation (EC) No. 178/2002" (2006) 3 European Food and Feed Law Review 146, 146–53.

34 Henson & J. Caswell, *supra* note 32.

B. Risk Assessment in EU Food Law

The scientific process of analyzing whether something could present a risk is based on four steps (Article 3(11) GFL): hazard identification, hazard characterization, exposure assessment, and risk characterization. Whereas a hazard (Article 3(14)) is purely the *potential* of an agent, such as a food or food ingredient, to cause an adverse health effect following consumption, a risk is in Article 3(9) defined as the probability of such an adverse health effect occurring, as well as the severity of this effect. Hazard identification concerns the process to identify potential biological or chemical hazards that can be present in foods; the characterization of hazards entails the specifications of the effects that these hazards could result in. By means of exposure assessment, the amount of hazard present in foods and how much these foods are consumed by specific groups of people will be identified. In the fourth stage of risk assessment (risk characterization), a conclusion on the risk is drawn to conclude whether there could be a safety concern for the general population or specific groups. These four stages of risk assessment were first published in 1983 by the USA's National Research Council (NRC) as a systematic procedure to analyze environmental risks of chemicals and to allow for weighting different policy options to address identified risks.[35] From the publishing of the now well-known Red Book of the NRC, risk assessment and risk management have been put in practice to deal with a range of different exposures, such as to chemical substances, medicinal products, and foods.

In EU food law, the tasks of risk assessment and risk management are functionally separated: Article 6(2)[1] describes that risk assessment must be based on "available scientific evidence and undertaken in an independent, objective and transparent manner." Risk assessment was already described in the White Paper on Food Safety to encompass scientific advice and information analysis, which should be based on accurate and up-to-date scientific evidence. This same White Paper suggested that risk assessment and risk management should be functionally separated, for which the to-be-established European Food Authority would be essential in providing scientific advice as risk assessor.

C. Risk Management in EU Food Law

The roles of risk assessor and risk manager are explicitly separated in EU food law. Based on the submitted scientific evidence with its uncertainty and variability, EFSA's assessment proposes a range of policy measures with differing levels of scientific support. In political risk management decisions, these findings are combined with legitimate other concerns to decide upon a policy measure,

35 de Boer, *supra* note 32; National Research Council (US). (1983). *Risk Assessment in the Federal Government: Managing the Process*. (Washington, DC, National Academies Press (US) 1983); Zwietering, *supra* note 4.

which includes, *inter alia*, public health considerations.[36] As Article 3 of the GFL lays down, weighing the policy alternatives (conducted in consultation with interested parties) should allow for the selection of appropriate prevention and/or control options.[37] For this broad range of tasks (from prevention to control measures), a wide array of decisions are available: from commissioning research projects or recommendations, to informing the general public, and of course to legally binding measures such as administrative decisions.[38]

The risk management role is fulfilled by the different bodies that develop European policies and by those bodies that make decisions upon prevention and control of risks within the food system: the European Commission, the European Parliament, and individual Member States. The European Commission is the sole body that is able to take the initiative for making EU law (known as the full legislative initiative), as defined in Article 17(2) of the Treaty on European Union (TEU).[39] Since the European Parliament and the Council need to adopt the laws that are drawn up by the Commission in the ordinary legislative procedure (Article 294 of the Treaty on the Functioning of the European Union [TFEU]),[40] these institutions can also be considered risk managers. With European Union law being part of the legal systems of the Member States that these Member States enforce within their own jurisdictions, the Member States can also function as risk managers in EU food law.

The roles of the risk management bodies involved in decision-making processes in the European Union thus result from the fact that their roles and responsibilities are laid down in the European Treaties. Although the description and especially the separation of tasks within the risk analysis procedure becomes very clear from the GFL, the European bodies involved in risk management are almost not touched upon. Only Article 22(8) and Article 40(1) of the GFL specify the organizations involved in risk analysis: Article 22(8) requires the different organizations (EFSA, the Commission, and the Member States) to cooperate to ensure that risk assessment, risk management, and risk communication functions are well connected; from Article 40(1), it becomes clear that EFSA is able to provide communications related to its mission, while it is defined as the Commission's role to communicate its risk management decisions. Article 17(2) touches upon the responsibility of the Member States to enforce food law throughout the food chain.

36 Meyer, *supra* note 33.

37 Evan Kleef, L. J. Frewer, G. M. Chryssochoidis, J. R. Houghton, S. Korzen-Bohr, T. Krystallis, J. Lassen, U. Pfenning & G. Rowe, "Perceptions of Food Risk Management Among Key Stakeholders: Results from a Cross-European Study" (2006) 47(1) Appetite 46, 46–63.

38 Meyer, *supra* note 33.

39 Treaty on European Union. *Consolidated version 1 March 2020.*

40 Treaty on the Functioning of the European Union. *Consolidated version 1 March 2020.*

IV. EFSA as Risk Assessor

As highlighted previously, the GFL emphasizes the need for independent and objective scientific advice in decision-making processes related to foods. Additionally, the GFL is the founding regulation of EFSA (Article 1). Article 22 describes that the mission of EFSA is to provide scientific advice and scientific and technical support for all European legislation and policies that affect food and feed safety. For that purpose, they are required (Article 22(4)) to collect and analyze data. Whereas the first few elements within this mission statement focus on the contribution of EFSA to a high level of (consumer) health protection, Article 22(5) also details that advice and support regarding human nutrition, when related to European legislation, is part of this mission.

As described in Article 23, the tasks of EFSA all relate to this mission. These tasks range from providing Community institutions and Member States with the best possible scientific opinions when this is laid down in legislation or upon request to commissioning scientific studies that are related to its mission. However, by defining in Article 23(l) that any other task assigned to EFSA by the Commission that can be placed within its mission could become part of EFSA's work, the potential for the Authority to provide advice related to food issues is highly broadened.

Article 24 describes the different bodies within the Authority, which include a scientific committee and scientific panels ((Article 24(d)). As described in Article 28(4), these scientific panels are composed of independent scientific experts. Currently, ten permanent scientific panels with independent experts work on a broad range of topics and issues of food and feed safety. Upon request of EFSA, the number and the names of the panels can be adjusted. This is mainly seen to happen when the three-year mandates of the involved scientific experts end. Of the ten panels, one is mainly focused on nutrition in general, the panel currently known as the Panel on Nutrition, Novel Foods and Food Allergens (Article 28(4)(e)), often abbreviated as the NDA Panel. Scientists in this panel bring a range of expertise to the table and, for example, study (infant) nutrition, food allergy, epidemiology, food technology, and toxicology. The NDA Panel is tasked with providing advice related to different aspects of human nutrition, including (1) the tolerable upper intake levels for nutrients (maximum intake levels), (2) safety of novel foods, (3) food allergens, (4) dietetic products (products that currently fall within the category of foods for specific groups),[41] (5) population reference intakes for nutrients, and (6) nutrition and health claims on foods.[42] Together with the Scientific Committee of EFSA, the panels are responsible for issuing scientific advice within their competence (Article 28(1)). The ten chairs of the scientific panels, together

41 Regulation (EU) No 609/2013 of the European Parliament and of the Council of 12 June 2013 on food intended for infants and young children, food for special medical purposes, and total diet replacement for weight control. OJ L 181, p. 35–56. *Consolidated version 28 April 2021.*

42 A. Flynn & J. Kleiner, "Scientific Advice on Human Nutrition" (2012) 10(1)0 EFSA Journal s1009.

with six independent scientific experts, form this Scientific Committee (Article 28(3)). This Committee is tasked (Article 28(2)) with ensuring consistency of the procedures to issue such advice and to harmonize working methods, next to issuing advice upon "multisectoral" or cross-sectional issues.

The scientific advice that EFSA is tasked to provide for the decision-making process related to EU food law is published in so-called scientific opinions (Article 29). A scientific opinion can be developed at the request of the Commission, the European Parliament, or Member States, and EFSA can be tasked to issue such opinions under specific regulatory procedures. It is also possible for EFSA to issue scientific opinions on its own initiative, as long as it deals with aspects within the mission of the Authority. The GFL, in describing the aim of EFSA together with specific elements related to its operations and functions, strictly limits the competence of the Authority to a scientific role and thereby excludes any decision-making powers being attributed to EFSA.[43]

A. EFSA's Activities

Within the relatively short period of time that the EFSA has existed, the Authority has become a well-recognized institute for scientific advice related to food and food safety issues.[44] EFSA publishes all its scientific outputs, which include scientific opinions as well as various other publications to support their work. This includes (1) other scientific outputs of EFSA, either statements of the Scientific Committee or scientific panels (containing fewer details then opinions) or guidance documents of the Scientific Committee or scientific panels (to explain the principles behind the approaches of EFSA); (2) other scientific outputs which include the results of a peer review process on scientific evidence related to pesticides; and (3) supporting publications that are either describing technical processes (so-called Technical Reports), External Scientific Reports related to risk assessment and its methodologies, or Event Reports.[45]

All the scientific output of EFSA can be found in the *EFSA Journal*, in which various supporting publications are also published. On December 12, 2021, a total of 8,659 publications were published within the *EFSA Journal*, all related to the following 15 topics: animal feed, animal health and welfare, biological hazards, chemical contaminants, contaminants in feed, cross-cutting science, data, emerging risks, feed additives, food ingredients and packaging, genetically modified organisms (GMOs), methodology, nutrition, pesticides, and plant health (available via www.efsa.europa.eu/en/publications). With only

43 Silano, *supra* note 4.

44 V. Ludden, E. Godfrey, A. Kobilsky, F. Hahn & L. Jansen, *External Evaluation of EFSA 2011–2016 Final Report* (Parma, European Food Safety Authority (EFSA) 2018); M. Silano & V. Silano, *Ensuring Food Safety in the European Union* (Boca Raton, CRC Press 2021).

45 European Food Safety Authority, *Definitions of EFSA Scientific Outputs and Supporting Publications* (2010), *available at*, https://www.efsa.europa.eu/en/efsajournal/scdocdefinitions.

five publications, contaminants in feed is the issue that was published upon the least in 2021. Pesticides (with 2,186 publications), feed additives (1,195 publications), food ingredients and packaging (1,156 publications), and nutrition (1,105 publications) are the four subjects upon which the most publications were issued by the panels and the Scientific Committee. Selecting the term "health claim" in the publications related to nutrition results in a total of 1,006 publications (91%).

All questions asked of the EFSA by the different EU institutions (which includes chairs of panels, EFSA itself, the European Parliament, the European Commission, or Member States) are listed in the portal OpenEFSA. The portal can be accessed via open.efsa.europa.eu and is described as "the single public interface for all information related to EFSA's scientific work." On December 12, 2021, a total of 6,735 questions were listed in the portal as open to be answered. Before January 21, 2021, all questions directed to EFSA were listed in the Register of Questions. A total of 20,035 questions were listed as finalized by January 21, 2021, which contained 5,909 questions for the Nutrition Unit. Interestingly, of these almost 6,000 questions, 1,531 were related to health (keyword search "health"), while "novel" as keyword merely resulted in 205 hits; "safe" showed 150 questions (of which many are also related to novel foods), and "tox*" as search term (for toxicity-related questions) found 28 questions. "Aller*", as a keyword for allergy-related matters, resulted in a total of 25 finished (or withdrawn) questions by January 2021. Even though this explorative search through the former Register of Questions merely addressed questions in English that are considered finalized, these findings do highlight that a large amount of the workload of the NDA Panel so far has been dealing with health claims (almost 26% of the completed questions). EFSA's Annual Activity Report of 2020 also emphasizes the high interest of the public in the nutrition work of EFSA, specifically health claims.[46] This workload, especially with the increasing complexity of assessments, cannot be underestimated.[47]

V. EFSA's Role in Scientific Assessment

A. The Functional Separation of Risk Assessment and Risk Management

The roles of risk management and risk assessment are described as functionally separated by the founding of EFSA by the GFL in EU food policies and decisions related to food, food safety, and the food chain.[48] This strict separation

46 J. Husu-Kallio, *EFSA Consolidated Annual Activity Report 2020* (Luxembourg, Publications Office of the European Union 2021).

47 Flynn & Kleiner, *supra* note 42.

48 S. Gabbi, "The Interaction between Risk Assessors and Risk Managers" (2007) 2(3) European Food and Feed Law Review, 126, 126–35.

should ensure that the scientific advice is completely independent and is purely an objective, transparent assessment of scientific evidence related to the question that needs to be answered. The functional separation of the assessment from the management decision has, however, been debated in literature: the practical reality of the risk analysis procedure requires a certain amount of interaction between risk assessors and risk managers, and the separation is therefore not always clear cut.[49] The influence of the risk manager on the work of EFSA as assessor is highly relevant, already shown by the risk manager providing the mandate to EFSA and thereby the framing or terms of reference within which the Authority needs to operate.[50] The effect of risk assessment on risk management decisions also cannot be underestimated: although scientific opinions issued by EFSA are not binding for the European Commission, motivations have to be provided when the EFSA opinion is not complied with.[51] The importance attributed to knowledge underlying EU food policy enlarges the dependence on EFSA's scientific advice.[52] The separation of tasks within the GFL, however, does give rise to various effects that aid in unraveling assessment and management, such as ensuring that individuals involved in risk assessment are not engaged in risk management.[53] A transparent dialogue to ensure understanding of, on the one hand, the risk manager's questions asked to the assessor and, on the other hand, the assessor's advice provided to the manager becomes even more essential for useful risk analysis.[54] To what extent risk assessment and risk management are still intertwined in spite of this legal functional separation laid down in the GFL requires further review.

B. The Legal Status of Scientific Opinions

As EFSA is a scientific authority and does not function as risk manager, no legally binding decisions are adopted or published by EFSA, nor does the

49 A. Ely, A. Stirling, M. Dreyer, O. Renn, E. Vos & F. Wendler, "The Need for Change" in Marion Dreyer & O. Renn (eds.), *Food Safety Governance – Integrating Science, Precaution and Public Involvement* (Berlin Heidelberg, Springer-Verlag 2009), at 11–28; J. R. Houghton, G. Rowe, L. J. Frewer, E. Van Kleef, G. Chryssochoidis, O. Kehagia, S. Korzen-Bohrd, J. Lassend, U. P. Fenninge & A. Stradaf, "The Quality of Food Risk Management in Europe: Perspectives and Priorities" (2008) 33(1) Food Policy 13, 13–26; M. Pagano, "The Italian Xylella Case: The Role of EFSA in the EU Decision-making on Risk" (2017) 8(3) European Journal of Risk Regulation 599, 599–605.

50 M. Dreyer, O. Renn, A. Ely, A. Stirling, E. Vos & F. Wendler, (2009). "Summary: Key Features of the General Framework" in M Dreyer & O. Renn (eds.), *Food Safety Governance – Integrating Science, Precaution and Public Involvement* (Berlin Heidelberg, Springer-Verlag 2009), at 159–66; Houghton et al., *supra* note 49; E. Vos & F. Wendler, "Legal and Institutional Aspects of the General Framework" in M Dreyer & O. Renn (eds.), *Food Safety Governance – Integrating Science, Precaution and Public Involvement* (Berlin Heidelberg, Springer-Verlag 2009), at 83–110.

51 Silano, *supra* note 4; Szajkowska, *supra* note 24.

52 Szajkowska, *supra* note 24.

53 Houghton et al., *supra* note 49.

54 Gabbi, *supra* note 48.

Authority have any controlling responsibilities.[55] However, as previously indicated, in cases where the risk manager does not follow the risk assessor's opinion, this needs to be justified by the decision maker. In practice, very little divergence seems to exist between the issued scientific opinion and the subsequent authorization or other legal decision made by the risk manager.[56] As put forward in the previous sections, the current potential entanglement between the risk assessor and risk manager therefore requires careful analysis.

Within the different documents that are issued by EFSA, it is also emphasized that these cannot be considered to have any legal status. This is exemplified by the disclaimer found in the annex of a scientific opinion addressing the assessment of Vitamin E–related health claims by the NDA Panel: "The present opinion does not constitute, and cannot be construed as, an authorization of the marketing of the food/food constituent".[57] In EFSA's general scientific guidance on health claim applications, the section on the legal framework reemphasizes this by detailing that "decisions regarding the authorisation of health claims . . . are taken by risk managers".[58] The GFL in itself does not seem to introduce any possibility for legal review of any opinions issued by EFSA[59]. The opinions of EFSA are considered an intermediate step in a procedure, while only the final decisions can be brought to court. This implies that merely the usage of the scientific assessment by the risk manager, and not the scientific assessment itself, can be contested.[60] EFSA has, however, been brought to the European Court of Justice related to the use of specific documents, regarding the confidentiality of data submitted to the Agency, among others.

C. *Scientific Assessment Versus Risk Assessment*

The work of EFSA is based on the mandates given by the different risk managers and can also originate from their own initiative (often referred to as "self-mandate"). Even though throughout the GFL, the concept of "risk assessment" and the role of "risk assessor" are used to describe the Authority's activities, one of the elements that falls within the mission of EFSA according to Article 22(5) of the GFL is the provision of advice and support on human nutrition–related issues within the European Union. This provides the legal basis to also provide

55 Silano, *supra* note 4.

56 Silano, *supra* note 4.

57 EFSA NDA Panel. "Scientific Opinion on the Substantiation of Health Claims Related to Vitamin E and Protection of DNA, Proteins and Lipids from Oxidative Damage (ID 160, 162, 1947), Maintenance of the Normal Function of the Immune System (ID 161, 163), Maintenance of Norm" (2010) 8(10) EFSA Journal 1816.

58 EFSA NDA Panel, "General Scientific Guidance for Stakeholders on Health Claim Applications (Revision 1)" (2021) 19(3) EFSA Journal 6553.

59 A. Alemanno & S. Mahieu, "The European Food Safety Authority Before European Courts – Some Reflections on the Judicial Review of EFSA Scientific Opinions and Administrative Acts" (2008) 5 European Food and Feed Law Review 320, 320–33.

60 Alemanno & Mahieu, *supra* note 59; Pagano, *supra* note 49.

scientific advice related to health benefits (or efficacy) when mandated to do so within European food laws or upon request of one of the risk management bodies. The interesting difference in terminology of "scientific assessment," as it is referred to by EFSA itself[61] versus the use of "risk assessment" as main term in the GFL can therefore not be explained by the mandate itself, which entails all aspects of scientific assessment related to food.[62]

As risk assessor, EFSA is not tasked with conducting scientific experiments for specific authorization procedures. As laid down in various specific food regulations that require foods,[63] food improvement agents,[64] or health effects of foods[65] to be based on scientific evidence, these safety or efficacy considerations need to be proven by the food business operator who is interested in placing the product on the market or using the claim on a food label.[66] Even though EFSA is involved in research projects, the main role of EFSA and the scientific experts involved in the different panels is therefore based on scientific evidence gathered by such food industrials. This has resulted in the work of EFSA being referred to as "peer review" rather than risk assessment: reviewing whether the scientific evidence is of the highest standard seems a limited interpretation of conducting risk assessment.[67] Whether this role of EFSA as rather young scientific agency will change in the future can be questioned.

D. Assessing Risks or Benefits

In the past, nutrition science and nutritional research were mainly focused on studying the safety of foods and analyzing how undernourishment should be prevented by providing sufficient nutrients in foods.[68] Because of both technological and economic developments, during the last decades, the effects of nutrition in maintaining and improving health gained increasing interest.[69] Risk assessment was already employed to deal with safety risks of, for example,

61 EFSA Scientific Committee et al., *supra* note 9.

62 A.de Boer, *supra* note 4.

63 Novel Food Regulation, *supra* note 7.

64 Regulation (EC) No 1331/2008 of the European Parliament and of the Council of 16 December 2008 establishing a common authorisation procedure for food additives, food enzymes and food flavourings. OJ L 354, p. 1–6. *Consolidated version 27 March 2021.*

65 Regulation 1924/2006, *supra* note 6.

66 de. Boer, *supra* note 7.

67 A.de Boer, *supra* note 4; A. de Boer & A. Bast, "Stakeholders' Perception of the Nutrition and Health Claim Regulation. International Journal of Food Sciences and Nutrition" (2015), 66(3) International Journal of Food Sciences and Nutrition 321, 321–28.

68 L. Afman & M. Müller, "Nutrigenomics: From Molecular Nutrition to Prevention of Disease" (2006) 106(4) Journal of the American Dietetic Association 569, 569–76; de Boer, *supra* note 10; N. A. Georgiou, J. Garssen & R. F. Witkamp, "Pharma-Nutrition Interface: The Gap Is Narrowing" (2011) 651 European Journal of Pharmacology 1, 1–8.

69 B. Bigliardi & F. Galati, "Innovation trends in the food industry: The case of functional foods" (2013) 31(2) Trends in Food Science & Technology 118, 118–29; de Boer, *supra* note 10; Georgiou et al., *supra* note 68.

microbiological contamination, while it is also increasingly used to analyze the two-sided risks (of under- and overconsumption) of essential nutrients.[70] The approaches focus on determining a threshold or maximum level above which the dose of an ingredient or compound would present a risk or a minimum level below which the intake of a nutrient is inadequate.[71] Assessing benefits of nutrients is concerned with the range beyond which there is a risk, that is, within the range between inadequate and excessive intake.[72]

The benefit assessment of nutrition under EU food law as employed within the Nutrition and Health Claim Regulation has, however, taken a slightly different approach: subsequent to the identification and characterization of the ingredient, the effect needs to be characterized, and the benefit of this effect for human health will be analyzed. The third step in this analysis is to identify the cause-and-effect relationship between consuming the ingredient (identified in step 1) and the beneficial health effect (characterized in step 2).[73] This difference illustrates that, even though in risk assessment of single nutrients for, among others, dietary reference values, a "window of benefit" is identified, and a dose-effect relationship is essential,[74] while for the analysis of benefits of nutrients under the Nutrition and Health Claim Regulation, a cut-off point is identified above which the health effect is considered sufficiently characterized.[75] While the scientific basis of this distinction should be investigated, and methods to assess benefits and safety of foods need further clarification, the combination of these different assessment approaches into the single term "scientific assessment" also requires reflection.

There are two main considerations in this reflection. First, the type of data used in assessing whether a component could affect the human population (either positively or negatively) should be considered. The data requirements for both safety and efficacy assessments differ from each other: whereas safety assessments are mainly conducted with *in vitro* and animal studies, for efficacy assessments, it is required to study the effects of compounds in human trials.[76] As summarized by Nauta et al., already within the type of assessments, there are differences when it comes to scientific evidence requirements: for health

70 Nauta et al., *supra* note 32.

71 Nauta et al., *supra* note 32.

72 Nauta et al., *supra* note 32.

73 A. de Boer, E. Vos & A. Bast, "Implementation of the Nutrition and Health Claim Regulation – The Case of Antioxidants" (2014) 68(3) Regulatory Toxicology and Pharmacology, 475, 475–87; G. M. K. Lenssen, A. Bast & A. de Boer, "Clarifying the Health Claim Assessment Procedure of EFSA Will Benefit Functional Food Innovation" (2018) 47 Journal of Functional Foods 386, 386–96.

74 Nauta et al., *supra* note 32.

75 de Boer et al., *supra* note 73, 375–487.

76 Lenssen et al., *supra* note 73; I. Pravst, A. Kušar, K. Žmitek, K. Miklavec, Ž. Lavriša, L. Lähteenmäki, V. Kulikovskaja, R. N. Malcolm, Charo Hodgkins, Monique M. Raats & REDICLAIM Consortium, "Recommendations for Successful Substantiation of New Health Claims in the European Union" (2018) 71 Trends in Food Science and Technology 259, 259–63.

claims, a positive physiological effect should be clearly established with sufficient well-established data, while dietary guidelines are based on probable associations between intake and potential benefits.[77]

Second, the methodology used to conduct the assessment itself is of importance. Is it necessary to establish one single methodology for all three types of assessments (risk assessment, benefit/efficacy assessments, and risk-benefit assessments)? Currently, risk-benefit assessments are mainly conducted for those substances that are known as essential food components to maintain health, while overconsumption could result in toxic health effects. The 2010 Guidance on human health risk-benefit assessment of foods by EFSA advises mirroring the risk assessment procedures that are already used [(1) hazard identification, (2) hazard characterization, (3) exposure assessment, (4) risk characterization] with the four following steps: (1) positive health effect identification, (2) positive health effect characterization (dose-response assessment), (3) exposure assessment, and (4) benefit characterization.[78] The initial assessment in this combined procedure should then identify whether the health risks far outweigh the health benefits or vice versa, which should be followed by a more refined assessment for quantitative estimates of the risk and benefits and finally result in a single "net health impact value," using metrics such as disability-adjusted life years (DALYs) an quality-adjusted life years.[79] Even though in both risks and benefits, exposure to the compounds will be key, it is questionable whether this mirroring methodology is the most accurate way of identifying an optimum or optimal range of intake of substances. The rapid developments in risk-benefit assessments are expected to address important underlying questions, including imbalances for scientific evidence requirements, the use of quantitative measures (such as DALYs), and the exact scope of the assessments.[80] Not only will this young scientific field of risk-benefit assessments benefit from these findings, but also the pure risk assessment and benefit assessment that are conducted separately will be able to build upon these findings.

It is questionable whether all three types of assessment should be conducted in the exact same way, and it may be very reasonable for them to differ in the type of data requested for assessing risks or benefits of foods and food ingredients. However, a shared overall methodology as approach to these assessments is expected to benefit all involved parties: one basic method in which the submitted data is systematically gathered, critically reviewed by the applicant, and subsequently assessed by experts who follow a transparent, step-by-step procedure will further benefit the quality and efficiency of the procedure.[81]

77 Nauta et al., *supra* note 32.

78 EFSA Scientific Committee, "Guidance on human health risk-benefit assessment of foods" (2010). 8:7 EFSA Journal, 1673.

79 EFSA Scientific Committee, *supra* note 78.

80 Nauta et al., *supra* note 32.

81 A.de Boer, *supra* note 4.

VI. Concluding Remarks and Future Considerations

By analyzing the legal basis of the work conducted by the EFSA, this chapter aims to build on existing literature that reviews the tasks, activities, and even legitimacy of EFSA[82] and reflect on essential issues that seemingly result from these practices. First, the analysis presented in this chapter clarifies that the legal basis for conducting assessments related to risks and beneficial effects of food (ingredients) is clearly put forward in the GFL. Still, the reasons to consistently use the term "risk assessment" in legislation versus "scientific assessment" in EFSA's corporate documents still need to be unraveled. Interestingly, a large amount of the work conducted by EFSA is shown to be related to the assessment of health claims, which is only one of the areas of regulated products within which EFSA is functioning as risk assessor. And, more importantly, "risk assessment" may be a debatable term when the main purpose of assessment is actually an *efficacy* assessment. This is not merely the case for the work that EFSA's NDA Panel is conducting for health claims but is, for example, also seen in assessing the efficacy of feed additives under Regulation 1831/2003.[83]

This analysis also highlights the need to further review the term "assessment" for the issued opinions under specific sectoral food legislation: it refers to "risk assessment," "benefit/efficacy assessment," and even to "risk-benefit assessment," especially since the procedure itself is focused only on reviewing submitted scientific evidence rather than presenting a systematic approach to gather scientific evidence. This chapter has identified various questions and considerations that need to be addressed before a shared approach may be developed for the different types of assessments. This includes, among others, questions as to what type of data is required for a complete assessment. Further research into already conducted scientific assessments, as published by EFSA, can be seen as an important next step to advance this debate. Whereas this chapter has further unraveled the legal basis of EFSA's work and activities as laid down in European food law, future research is necessary to advance the debate regarding both the terminology used for the different types of assessment and to foster optimizing the processes to conduct these assessments.

82 Including, but not limited to: Alemanno & Mahieu, *supra* note 59; S. Chatzopoulou, "Unpacking the Mechanisms of the EU 'Throughput' Governance Legitimacy: The Case of EFSA" (2015) 16(2) European Politics and Society 159, 159–77; H. Deluyker,. "Is Scientific Assessment a Scientific Discipline?" (2017) 15(11) EFSA Journal e15111; Silano, *supra* note 4.

83 Regulation (EC) No 1831/2003 of the European Parliament and of the Council of 22 September 2003 on additives for use in animal nutrition. OJ L 228, p. 29–43. *Consolidated version 27 March 2021.*

4 Regulating Gene Technology in Food

The American Approach and Practice

Neal D. Fortin

I. Introduction

A common perception is that the United States has lax regulation of gene technology. If one examines the *direct* regulation of gene technology in the United States, it seems as if gene technology is relatively unregulated. On the other hand, if one examines the regulation of the finished products of gene technology, it is clear that the products are extensively regulated.

This dichotomy reflects how United States food law is organized around *product* characteristics rather than *process* characteristics. To be clear, processes are regulated, but this is largely as an effective means to regulate product characteristics. In addition, U.S. laws regulate products based on their specific intended uses. For instance, a pharmaceutical is regulated differently than a food, which is regulated differently than an industrial chemical.

There is strength in this approach. The main strength of this regulation by characteristic and use is that it allows science-focused attention on potential risk. Agencies and their scientists in respective areas of expertise are assigned to evaluate particular aspects of gene technology. For example, when protectant properties are introduced into a plant, the U.S. Environmental Protection Agency (EPA), the federal agency with the expertise and responsibility for regulating pesticides, is assigned to review the pesticidal properties of the new plant variety.

However, there is also weakness in this approach. The main weakness of regulation by characteristic is that this approach may be obtuse to the public and fail to generate public confidence. There are three main federal agencies involved in the oversight of biotechnology, the U.S. Department of Agriculture (USDA), the Food and Drug Administration (FDA), and the Environmental Protection Agency. However, seven offices or centers within those three agencies handle different aspects of oversight. Moreover, rather than a single, simple unitary statute on the regulation of biotechnology related to food, there are nine different statutes. See Table 4.2. Although there are historical and sound organizational reasons for this dispersed authority and responsibility, the piecemeal or fragmented structure can give an appearance to the public of being a disorganized and haphazard approach. In addition, because the U.S. regulatory

DOI: 10.4324/9781003271918-5

framework for biotechnology products relies on several different laws, the nomenclature in these statutes for various actions is sometimes inconsistent, but this inconsistency in terms does not indicate that the reviews conducted by the different regulatory agencies are less rigorous.

Tables 4.1 and 4.2 illustrate the complex structure of the U.S. regulation of gene technology for food production. For instance, the FDA Center for Food Safety and Applied Nutrition (CFSAN) has oversight of the safety of foods derived via gene technology in plants or cultured cells, but the FDA Center for Veterinary Medicine (CVM) has responsibility for the oversight of the safety of food derived from gene technology in animals, along with the USDA Food Safety Inspection Service (FSIS) when the animal is one of the amenable species under the three inspection acts enforced by FSIS. The USDA Animal and Plant Health Inspection Service (APHIS) also becomes involved in oversight and approval when an animal- or plant-derived product from gene technology might pose a plant pest risk. The EPA Office of Pesticide Programs (OPP) has responsibility for the regulation of pesticide substances and related genetic material for human and environmental safety, including the safety of dietary exposure to pesticide residues in human and animal food. See Table 4.1.

Each agency uses already existing statutory authorities to ensure the safety of biotechnology products. These statutes define the boundaries and the scope of

Table 4.1 Oversight of gene technology in food products by EPA, FDA, and USDA[1]

Source of Genetically Engineered Organism or Culture		
Plant	*Animal*	*Microbe or Cultured Cell*
USDA, APHIS—If plant poses a plant pest risk FDA, CFSAN EPA, OPP—If a plant-incorporated protectant is produced by a plant, EPA, OPP regulate the pesticide substance and related genetic material for human and environmental safety, including the safety of dietary exposure to pesticide residues in human and animal food	FDA, CVM USDA, APHIS—If an animal poses a plant pest risk USDA, APHIS, VS—If an animal poses a health risk to livestock FDA, CFSAN USDA, FSIS	FDA, CFSAN USDA, FSIS

1 Adapted from FDA, USDA, EPA, "Modernizing the Regulatory System for Biotechnology Products: Final Version of the 2017 Update to the Coordinated Framework for the Regulation of Biotechnology", Jan. 4, 2017, *available at*, https://usbiotechnologyregulation.mrp.usda.gov/biotechnologygov/home/modernizing/modernizing_biotechnology_framework.

oversight granted to each regulatory agency. However, the agencies endeavor to follow a risk-based approach to regulation, to the extent permitted under their statutory authority, and to operate in an integrated and coordinated fashion with each other.

The primary food safety statute is the Federal Food, Drug, and Cosmetic Act (FD&C Act). The statute mandates that the FDA ensure that all human food and animal feed is safe and that the EPA ensure that no harm will result from aggregate exposure to any pesticide residue, including all anticipated dietary exposures and all other exposures for which there is reliable information. The EPA also bears responsibility under the Federal Insecticide, Fungicide, and Rodenticide Act (FIFRA) for preventing and eliminating unreasonable adverse effects on the environment from any pesticidal property resulting from gene technology. For environmental and occupational risks, the EPA compares economic, social, and environmental risks to human health and the environment and benefits associated with pesticide use. However, for dietary or human health effects, the sole standard is the safety of all combined exposures to the pesticide and related compounds.

The USDA under the Animal Health Protection Act (AHPA) protects livestock from animal pest and disease risks, and under the Plant Protection Act (PPA), it protects agricultural plants and agriculturally important natural resources from damage caused by organisms that pose plant pest or noxious weed risks. The USDA under the Federal Meat Inspection Act (FMIA), the Poultry Products Inspection Act (PPIA), and the Egg Products Inspection Act (EPIA) ensures that meat, poultry, and egg products are safe and wholesome. The National Environmental Policy Act (NEPA) requires that all federal agencies ensure that they give proper consideration to the environment before any major federal action, including approval of a product of biotechnology.

Table 4.2 Main statutes in food regulation of gene technology food products[2]

Agency	*Statute*	*Regulatory Goal*
EPA	Federal Insecticide, Fungicide, and Rodenticide Act (FIFRA)	Prevent and eliminate unreasonable adverse effects on the environment. • For environmental and occupational risks, this involves comparing economic, social, and environmental risks to human health and the environment and benefits associated with the pesticide use. • For dietary or residential human health effects, the sole standard is the "safety" of all the combined exposures to the pesticide and related compounds.

2 Ibid.

EPA	Federal Food, Drug, and Cosmetic (FD&C) Act	Ensure that no harm will result from aggregate exposure to the pesticide residue, including all anticipated dietary exposures and all other exposures for which there is reliable information.
EPA	Toxic Substance Control Act (TSCA)	Prevent the manufacture, processing, distribution in commerce, use, or disposal of chemical substances, or any combination of such activities with such substances, from presenting an unreasonable risk of injury to health or the environment, including an unreasonable risk to a potentially exposed or susceptible population, without consideration of costs or other non-risk factors.
FDA	Federal Food, Drug, and Cosmetic (FD&C) Act	Ensure human and animal food is safe, sanitary, and properly labeled.
USDA	Animal Health Protection Act (AHPA)	Protect livestock from animal pest and disease risks.
USDA	Plant Protection Act (PPA)	Protect agricultural plants and agriculturally important natural resources from damage caused by organisms that pose plant pest or noxious weed risks.
USDA	Federal Meat Inspection Act (FMIA)	Ensure that the United States' commercial supply of meat, poultry, and egg products is safe, wholesome, and correctly labeled.
USDA	Poultry Products Inspection Act (PPIA)	
USDA	Egg Products Inspection Act (EPIA)	
EPA FDA USDA	National Environmental Policy Act (NEPA)	Requires federal agencies ensure they give proper consideration to the environment before any major federal action, including approval of a GMO.

II. Regulating Food Safety Risks

A. FDA Oversight

The FDA regulates the safety of food and animal feed through the general safety requirements of the Food, Drug, and Cosmetic Act. This authority derives largely from two provisions of the act: the section 402(a)(1) adulteration standard and the section 409 food additive requirements. In addition, animals altered by gene technology are regulated under the new animal drug provisions of the FD&C Act.

1. Adulteration

Under section 402(a)(1) of the FD&C Act, a food that bears or contains any added poisonous or deleterious substance that may render it injurious to health is deemed adulterated.[3] "Added" under this section includes additions by gene technology.

3 21 U.S.C. § 342(a)(1).

The sale of such adulterated food is a violation of the FD&C Act, and under the authority of the Act, FDA has the power to remove the food from commerce.

2. *Food Additive Requirements*

The FD&C Act section 409 food additives provisions require an FDA premarket approval of any food additive, which includes products of gene technology.[4] An unapproved food additive is automatically deemed food unsafe, and any food containing an unapproved food additive is adulterated under section 402(a)(2)(C) of the FD&C Act. The proponent of a new food additive must prove with a reasonable certainty that the substance is not harmful under the conditions of intended use.[5] When the FDA approves a new additive use, it is published in the *Federal Register*. The public has a comment period for submission of objections and requests for a hearing.[6]

The procedure of obtaining pre-market approval requires the submission of safety data, including animal studies, toxicological studies, and other such evidence of safety by the proponent of the additive. FDA reviews the submissions and makes a determination regarding the safety of the additives under the conditions of their intended use. Briefly stated, the process for approval of a food additive begins with the submission of a food additive petition that includes at a minimum:

- The identity and composition of the additive
- The proposed use in food
- The amount to be added to food
- Data establishing the intended effect
- Quantitative detection methods in food
- Full reports of all safety studies (e.g., toxicology, allergenicity, nutrition)
- Proposed tolerances (if needed)
- Environmental review information

Additive approvals issued are generic; therefore, anyone in compliance with the conditions of use laid out in the regulation may use the additive in food. Approvals are safety based only. There is no balancing of risks versus benefits.

However, the law specifically excludes from food additive review pesticide residues and new animal drug residues because their safety is reviewed under different requirements of the FD&C Act.[7] Also excluded from food additive approval are uses of substances that are generally recognized as safe (GRAS) among experts qualified by scientific training and experience to evaluate the

4 21 U.S.C. § 348.
5 21 C.F.R. §§ 170.3(i) and 570.3(i).
6 21 C.F.R. § 171.110.
7 21 U.S.C. § 321(s).

safety.[8] The safety standard for both food additive and GRAS substance uses is a reasonable certainty that the substance is not harmful under the conditions of intended use.[9] Although the safety standard is the same, the GRAS standard requires publicly available proof that is accepted by most scientific experts qualified to evaluate the safety.

Because GRAS determination is based on the consensus of experts in the field rather than FDA approval or acceptance, no submission to FDA is required for GRAS use. Therefore, a company may self-determine GRAS status without notifying the FDA. This intentional loophole in the law creates a lack of certainty and oversight.

Consequently, FDA established a voluntary premarket consultation process to encourage the use of the FDA-premarket review and ensure that any safety issues associated with a food derived from gene technology are resolved.[10] This includes the potential for allergenicity, toxicity, and anti-nutrient effects. It also includes a review of whether a substance in the food requires approval via a food additive petition. The FDA consultation also looks at whether any important characteristics of a food changed in a way that is relevant to food safety or nutrition. Although FDA regulates based on the characteristics of the food rather than the breeding method, during the consultation, the FDA examines the sources, identities, and functions of introduced genetic material because this informs the expected effect on the composition or characteristics of the food.

The FDA posts the results of completed consultations on its website. Although the FDA consultation is voluntary, it appears that all genetically engineered food crops intended for marketing have been submitted to FDA for a consultation or other relevant premarket process prior to marketing. Completion of the voluntary consultation provides a company with an assurance that their product is in compliance with the law, and a satisfactory FDA consultation is important for marketing. Moreover, if a company were to skip the FDA consultation and be wrong about the safety or the need for food additive, color additive, or pesticide residue approval, enforcement action could ensue, including warning letters, product recalls, seizures, injunctions, and criminal prosecution.

3. Genetically Altered Animals

The definition of "drug" under FD&C Act section 201(g)(1)(C) includes "articles (other than food) intended to affect the structure or any function of the

8 Ibid.

9 21 C.F.R. §§ 170.3(i) and 570.3(i).

10 *See* FDA, Consultation Procedures under FDA's 1992 Statement of Policy for Foods Derived from New Plant Varieties (June 1996; Revised Oct. 1997), *available at* www.fda.gov/food/ingredients-additives-gras-packaging-guidance-documents-regulatory-information/consultation-procedures-under-fdas-1992-statement-policy-foods-derived-new-plant-varieties (last accessed Oct. 29, 2020).

body of man or other animals."[11] The use of technology to alter the genetic material of an animal is a use that is intended to affect the animal's structure or function, which, therefore, meets the Act's definition of drug. The FD&C Act generally makes it unlawful to introduce new animal drugs into commerce without FDA's approval.[12]

It is the FDA Center for Veterinary Medicine that is responsible for evaluating the safety and effectiveness of any genetic engineering of an animal. CVM evaluates both the safety of any food derived from the genetically engineered animal as well as the safety of the genetic engineering to the target animal. In addition, CVM evaluates whether the claims submitted by the applicant are valid.[13]

B. EPA Oversight

Under the Federal Insecticide, Fungicide, and Rodenticide Act, the EPA regulates the labeling, sale, distribution, and use of all pesticides, including those produced through gene technology.[14] Under FIFRA, a pesticide may not be sold or distributed unless it is registered by EPA. Thus, "register" is equivalent in meaning to the term "authorize." There are two separate tests to meet before the EPA may register a pesticide for use. EPA may register a pesticide only if (1) it has no unreasonable adverse effect to man or the environment, taking into account the economic, social, and environmental costs and benefits of the use of a pesticide, *and* (2) no human dietary risk results from food residues from the use of a pesticide; specifically, the use of the pesticide cannot be inconsistent with the pesticide residue tolerances established for food under section 408 of the Food, Drug, and Cosmetic Act.[15]

An application to EPA for a pesticide registration requires extensive scientific data and information on the potential effects of a pesticide. The safety of pesticide residues and other substances resulting from the use of a pesticide on a crop or food, which includes any metabolic or other degradation products of the pesticide, must be proven safe under section 408 of the FD&C Act. The act makes it unlawful to enter into interstate commerce any food that has a pesticide residue that has not been registered or for a food to have a pesticide residue for which a tolerance has not been set.[16]

11 21 U.S.C. § 321(g)(1)(C).

12 21 U.S.C. §§ 331(a), 351(a)(5).

13 *See*, FDA, CVM GFI #187 Regulation of Intentionally Altered Genomic DNA in Animals (Jan. 2017), *available at* www.fda.gov/regulatory-information/search-fda-guidance-documents/cvm-gfi-187-regulation-intentionally-altered-genomic-dna-animals (last accessed Oct. 29, 2020).

14 7 U.S.C. § 136a(a).

15 7 U.S.C § 136(bb).

16 EPA use the term "tolerance" for what much of the world refers to as maximum residue limits (MRLs).

The tolerance must be set to ensure "a reasonable certainty that no harm will result from aggregate exposure to residues of the pesticide" in food for humans or animals, including all anticipated dietary exposures and all other exposures for which there is reliable information.[17] EPA in response to a petition or on its own initiative may modify or revoke a tolerance. FIFRA requires that EPA re-evaluate each registered pesticide at least every 15 years to determine whether the pesticide continues to meet the FIFRA standard for registration. However, FDA enforces the tolerances established by EPA for pesticide chemical residues in food and animal feed.

C. USDA FSIS

The USDA Food Safety and Inspection Service is responsible for ensuring the safety of meat, poultry, egg products, and fish of the order Siluriformes. While FDA oversees the safety of substances added to these FSIS-regulated products, including additions via gene technology, the FSIS reviews whether the use of these additions in meat, poultry, egg, and or fish of the order Siluriformes is suitable under FMIA, PPIA, and EPIA. Therefore, FDA informs FSIS of any reviews of the safety of any genetic engineering related to meat, poultry, eggs, or fish of the order Siluriformes when intended to be used for human consumption, as well as the safety of any substances added as a result of the gene technology.[18]

III. Regulating the Environmental Risks

A. National Environmental Policy Act

The National Environmental Policy Act establishes the consistent process by which federal agencies must consider the consequences of their proposed actions on the human environment before a decision.[19] NEPA requires federal agencies to prepare a detailed "environmental impact statement" (EIS) for all major federal actions significantly affecting the quality of the human environment.[20]

Food additive approvals are also subject to the National Environmental Policy Act requirements. Similarly, the potential environmental impacts of genetically engineered animals must be examined before they are approved

17 21 U.S.C. § 346a(b)(2)(A)(ii) *or* 346a(c)(2)(A)(ii).

18 *See* MOU No. 225-00-2000 Amendment 1, Memorandum of Understanding between the U.S. Department of Agriculture Food Safety and Inspection Service and the U.S. Department of Health and Human Services Food and Drug Administration (Mar. 24, 2015), *available at* www.fsis.usda.gov/wps/portal/fsis/topics/regulations/directives/7000-series/MOU-FSIS-FDA (last accessed Oct. 29, 2020).

19 2 U.S.C. § 4321 et seq.

20 42 U.S.C. § 4332(2)(C).

under the NEPA. However, confidential requirements for new drug applications generally prevent FDA from releasing information in a new animal drug application before approval of the new animal drug. To encourage public transparency, FDA has sought permission of the drug sponsor to allow and consider public input in the agency's evaluation of the potential effects on the environment from an investigational use or approval of a genetically engineered animal.

B. EPA

1. Federal Insecticide, Fungicide, and Rodenticide Act

Under FIFRA, the EPA regulates the sale, distribution, and use of all pesticides, including those produced through gene technology.[21] An application to EPA for a pesticide registration requires extensive scientific data and information on the environmental effects of a pesticide. EPA must establish that the pesticide cannot harm non-target organisms, including humans, wildlife, and plants, and cannot harm endangered species. For an applicant to generate data, the EPA may allow field testing through an experimental use permit (EUP). The EUP will require controls be put in place to prevent unreasonable adverse effects on health and the environment. When the pesticide is a genetically engineered microorganism, the applicant must notify EPA before testing. EPA may issue an EUP only when the test will not cause unreasonable adverse effects on the environment.[22] As needed to protect the environment, the EPA may place obligations in connection with the registrations, which may include, among other things, record-keeping requirements and limits on sale, distribution, and use.

2. Toxic Substances Control Act

Under the Toxic Substances Control Act (TSCA), the EPA has oversight authority and responsibility for non-food commercial and industrial applications of microbial gene technology.[23] All "new chemical substances," including microorganisms subjected to gene technology, are under TSCA pre-manufacturing review to prevent the manufacturing, processing, distribution in commerce, use, or disposal from presenting an unreasonable risk of injury to health or the environment, including to a potentially exposed or susceptible population.

21 7 U.S.C. § 136a(a).

22 40 C.F.R. § 172.3.

23 15 U.S.C. § 2601 *et seq.*, as amended by the Frank R. Lautenberg Chemical Safety for the 21st Century Act, P.L. No. 114-182 (June 22, 2016).

C. USDA

The USDA Animal and Plant Health Inspection Service is responsible for protecting agriculture from pests and diseases. The Animal Health Protection Act (AHPA) and the Plant Protection Act (PPA) give USDA the authority and responsibility to regulate products of gene technology that may pose a risk to agricultural plant and animal health. The AHPA gives USDA regulatory oversight over any products of gene technology that are pests to or cause disease in livestock. The PPA gives USDA regulatory oversight over products of gene technology deemed plant pests or noxious weeds.

In addition, the USDA must comply with the provision of NEPA in its decision making. Thus, for example, before authorizing a genetically engineered plant, the USDA must take a hard look at the environmental impact of that decision. The USDA APHIS prepares either an environmental assessment (EA) or the more comprehensive environmental impact statement before making decisions about issuing permits. Draft EAs and EISs are published in the *Federal Register*, and the public has an opportunity to comment, which the agency considers before publishing the final version of the EA or EIS.

IV. Hypothetical Case Study

The following hypothetical case study is designed to illustrate the navigation of a developer of a genetically engineered plant intended for food through research and development to regulatory steps before commercialization. No actual product is represented, but rather a typical pathway for such a product is presented. Although typical, differences in gene technology products and product traits can affect the course of regulation. This example does not comprehensively include all requirements or policies of the relevant agencies.

A. Hypothetical Genetically Engineered Corn With Pesticidal Properties[24]

This hypothetical crop intended for human food and animal feed is genetically engineered with pesticidal activity against certain insects.

1. The Product

Corn (*Zea mays*) is genetically engineered to express a protein with pesticidal activity. The gene encoding the protein is isolated from the bacterium *Bacillus thuringiensis* and controlled by the cauliflower mosaic virus-derived 35S

24 Adapted from FDA, USDA, EPA, *supra* note 1.

promoter. The construct is integrated into a binary vector and introduced into the corn genome using *Agrobacterium*-mediated transformation. Also encoded on the vector and stably incorporated into the corn genome is a gene that enables the selection of transformants during research and development.

2. *Agencies With Oversight*

EPA regulates the pesticidal trait in the plant. FDA regulates the safety of the corn because it will be used for food for humans and animals. USDA regulates the growing of the corn plant engineered with plant pest components.

3. *Developer Responsibilities During Research and Development*

Research and development will be in contained systems (such as the laboratory and greenhouse). Research and development activities in contained systems are outside the regulatory authority of USDA APHIS under the Plant Protection Act. However, if the corn will be imported into the United States or transported across state lines, the developer must obtain an import or interstate shipment authorization from USDA APHIS.

4. *Developer Responsibilities Before Starting Field Trials*

Environmental release triggers USDA APHIS regulatory requirements. Therefore, under the Plant Protection Act, before starting small-scale, non-contained field trials, the developer must obtain an authorization for environmental release from USDA APHIS. If the corn involves genetic engineering from a new species or novel modifications that potentially raise new issues, then USDA APHIS must prepare an appropriate environmental analysis. This will be either an environmental assessment or an environmental impact statement.

Because the corn is intended for food use, at this stage, the developer must either obtain a tolerance for the residues of the pesticide in the food from EPA under the Federal Food, Drug, and Cosmetic Act or destroy any crops with residues of the pesticide. Additionally, the developer must ensure that the corn and any derived products to be used for food for humans or animals are safe and meet all other applicable FDA requirements. The developer should provide relevant scientific and technical information to FDA and begin a voluntary consultation about food safety and other FDA-related regulatory issues that may be associated with food from the corn.

5. *Additional Responsibilities Before Starting Large-Scale Field Trials*

If the field trial cumulative plot size is 10 acres or more, the developer must obtain an experimental use permit from EPA under the Federal Insecticide, Fungicide, and Rodenticide Act. If the developer has not already done so, it must obtain a pesticide tolerance or tolerance exemption from EPA or ensure that all experimental crops with residues of the pesticide are destroyed.

6. *Before Commercialization*

The developer must ensure that all regulatory requirements have been met prior to the commercialization of the corn. The developer must receive either an authorization for importation, interstate movement, or environmental release prior to commercialization. During the review process, USDA APHIS prepares a Plant Pest Risk Assessment and either an EA or an EIS to address the environmental impacts associated with the unconfined release of the corn. The developer must receive an EPA-issued pesticide registration and tolerance for the residues of the pesticide in the food. The developer must also ensure that the corn and any derived products to be used for food are safe and meet all other applicable FDA requirements.

7. *Public Engagement*

The EPA, under its FIFRA and FD&C Act responsibilities, will offer the public opportunities to comment at several points, including public notices at the receipt of an application, prior to preliminary decisions, and prior to final decisions.

FDA posts the results of the completed consultation on its website. If a food additive review is required, a proposed food additive approval will be published in the *Federal Register* for public comment. Comments will be considered and answered when the final food additive rule is published in the *Federal Register.*

The public is given an opportunity to comment to APHIS as it develops the EA or EIS and the Plant Pest Risk Assessment (PPRA). If an EIS is prepared, the public may have as many as three additional opportunities to provide input into the decision-making process.

Part II

Emerging Technologies and their Ramifications for Food Safety Governance

5 The Impacts of Cross-Border E-Commerce Activities on the Enforcement of SPS Measures

The Chink in the Armor?

Kai-Chih Chang[*]

I. Introduction

The world economy mainly consists of small and medium-sized enterprises (SMEs).[1] Although less visible, SMEs are the main thrust of economic development in most developing countries[2] and are responsible for maintaining sustainable growth and export earnings.[3] Nevertheless, due to the scale of their operations, SMEs are vulnerable to trade obstacles that can easily reduce SME competitiveness in the global market. For this reason, only a small portion of SMEs are involved in cross-border business or operate internationally,[4] and international trade remains primarily dominated by large multinational enterprises (MNEs) and transnational corporations (TNCs).[5] Under the impression

* An earlier version of this chapter was presented at the 4th Conference on Food Law& Policy organized by Center for Trans-Pacifi c Partnership and Transnational Trade Laws, School of Law, National Yang Ming Chiao Tung University. The author would like to thank the participants at the conference for very helpful comments.

1 *See* World Trade Organization, *World Trade Report 2016: Levelling the Trading Field for SMEs* (Geneva, World Trade Organization 2016), at 14–20; Viral Pandya, "Comparative Analysis of Development of SMEs in Developed and Developing Countries", *2012 International Conference on Business and Management*, Sept. 6–7, 2012, Phuket, Thailand, *available at* www.researchgate.net/publication/266594413_Comparative_analysis_of_development_of_SMEs_in_developed_and_developing_countries.

2 Musara Mazanai & Olawale Fatoki, "The Effectiveness of Business Development Services Providers (BDS) in Improving Access to Debt Finance by Start-up SMEs in South Africa" (2011) 3(4) International Journal of Economics and Finance 208.

3 Normah M. Aris, *SMEs: Building Blocks for Economic Growth*, at 1–13, National Statistics Conference Department of Statistics, Malaysia, Sept. 4–5, 2006.

4 Arancha González, "Leveraging Trade Facilitation Reforms for Increased SME Competitiveness" in Thilo Rensmann (ed), *Small and Medium-Sized Enterprises in International Economic Law* (Oxford, Oxford University Press 2017), at 38, 39. The United States may be an exception, as 98% of its exporters are SMEs and accounted for 33% of export in value. *See* U.S. Department of Commerce, "National Export Initiative Fact Sheet" (2014), *available at* http://trade.gov/nei/nei-fact-sheet.asp (last accessed Apr. 12, 2019).

5 World Trade Organization, *supra* note 1, at 31–55.

DOI: 10.4324/9781003271918-7

that MNEs and TNCs are the main actors in international trade, international economic law governing the transboundary movement of goods, services, and capital has long focused on the needs of MNEs.[6] The needs of SMEs are largely ignored.[7]

Although the predominant portion of SME operations are geographically limited and rarely extend beyond borders, SMEs are increasingly able to operate beyond their domestic habitat. By becoming part of global value chains (GVCs), suppliers to MNEs, or directly participating in international trade, SMEs have become more visible and active in international trade practices. States have also gradually realized that sustainable development of SMEs would help states achieve economic growth and employment and improve wages and working conditions. A consensus to adopt policies that would encourage the growth of SMEs and facilitate their integration into the value chain has gradually emerged and was eventually reflected in the adoption of the United Nations 2030 Agenda for Sustainable Development.[8] In the G20 Strategy for Global Trade Growth, adopted in 2016 at the Hangzhou Summit, leaders also encouraged states to explore the possibility of facilitating SME participation in global business, in particular through e-commerce.[9]

E-commerce is a product of technology development. In the Organisation for Economic Co-operation and Development (OECD) definition, e-commerce is a business model where all commercial transactions between the supplier and consumer are done through a communications network with wireless devices.[10] Depending on the states' preferences and how the term is applied, elements such as cross-border data flows, information exchange, cybersecurity, and artificial intelligence are also covered under the umbrella of e-commerce.[11] One of the most prominent features of e-commerce is that it reduces the physical presence requirement for business operations. Unlike the traditional perception that production, distribution, marketing, sale, or delivery of goods and services requires the physical presence of a person or in-person contacts, technology developments now allow transactions to be done via electronic means. Except in countries where the internet remains under

6 *See e.g.* Mattias Herdegen, *Principles of International Economic Law* (2nd ed. 2016), at 41–44.

7 Thilo Rensmann, "Introduction" in Thilo Rensmann (ed), *Small and Medium-Sized Enterprises in International Economic Law 1* (Oxford, Oxford University Press 2017), at 1.

8 UN General Assembly, Transforming Our World: The 2030 Agenda for Sustainable Development, UNGA Res. 70/1 (Sept. 25, 2015), UN Doc. A/RES/70/1.

9 G20 Leaders' Communique Hangzhou Summit, Sept. 4–5, 2016, para. 29, *available at* http://g20.org/English/Documents/Current/201607/t20160715_3057_2.html.

10 Organization for Economic Co-Operation and Development, Mobile Commerce, Directorate for Science, Technology and Industry Committee on Consumer Policy, DSTI/CP(2006)7/FINAL (2008), OECD Publishing, *available at* www.oecd.org/sti/38077227.pdf (last accessed Oct. 21, 2017).

11 *See* the provisions under (E-Commerce) of the Comprehensive and Progressive Agreement for Trans-Pacific Partnership (CPTPP) Chapter 14.

intensive surveillance and control, or in places lacking the infrastructure to support internet connection, e-commerce breaks down the territorial and geographical limits for businesses to operate and thus facilitates the free flow of goods and services.

Since e-commerce significantly undercuts the cost for a business to operate beyond the border and expand its operation, it is also considered an effective means to strengthen SMEs' ability to participate in international trade. To better assist SMEs in participating in global business via e-commerce and eventually creating revenues and economic development for the country, trade regulations are currently being reassessed and are under reform at both the multilateral and regional levels. It is hoped that SMEs can achieve greater success and sustain economic developments by operating through e-commerce.

The promotion of SMEs and e-commerce performance are indisputably important, but so is the necessity to protect other equally essential interests. Because SMEs operate on a small scale and through disaggregated means, their distinctive operation features also create regulatory challenges for government authorities. Compared to traditional large bulk importations that are easier to identify and examine, SMEs' disaggregated transport of goods is more difficult to trace and track. SMEs' frequent use of parcel package shipping methods also creates difficulties for customs authorities to enforce sanitary and phytosanitary (SPS) measures. Consequently, it may create challenges for states to protect human, animal, and plant life and health in their territory. As the current normative reform discussion primarily focuses on helping to promote the operation of SMEs and eliminate barriers unfriendly to SMEs, this chapter calls to mitigate or manage the risks and problems associated with the development of SMEs and e-commerce.

In five parts, this chapter discusses how the development of e-commerce and SME operations brings challenges to states' SPS enforcement over imported food products. Taking Taiwan's recent experience in preventing the spread of the African swine fever epidemic as a case study, this chapter highlights the risks associated with the flourishing development of cross-border SME operations and how current border control measures are unequipped to address such threats. Following the introduction section, the second part of this chapter starts by introducing the standard border measures adopted by states, including the customs clearance procedure for goods and parcels. As the theme of this chapter focuses on the customs enforcement of SPS measures, the analysis mainly centers on practices relating to the importation of food and agricultural goods. In the third section, we then turn to discussing the rapid development of SMEs and how e-commerce helps SMEs expand their participation in international trade. Section IV of this chapter explains how the new trade models weaken the effectiveness of the current SPS regulations and enforcement mechanisms. Again, centering on Taiwan's recent experience in preventing the African swine fever epidemic, this section highlights the current border control mechanism's weakness and discusses how the regulatory framework can be better reformed. Section V concludes.

II. Border Measures and Importation Regulations

A. General Importation Procedures

As the supreme governing power of the land, states hold judicial, legislative, and executive jurisdiction over subjects within their territory and can also regulate and decide who and what may enter into their territory and set the conditions of their entrance. The rules governing the flows of goods in and out of a state's territory are usually implemented and enforced by the customs authorities. All goods to be imported into a state must comply with the import requirements and shall be subjected to examination and inspection at the border to ensure their safety.

Although the customs regulations of each country are different, they share similar features. Typically, the importers are required to produce required paperwork, give prior notice, and file and declare the content and value of the goods. Then, the customs officials will determine the amount of the duties owed and inspect the shipment when necessary. Taking the U.S.'s practices as an example, importers must complete the following steps to ensure their shipments arrive legally. First, before the arrival of the goods, importers are required to make arrangements with the Customs and Border Protection at the port of entry where the goods will arrive. Second, once the shipments have arrived, importers shall then declare the entry of goods;[12] file an entry summary, which includes the goods' classification, country of origin, and value and demonstrates that the importer has the right to make entry; and file for release. Finally, after these steps are completed and the estimated duties are paid, the importers may acquire an entry document indicating that all required procedures and requirements have been fulfilled. The goods will then be released for entrance.

Customs and Border Protection (CBP) is given absolute discretion to determine which shipments shall be subjected to inspection. The exact algorithms used to evaluate the shipments' degree of risk remain unknown. Still, some of the known factors include the nature of the goods, the record of the importer and shipper, and the country of origin.[13] The main examination methods used by the CBP include the vehicle and cargo inspection system (VACIS) exam (non-intrusive x-ray inspection, NII), tail gate exam, and intensive exam.[14] In the VACIS exam, the cargo container is placed into a unit and scanned with gamma-ray technology. The VACIS exam can only be conducted at a CBP-approved inspection site since special equipment is required. Compared to the

12 Including if the goods will be entered for consumption, entered for warehouse storage, or transported to and entered at another port of entry.

13 Dimitri Konstantinidis, "Why Me? What Triggers a Customs Inspection?", May 17, 2017, *available at* www.morethanshipping.com/triggers-customs-inspection/.

14 Understanding US Customs Inspections, Australian Int'l Movers Ass'n, July 18, 2018, *available at* www.aima.com.au/understanding-us-customs-inspections/.

other exam methods, VACIS is less invasive and can be performed relatively quickly.

On the other hand, the tail gate exam is usually performed at the port. A CBP officer will break the seal of the container and inspect its contents. If suspicious substances are found, the inspection might further escalate to the highest degree of inspection: the intensive exam. The intensive exam is an exam performed by an anti-terrorism contraband enforcement examination team (A-TCET). The A-TCET exam is used less frequently and is usually performed after the cargo fails to pass the VACIS or tail gate exam. When an intensive exam is required, the shipment will be moved to a customs examination station (CES) and emptied for CBP officers to inspect its content.

Regardless of being subjected to the VACIS, tail gate, or A-TCET exams, all inspection costs and incurred fees shall be borne by the owner of the goods (the shipper). Although being inspected by the CBP may be costly and frustrating to those exporting to the U.S., checks and inspections occur less frequently than expected. In general, only 3–5% of the cargo entering the U.S. is selected for examination. Although importers are not required to hire a customs broker to clear the goods, customs brokers are helpful and may prevent importers from making costly mistakes.

Aside from the standard customs clearance and inspection procedures, additional compliance requirements may be added to particular commodities such as food, pharmaceutical products, firearms, and other goods subject to the regulation of other federal agencies. Working together with the CBP, other agencies help to flag and signal shipments that ought to be subjected to a higher degree of inspection. For the importation of agricultural and animal products, special import regulations and inspections apply to mitigate the risk associated with these particular types of shipments. Agricultural quarantine inspection (AQI) is mainly used to facilitate the safe trade of agricultural goods and ensure the protection of the U.S. from unwanted plants, pests, and diseases. The AQI programs are enforced collaboratively at the border and ports of entry by the plant protection and quarantine (PPQ) and the CBP officers.

Meanwhile, the importation of meat, animal products, by-products, and live animals are subject to Animal and Plant Health Inspection Service (APHIS) regulations and are enforced together by the CBP and the United States Department of Agriculture Food Safety and Inspection Service (FSIS) officers. Permits, sanitary certificates (for animal products), and phytosanitary certificates (for plant products) are generally required for agricultural and food product shipments. APHIS officers also check local markets and stores regularly in search of illegally imported commodities.

When importers fail to fulfill the required procedure and requirements, the goods may be subjected to suspension of entry, confiscation, and return. In addition, importers may face civil penalties and criminal fines and may even be criminally prosecuted if the goods relate to restricted or prohibited items.

B. Importation and Clearance Procedures for Postal and Parcel Shipments

Compared with the sophisticated clearance requirements and procedures that cargo shipments must comply with, the customs clearance requirements and procedures for postal/parcel shipments are relatively simple.[15] Two reasons explain and justify such differential treatments. First, from a historical perspective, the usage of international postal services is different from cargo shipments. Before the invention of the telephone and other modern communication methods, international mail was the primary way people communicated internationally. In order to relieve the customs and postal authorities from the heavy burden caused by the large quantity of in-flow postal shipments, the procedures and rules for handling mail and parcels were therefore streamlined and simplified. Second, the differences between postal packages and commercial cargo shipments also justify the differential treatment imposed. In contrast with international mail, which at that time was primarily letters and low-value packages that were mainly unrelated to trade, cargo shipments are used to transport commercial goods. Therefore, while there is no economic incentive for states to impose strict customs regulations and procedures upon postal deliveries since there is a little tariff to be collected, states have the incentive to collect tariff from cargo shipments and perhaps even the incentive to deter the importation of foreign goods to protect their domestic producers.

The United Nations Universal Postal Union (UPU) also helps streamline the customs procedures for international mail and parcels. International agreements and regulations were adopted under the UPU to ensure that all members use standard declaration forms for their international shipments. Although the shipper is also required to provide information about the parcel's contents, weight, and value and the recipient's name and address, the requirement is significantly less burdensome than for cargo shipments. In addition, international mail shippers are not required to make pre-arrival notifications, and the shipments can be released before the duties are collected.

As transportation technology developed and new forms of shipping demand emerged, private express carriers such as FedEx and DHL also joined and became part of international transport. Although private express couriers are treated no differently from usual cargo and baggage, the decision to have separate customs procedures for private express carriers emerged as shipments increased. In 1989, the U.S. CBP published a new set of regulations and guidelines addressing private express carrier needs. Under the new regulation, express couriers are required to reimburse the U.S. Customs for enjoying expedited clearances. Nonetheless, private express couriers are still required to provide pre-arrival document filing and fulfill the obligations to declare the content and value of

15 *U.S. Postal Service Competitive Concerns About Global Package Link Service*, United States General Accounting Office, Report to the Chairman, Subcommittee on the Postal Service, Committee on Government Reform and Oversight, House of Representative, GAO/GGD-98-104, June, 1998.

the shipment. Nowadays, express carriers such as FedEx or DHL usually use customs brokers to clear the goods. Currently, the import clearance procedures for postal shipments and carrier shipments are very different.[16]

III. The Development of SMEs, E-Commerce, and their Impact on SPS Enforcement

A. SME Involvement in International Trade

SMEs are the backbone of many economies. According to a study jointly conducted by the OECD and the World Bank Group in 2015, SMEs are estimated to account for almost 95% of all firms, over 50% of global GDP, and up to 70% of employment.[17] Although SMEs are large in number, they often lack efficiency and are less competitive in international trade.[18] Due to lags in productivity and the inability to benefit from economies of scale, the economic performance of SMEs is also found to be less impressive compared to their larger peers.[19] The positive correlations found between a firm's size and its involvement in international trade also indicate that SMEs are less capable of participating in international trade.

Even though most SMEs rarely participate in international trade, they are not exempt from being affected by the rapidly emerging global market. As trade barriers are gradually removed under the WTO and free trade agreements, SMEs now face competition from foreign firms. Large MNEs like Wal-Mart and Costco outcompete local businesses in many countries since they enjoy economies of scale and operate at a lower cost. Although SMEs may also benefit from reducing trade barriers and may gain through participating in international trade by becoming part of the global value chain, they remain vulnerable to trade barriers due to their inherent capacity restraints. Even customs requirements and costs may prevent SMEs from entering the market.[20] The vast and complicated SPS and technical regulation requirements adopted

16 For a comparison between the import clearance procedures for postal shipments and carrier shipments, *see* U.S. Postal Service Competitive Concerns About Global Package Link Service at 31, United States General Accounting Office, Report to the Chairman, Subcommittee on the Postal Service, Committee on Government Reform and Oversight, House of Representative, GAO/GGD-98-104, June 1998.

17 Organization for Economic Co-Operation and Development (OECD) and World Bank Group, "Inclusive Global Value Chains, Report Prepared for Submission to G20 Trade Ministers Meeting", Oct. 6, 2015, *available at* www.oecd.org/trade/OECD-WBG-g20-gvc-report-2015.pdf.

18 González, *supra* note 4, at 44.

19 Rudolf Adlung & Marta Soprana, "Trade Policy for SMEs from a GATS Perspective" in Thilo Rensmann (ed), *Small and Medium-Sized Enterprises in International Economic Law* (Oxford, Oxford University Press 2017), at 13, 15.

20 Bernard Hoekman & Allesandro Nicita, *Trade Policy, Trade Costs, and Developing Country Trade*, at 18, World Bank Policy Research Working Paper 4797, Dec. 2018, http://elibrary.worlbank.org/doi/pdf/10.1596/1813-9450-4797.

by states, in particular, cause tremendous difficulties for exporters, especially SMEs, to enter the market.[21] Given that SMEs and producers in developing and least developed countries often lack the capacity to overcome trade obstacles, states have cooperated in various ways hoping to increase SME involvement in international trade.[22] As a result, numerous SME-facilitating efforts and arrangements have been made under the multilateral WTO and regional trade agreements.

The most recent achievement in the multilateral arena that facilitates SME participation in international trade is the Trade Facilitation Agreement (TFA), which entered into force on February 22, 2017, following ratification by two-thirds of WTO members. In the TFA, states commit to expediting the movement, release, and clearance of goods at customs.[23] Customs authorities and other agencies whose function relates to implementation and enforcement measures, such as the SPS and technical barriers to trade bodies, are also called to cooperate and reduce the miscellaneous and burdensome requirements.[24] For transparency purposes, states are also required to reveal the pre-arrival processing procedures and publish the average release times. In addition, they shall review and make known the possible incurred fees under the TFA.[25] Guidelines and best practices are also published and shared among the members to benefit from each other's experiences and take advantage of capacity-building opportunities available to support the implementation of the TFA.[26] Although the benefits of the TFA apply to both SMEs and other trade participants, it nevertheless significantly helped SMEs overcome the obstacles limiting their performance.

Besides the TFA, scholars have also urged the use of existing WTO provisions to assist SME development. For instance, Karsten Pötschke digs into Article 6.13 of the Anti-Dumping Agreement and Article 12.11 of the Agreement on Subsidies and Countervailing Measures (SCM). He argues that these provisions may be used to assist SMEs when they face anti-dumping and SCM investigations.[27] Although the provisions under the Anti-Dumping Agreement or the SCM do not exempt SMEs from anti-dumping investigations, they urge authorities to consider SMEs' needs. By calling on the authorities to provide proactive support and more flexible procedures to the SMEs, Article 6.13 of

21 United Nation Food & Agriculture Organization & World Trade Organization, *Trade and Food Standards* (Geneva, World Trade Organization 2007), at 29.

22 Ibid at 30.

23 TFA, preamble, art. 7.

24 Ibid, art. 5.

25 Ibid, arts. 1–3.

26 Ibid, arts. 5, 10.

27 Karsten Pötschke, "Rediscovering the Forgotten Article of the WTO Anti-Dumping Agreement: How Article 6.13 Protects SMEs" in Thilo Rensmann (ed), *Small and Medium-Sized Enterprises in International Economic Law* (Oxford, Oxford University Press 2017), at 61, 65.

the Anti-Dumping Agreement prevents SMEs from being negatively discriminated against.

Regarding the new developments in regional trade agreements, many of the recently concluded regional trade agreements (RTAs), such as the Comprehensive and Progressive Agreement for Trans-Pacific Partnership, and the United States-Mexico-Canada Agreement contain provisions or even a chapter dedicated to promoting and facilitating the development of SMEs. In the comprehensive studies done by José-Antonio Monteiro, which assess the 270 RTAs currently in force, it is noted that more than half of the RTAs contain at least one provision explicitly mentioning SMEs. It is also recorded that the number of SME-related provisions within RTAs is increasing.[28] Although the treaty language in most SME-related provisions remains relatively soft, and the parties are only asked to act to the best of their ability, the existence of these provisions signals the emerging consensus that states shall take notice of SMEs' particular needs and support their development.

In addition to the rules and regulations developed at the multilateral and regional level, it is proposed that SMEs would greatly benefit if their operations could be further integrated with cross-border e-commerce.

C. *Promoting SME Development Through E-Commerce*

E-commerce has a variety of definitions. In the 1998 Work Program for Electronic Commerce, e-commerce is understood as "the production, distribution, marketing, sale or delivery of goods and services by electronic means."[29] In the OECD definition, e-commerce refers to a business model where the commercial transaction between the supplier and consumer is done through communications networks with wireless devices.[30] As technology has further evolved and business models developed, cross-border data flows, information exchange, cybersecurity, and intelligence also fall within the scope of the modern concept of e-commerce.

Despite the wide variety of e-commerce applications, the flexible and convenient features of e-commerce may significantly contribute to SME development.[31] Through e-commerce, SMEs are not only able to reduce operating

28 José-Antonio Monteiro, *Provisions on Small and Medium-Sized Enterprises in Regional Trade Agreements*, at 6–7, World Trade Organization, Economic Research and Statistic Division, Aug. 18, 2016, *available at* www.wto.org/english/res_e/reser_e/ersd201612_e.pdf.

29 World Trade Organization, "Electronic Commerce", *available at* https://www.wto.org/english/tratop_e/econ_e/ecom_e.htm.

30 Organization for Economic Co-Operation & Development, "Mobile Commerce, Directorate for Science, Technology and Industry Committee on Consumer Policy", DSTI/CP(2006)7/FINAL (2007), *available at* www.oecd.org/sti/38077227.pdf.

31 Rutendo Tavengerwei, "Using Trade Facilitation to Assist SMEs in E-Commerce in Developing Countries" (2018) 21(2) Journal of International Economic Law 349.

costs by adopting more efficient production procedures, but they may also provide new products and services such as online financial and streaming services to consumers. Furthermore, because new markets such as online transactions allow businesses to operate beyond the physical and territorial boundary, SME operations are no longer limited by their lack of resources. They may reach a broader scope of customers without being present in the export market.[32] As e-commerce reduces the physical and time-dependent distance between the producer and consumer, the barrier to market entry is also reduced, increasing market competition.[33]

There are various ways SMEs can use e-commerce to enhance their participation in cross-border trade.[34] For instance, SMEs can reach foreign consumers by merely creating a website and displaying their products on the webpage. With the help of cooperation between international financial institutions and the arrangements made thereunder, the entire checkout procedure can be completed online without dealing with matters like currency exchange. Alternatively, SMEs may also expand their operations by utilizing e-commerce platforms such as e-Bay, Amazon, or Google Shopping. Although some of these platforms have been limited territorially for taxation reasons, this problem has now mostly been resolved through taxation cooperation between the countries and tariff exemptions given to goods under a specific value.

Moreover, powerful internet search engines also connect and facilitate collaborations between different e-commerce platforms. For instance, e-Bay creates local websites in places it operates, such as e-Bay U.S., e-Bay U.K., e-Bay Israel, and so on. However, when consumers search for products on any of these websites, the search engines show goods listed on the local website and those in other countries. Thus, by surfing and exploring on a single website, consumers may have access to products listed all over the world. This can greatly help the SMEs expand their outreach distance.

Last, affordable international postal and express carrier services also lowered entire transaction costs and allowed SMEs to deliver goods even without having any local marketing channels. Furthermore, the arrangements made between countries to expedite the clearance procedures for postal and express carrier packages also benefited SMEs since small packages of goods can now be shipped more quickly. As a result, they may be delivered to customers in shorter periods.

32 Heinz Hauser & Sacha Wunsch-Vincent, "A Call for a WTO E-Commerce Initiative" (2000) 6 International Journal of Communications Law & Policy 1, 2.

33 Catherine Mann & Sarah Knight, "Electronic Commerce in the WTO" in J. Schott (ed), *The WTO after Seattle* (Washington, DC, Peterson Institute for International Economics 2000), at 253.

34 Chapter 14 (E-Commerce) of the CPTPP, for instance, noted that parties should cooperate on sharing experiences, exchanging information, and assisting SMEs to overcome obstacles. *See* CPTPP, art. 14.15.

IV. The Risks Associated With the Development of SME Operations via E-Commerce

A. Ignored Risks and Dangers

Undoubtedly, collaborations between states at both multilateral and regional levels have reduced the burden for SMEs to operate internationally. The TFA itself was reported to reduce members' trade cost by 14% and import and export time by an average of 1–2 days.[35] However, while the ongoing negotiation agenda focuses on streamlining import procedures and expediting customs processes, the negative impacts associated with these changes seem neglected. The risks and dangers that may be associated with expanding the operations of SMEs have also been left out of the discussion.

Indeed, sophisticated customs requirements prevent SMEs from actively participating in international trade. But excluding those imposed for trade protection purposes, most customs procedures and import requirements are set to protect certain legitimate objectives. For instance, a labeling requirement may be imposed to ensure that consumers acquire sufficient information about the product and thus preserve their "right to know"; standards and technical requirements may also be set to ensure the safety of the product and the protection of other people's legitimate objectives. When it comes to the trade of food and agricultural products, the SPS measures, which are sometimes abusively used and often viewed as non-tariff trade barriers, also play a critical role in preventing the entrance of unwanted pests and diseases. As the current trend pushes to reduce regulatory requirements and burdens on imports to support the operation of SMEs, we are left with the question of whether the simplified measures and procedures are still capable of maintaining the expected level of protection that the states aim to achieve.

In the following section, by studying the difficulties that Taiwan faced when combatting and preventing the cross-border spread of African swine fever (ASF), this chapter highlights how the development of SMEs, especially those conducting cross-border operations via e-commerce, weakens states' protection over their subjects.

B. Taiwan's Experience in Preventing the Outbreak of African Swine Fever

ASF is prevalent and endemic in the sub-Saharan Africa region. Historically, outbreaks have also occurred in Europe, some Caribbean countries, and South America. Since 2007, ASF has been reported in multiple countries across Africa, Asia, and the European continents.[36] A significant increase in the

35 Tavengerwei, *supra* note 31, at 353.

36 African Swine Fever (ASF), "World Animal Health Information and Analysis Department", *available at* www.oie.int/en/animal-health-in-the-world/animal-diseases/african-swine-fever/#A (last accessed Apr. 25, 2019).

number of outbreaks has been identified since 2016, with the disease being found in Moldova, Czech Republic, Romania, Hungary, Bulgaria, Belgium, and reported for the first time in the Peoples' Republic of China (PRC) in August 2018. According to the World Organisation for Animal Health (OIE), a severe outbreak has occurred in Asia, especially in the Peoples' Republic of China. Although the PRC reported nearly 55% of the world's losses,[37] it is speculated that the losses have been underreported, and the actual outbreak is much more severe than disclosed.[38]

The mortality rate of ASF can be as high as 100%. However, the mortality for moderately virulent forms of ASF still ranges from 30–70%. As there are no known treatments or vaccines for ASF, prevention relies entirely on import restrictions and enforcement. Also, the ASF virus may remain active after the host is deceased. Therefore, disease-free countries must ensure that neither infected pig livestock nor pork products are introduced into ASF-free areas via processed products.

Noticing the devastating impact of ASF and the ongoing epidemic outbreaks in the region, Taiwan quickly imposed importation bans on all pig livestock and processed pork products from ASF-affected areas, including those from the PRC. It is hoped that the strict importation restrictions can help Taiwan prevent the entrance of ASF and protect Taiwan's local animal husbandry, which has just started to revive from the destructive foot-and-mouth disease outbreak that happened almost 21 years ago. But despite the strict importation bans imposed, there are still numerous reports of processed pork products found in Taiwan carrying ASF from the PRC.

Although most of the processed pork products found in Taiwan carrying ASF from the PRC were brought by travelers and were intercepted at the border, many prohibited products unexpectedly entered into Taiwan via postal and express carrier packages. Consumers also reported that they received pork sausages and meat products as gifts when they made purchases from Taobao sellers.[39] Some consumers even disregard the prohibition rules and order pork products from individual vendors on Taobao and request to ship the products to Taiwan.[40] As of March 31, 2019, 71 instances of illegal mailed-in pork products (some carrying the ASF virus) have been detected at the postal service examination points.

37 African Swine Fever (ASF) Situation, Report N° 15: April 12–25, 2019, World Animal Health Information and Analysis Department, *available at* www.oie.int/fileadmin/Home/eng/Animal_Health_in_the_World/docs/pdf/Disease_cards/ASF/Report_15_Current_situation_of_ASF.pdf.

38 "China Probably Underreporting Swine Fever: U.S. Agriculture's Perdue", *Reuters*, Aug. 31, 2018, *available at* www.reuters.com/article/us-china-swinefever-usa/china-probably-underreporting-swine-fever-u-s-agricultures-perdue-idUSKCN1LF2AH (last accessed Apr. 25, 2019).

39 蘋果日報，豬瘟漏洞！網購收到中國香腸贈品 淘寶緊急公告禁止， Dec. 13, 2018, https://tw.appledaily.com/new/realtime/20181213/1483311/ (last accessed Apr. 21, 2019).

40 淘寶網購火腿腸 面臨重刑重罰，華視新聞， Sept. 11, 2018, https://news.cts.com.tw/cts/society/201809/201809111936719.html (last accessed Apr. 21, 2019).

The number of detected illegal pork products mailed in from the PRC may seem small; it nevertheless reveals the tip of the iceberg. With Taobao itself claiming to create more than one billion U.S. dollars of trade flow from PRC to Taiwan, it is hard to imagine the number of illegal goods that went through the customs and border control without being detected.[41] Taiwanese Customs also admits that given the number of shipments that came through customs, it is impossible to conduct inspections on all packages. The customs authority does not have enough resources to complete such tasks.[42] Furthermore, compared to traditional cargo shipments, which are required to follow a complete list of obligations and provide customs pre-arrival documents declaring the content, volume, and origin of the goods, postal and carrier packages are only required to follow a simplified process. Thus, to the customs authorities, shipments sent via postal and courier packages are more challenging to inspect since Customs lacks information about the packages' risk factors, thus preventing them from using algorithms to evaluate the degrees of risk and identify shipments that require additional attention. This is not to mention that small-scale operators may lack knowledge about the exportation process and their declaration obligations or may even intentionally provide false declarations to avoid their goods being subjected to inspections that may prolong the time for goods to pass through customs.

Currently, Taiwan customs authorities impose intensive inspection procedures to prevent the spread of ASF. After learning that pork products have penetrated through the quarantine defense line through postal and courier packages, more stringent rules and regulations were imposed. It is now required that all incoming mail packages go through x-ray scanning. Packages that are detected or suspected of carrying food products will be further manually inspected. Teams of quarantine detector dogs are also deployed at the ports to help detect meat products. Packages shipped from ASF-infected areas are separated and are subjected to more intensive inspections.

Meanwhile, the Taiwanese government also has requested Taobao prohibit its sellers from selling or shipping pork-related products to Taiwan. In addition, some merchants' web pages are also blocked to prevent cross-border transactions of pork products. According to the most recent statistics, the number of illegal packages has gradually decreased.[43]

C. Balancing Between Trade Facilitation and the Need to Protect

Although the Taiwanese government can temporarily strengthen the intensity of its inspections to prevent the import of goods that are potentially carrying

41 蔡紀眉、楊孟軒，淘寶攻台，momo總經理林啟峰：有國家這樣讓人侵門踏戶的嗎?，天下雜誌， Sept. 26, 2018, *available at* www.cw.com.tw/article/article.action?id=5092274 (last accessed Apr. 21, 2019).

42 Ibid.

43 查緝成果最新統計報表，中華郵政資訊網，*available at* www.post.gov.tw/post/internet/Group/index.jsp?ID=1548202358478 (last accessed Apr. 21, 2019).

ASF, these emergency measures are not the feasible final solutions to fix the problem.[44] As we have previously cited, only 3–5% of cargo shipments will be examined and inspected under the current practices. Furthermore, because intensive inspections require a massive amount of human and material resources, it is hard to imagine that the customs authorities and postal services are capable of bearing the burden if we decide to double or triple the inspection ratio, not to mention if we choose to increase the level of protection further. Moreover, even if the customs authorities and postal services can bear such burdens, it comes with the price of prolonging the time for goods to pass through customs. Also, since the disaggregated forms of SME sales prevent customs authorities from using algorithms to predetermine the risks of the shipment and impose the corresponding degree of inspection, alternative sampling and inspection methods need to be developed.

Of course, there are numerous ways that the current regulatory system can be revised to mitigate the arising challenges. For instance, states may require e-commerce platforms to bear joint responsibility to ensure the safety of the listed products. Digital sales platforms may also be required to remove or block the listing of prohibited and restricted goods. In order to ensure that the shipment of goods is duly declared following the rules and regulations, e-commerce platforms may also help generate uniform declaration forms for their users. E-commerce platforms may also require packages to be shipped by registered carriers to help shippers comply with all importation requirements. In addition to public and private collaboration, noticing that the roles of postal services have changed rapidly, and the shipment of letters and low-value personal belongings are no longer the mainstream of their business, states may also want to modify the current international postal agreements and the clearance procedures for express carrier packages to better meet the needs of modern society. In multilateral and regional trade agreements, states may also

44 In fact, it has been proven that the methods used by Taiwanese government were ineffective in preventing the illegal importation of goods carrying ASF. In August 2021, pork products illegally smuggled from Vietnam carrying ASF were found in Taiwanese markets. *See* 蔣濬浩，「非洲豬瘟」恐引爆2000億災損！嚴守三年，為何台灣終被「走私豬」攻陷？，遠見，2021年8月30日, *available at* www.gvm.com.tw/article/82056 (last accessed Oct. 31, 2021）. After learning that illegal pork products had been smuggled into the market, the Taiwanese customs authority strengthened its inspection ratio again. In less than two months, between August 2021 and October 2021, more than 340 kilos of illegal pork products were detected and seized at the border. Nearly 75% of these illegal pork products were sent via postal packages, and the rest were mostly via air express. *See* 海關1個半月查獲308件走私豬肉製品　雙11網購高峰期將加強查緝，民視，2021年10月12日，0https://tw.news.yahoo.com/%E5%BF%AB%E6%96%B0%E8%81%9E-%E6%B5%B7%E9%97%9C1%E5%80%8B%E5%8D%8A%E6%9C%88%E6%9F%A5%E7%8D%B2308%E4%BB%B6%E8%B5%B0%E7%A7%81%E8%B1%AC%E8%82%89%E8%A3%BD%E5%93%81-%E9%9B%9911%E7%B6%B2%E8%B3%BC%E9%AB%98%E5%B3%B0%E6%9C%9F%E5%B0%87%E5%8A%A0%E5%BC%B7%E6%9F%A5%E7%B7%9D-133918631.html（last accessed Oct. 31, 2021）. It should be noted that the illegal pork products found in Taiwan were unrelated to e-commerce. However, these illegal smuggling incidents via postal and air shipments still signal the weaknesses of the current border control measures.

incorporate provisions marking the need and necessity for states to cooperate and mitigate the risks associated with SMEs and e-commerce development. The SPS chapters may also adopt separate mechanisms for these matters.

V. Conclusion

The development of SMEs is critical for the sake of economic growth. As discussed, the business opportunities created by e-commerce, TFA adoption, and many other international instruments have facilitated SMEs' participation in international trade. However, while we celebrate the successes and wait to enjoy the fruit of such development, we also ought to think preemptively about the risks associated with SMEs' enlarging trade activities.

From Taiwan's recent experience, we witnessed how SMEs' cross-border operations can seriously challenge a country's quarantine and SPS efforts. From the case study, we have also learned how the current border control measures were unprepared for the challenges created by these new forms of trading activities. Although highly intensive inspection measures can be provisionally taken to confront the sudden outburst of an epidemic such as ASF, a systematic review and even revision is still required. The search for economic development should not come with the unbearable cost of lowering the level of protection of other equally or even more important interests. Either through international or regional collaboration or even unilateral efforts, the quarantine loopholes must be patched. The design of the entire border inspection and control mechanism may also need to be readjusted.

It is not within the scope of this chapter to indicate how the system can be better remodeled or to provide the best solution to resolve the problem, since bringing such a proposal would require a comprehensive assessment and examination of a country's customs and border control mechanisms. Nevertheless, this chapter still hopes to bring attention to the risks associated with rapidly developing trade activities and the urgent need to manage such risks. More fundamentally, regulators are expected to be more cautious when streamlining the designated measures to protect legitimate interests in order to foresee and manage the risks.

6 Blockchainizing Food Law

Promises and Perils of Incorporating Distributed Ledger Technologies to Food Safety, Traceability, and Sustainability Governance

*Ching-Fu Lin**

I. Introduction

As the production, distribution, and consumption of food have become globalized against the backdrop of trade liberalization, market integration, and technological development in recent decades, the question of how best to ensure the safety and sustainability of agri-food products across state borders poses significant challenges to regulators worldwide.[1] While food governance calls for a global, holistic, system-based approach,[2] the agri-food industry is one of the largest and most fragmented sectors in the world.[3] As a result, while more and more newly adopted food laws incorporate a global supply-chain approach,[4] exercising effective and efficient control of the entire supply chain remains a difficult and costly task.

* This chapter was originally published by the *Food and Drug Law Journal* and is included in this edited volume with the permission of the journal. The author thanks Laurie Beyranevand, Timothy D. Lytton, and Steph Tai for their comments and suggestions; Cesare Varallo for sharing his practical insights; and Pei-Jen Wang, Sharu Luo, and Shih Ting Wang for their research assistance. Usual disclaimers apply.

1 *See generally* C. F. Lin, "Global Food Safety: Exploring Key Elements for an International Regulatory Strategy" (2011) 51 Virginia Journal of International Law 637.

2 *See generally* L. J. Beyranevand & E. M. B. Leib, "Making the Case for a National Food Strategy in the United States" (2017) 72 Food and Drug Law Journal 225; S. Tai, "Food Systems Law from Farm to Fork and Beyond" (2015) 45 Seton Hall Law Review 109; C. F. Lin, "SPS-Plus and Bilateral Treaty Network: A 'Global' Solution to the Global Food Safety Problem?" (2012) 29 Wisconsin International Law Journal 694.

3 For example, the agri-food sector in Southeast Asia is significantly fragmented, with the majority of the players as small and medium-sized corporations. *See*, for example, Organization for Economic Co-Operation and Development (OECD), *Economic Outlook for Southeast Asia, China and India 2017: Addressing Energy Challenges* (OECD 2017), *available at* http://www.oecd.org/dev/asia-pacific/mpf.htm; C. F. Lin, "The Emergence of ASEAN Regional Food Safety Governance: Structure, Substance, and Context" (2019) 74 Food and Drug Law Journal 80, 82.

4 A supply-chain approach, for instance, has been adopted by the United States' Food Safety Modernization Act, China's Food Safety Law, and the European Union's General Food Law. For more discussion, *see* M. Wang & C. F. Lin, "Towards a Bottom-up SPS Cooperation: An Analysis of Regulatory Convergence in Food Safety Regimes" (2016) 8 Trade Law and Development 117, 123–26.

DOI: 10.4324/9781003271918-8

Indeed, the emergence of multinational agri-food corporations, the advancement of food science and transportation technology, and the advent of the World Trade Organization (WTO) and its liberalization efforts have made possible the global sourcing of food ingredients.[5] As a result, the global food supply chain has grown extensive and fragmented, creating room for foodborne risks, economic adulteration, and management inefficiencies.[6] Along the complex global supply chain, a misstep or regulatory failure at one node can spill over to others, with serious public health and economic consequences. Therefore, ensuring reasonable levels of transparency (sharing of correct information), safety and quality control, traceability, and collective, well-informed governance actions and institutional designs are essential.[7]

Myriad governance initiatives have been adopted by various public, private, and hybrid actors at the national, regional, and multilateral levels, incorporating command-and-control, as well as market-oriented approaches.[8] What has largely been absent in the regulatory landscape, however, is the active use of technology as a means to deliver good governance.[9] In the sphere of agri-food law and policy, distributed ledger technologies (DLTs, colloquially known as

5 *See* Lin, *supra* note 1, at 661–63.

6 *See*, for example, World Health Organization (WHO), "Global Health Observatory Data Repository", *available at* http://apps.who.int/gho/data/node.home (last accessed Apr. 20, 2021); WHO, *WHO Estimates of the Global Burden of Foodborne Diseases: Foodborne Disease Burden Epidemiology Reference Group 2007–2015* (2015) [hereinafter "WHO 2015"]; U.S. Food And Drug Administration (FDA), *FDA Strategy for the Safety of Imported Food* (2019), *available at* https://perma.cc/EA86-Y9BP; *see generally* S. M. Gavaravarapu et al., "A Case for Refining the WHO Global Strategy on Food Safety: Perspectives from India" (2013) 1 The Lancet: Global Health 254; M. Uyttendaele et al., "Food Safety, a Global Challenge" (2016) 13 International Journal of Environmental Research and Public Health 67; F. Fung et al., "Food Safety in the 21st Century" (2018) 41 Biomedical Journal 88.

7 The adoption of the Food Safety Modernization Act (FSMA) in the United States marked a move toward such multi-stakeholder, global supply chain, and public-private collaboration institutional designs. *See*, for example, C. S. DeWaal, "The Legal Basis for Food Safety Regulation in the USA and EU" in J. G. Morris & M. Potter (eds), *Foodborne Infections and Intoxications* (London, Academic Press 2013), at 521–22; *see generally* M. T. Oldfield, "Enactment of the Food Safety Modernization Act: The US FDA within the Context of Interacting Public-Private Governance Processes" (2015) 6 European Journal of Risk Regulation 488.

8 *See*, for example, Beyranevand & Leib, *supra* note 2, at 235–39; S. Halabi & C. F. Lin, "Assessing the Relative Influence and Efficacy of Public and Private Food Safety Regulation Regimes: Comparing Codex and Global GAP Standards" (2017) 72 Food and Drug Law Journal 262, 266–70; N. D. Fortin, "HACCP and Other Regulatory Approaches to Prevention of Foodborne Diseases" in J. G. Morris & M. Potter (eds), *Foodborne Infections and Intoxications* (London, Academic Press 2013); C. F. Lin, "Mega-Regional Transformation of Global Food Safety Governance: Normative Roots and Ramifications" in S. Y. Peng et al. (eds), *Governing Science and Technology Under the International Economic Order: Regulatory Divergence and Convergence in the Age of Megaregionals* (Northampton, Edward Elgar Publishing 2018); Lin, *supra* note 3, at 80, 82–6; M. Wang & C. F. Lin, "Ploughing Away Capacity Constraints in Global Agri-Food Trade" in J. Pauwelyn & M. Wang (eds), *Building Legal Capacity for a More Inclusive Globalization: Barriers to and Best Practices for Integrating Developing Countries into Global Economic Regulation* (Geneva, The Graduate Institute 2019).

9 It should be noted that the limited but growing use of Global Trade Item Numbers (GTINs) to strengthen product traceability in the agri-food industry. GTIN records information about a lot of

"blockchain") seem to be one of the most promising solutions (or "technical fixes") in addressing imminent governance challenges along the global food supply chain.

As will be analyzed in depth in Section III, blockchain refers to decentralized databases that can store, maintain, and update data collaboratively along a network of computing nodes.[10] With the help of cryptography, peer-to-peer networks, and consensus mechanisms, data input to the blockchain is simultaneously and permanently recorded and updated in all the nodes of the network, ensuring a high level of consistency and authenticity of such data.[11] For instance, IBM recently announced a collaboration with a few major food producers and retailers, such as Nestlé, Kroger, Unilever, and Wal-Mart, to leverage blockchain technologies to enhance quality control, food safety, management, and traceability.[12] Wal-Mart has further required its upstream suppliers of leafy greens to employ the cloud- and blockchain-based IBM Food Trust platform by September 2019.[13] Similarly, the United Nations' (UN) World Food Program (WFP) launched the Building Block program in 2017. Using iris-scanning technologies and blockchains, this program helped Syrian refugees verify their identities and directly deduct what they spend from the amount of aid they receive from the WFP.[14] Such initiatives have the potential to help retailers and consumers pinpoint sources of contamination at times of outbreak or provide production details and quality certifications (e.g. product origin, farm history, processing and shipping information, and fair trade or safety/sustainability standards).[15] Blockchains can also be combined with smart contract systems and other AI techniques to increase efficiency, simplify transactions, ensure compliance and security, and promote trade facilitation across borders.

While the far-reaching ramifications of blockchain technologies in the financial arena (such as fintech and cryptocurrency issues) have been discussed in media, literature, and politics in recent years, the opportunities and challenges

---

products in the form of numbers and a barcode. The GTIN system was endorsed by the Traceability Task Force—a multi-stakeholder group jointly created by the Produce Marketing Association (PMA) and the Canadian Produce Marketing Association (CPMA) in 2002—in its best practices guidelines. *See*, for example, T. D. Lytton, *Outbreak: Food Borne Illness and the Struggle for Food Safety* (Chicago, University of Chicago Press 2019), at 191–93; Food and Agriculture Organization of the United Nations (FAO), *Private Standards in the United States and European Union Markets for Fruit and Vegetables: Implications for Developing Countries* (New York, Renouf Publishing Co. Ltd. 2007), at 24–25.

10 *See* infra Part III.B.

11 Ibid.

12 Ibid.

13 Ibid.

14 Ibid.

15 *See* S. Charlebois, "How Blockchain Technology Could Transform the Food Industry", *The Conversation*, Dec. 20, 2017, *available at* https://theconversation.com/how-blockchain-technology-could-transform-the-food-industry-89348; *see also* infra Part III.A.

posed by blockchain to food safety, traceability, and sustainable development have been less analyzed.[16] The benefits of applying blockchain technologies in the global food supply chain seem salient: transforming paper-based documents into a blockchain-enabled identity to generate a high level of transparency and data integrity, enabling smaller farmers to bypass middlemen in crops trading and cash transfers, and providing an efficient and cost-effective way to manage the production system.

Blockchain, however, is not a silver bullet to solve all food governance issues; the use of the technology may create a new layer of challenges and arguably leave some key problems unaddressed. As will be further unpacked by this chapter, applying blockchain technologies to the governance of food safety, traceability, and sustainability triggers new regulatory questions of a technical capacity gap, standardization politics, cybersecurity and data protection, and technologically inherent limits of blockchain. In addition, "blockchainizing" the food supply chain may pose legal and policy challenges to both developed and developing (especially underdeveloped) countries in different ways—especially in terms of operational expertise and technical infrastructure, scalability and implementation costs, and power asymmetry in international standard-setting—which may, in turn, undermine the overall legitimacy and accountability of such techno-regulatory mechanisms.

This chapter, therefore, aims to explore the potential of blockchain technologies in revolutionizing the global food supply chain in terms of food safety, traceability, and sustainable development. More specifically, this chapter will examine concrete cases in which blockchains have been applied to transform how we conventionally think about food safety, certification, and traceability. Premised upon these cases, this chapter argues that blockchain technologies can indeed revolutionize the food supply chain by solving the information asymmetry problem and by increasing efficiency, transparency, and trust among all market players, as demonstrated by the recent pilots. If the recent pilot programs can be practically materialized and scaled up to real-world governance mechanisms, the participants in the global supply chain will be able to get connected and upload their data to the cloud-based system, which further generates a transparent, traceable, immutable, and shared record of production details; quality specifications and origin facts; sustainability and fair trade certifications; and storage, import/export, and logistics information.

Such transformation and benefits, however, do not come without costs or challenges. Blockchainizing governance of food safety, traceability, and sustainability pose another layer of regulatory questions about technical capacity and infrastructure gap, scalability and implementation costs, global standardization politics, cybersecurity and data protection, and technologically inherent limits of blockchain. Regulatory questions, as such, may call for a reconceptualization

16 Some relatively recent works have discussed the use of blockchain in regulation and the agri-food sector. *See* infra Part III.A.

of the forms and substances of conventional food law and policy (as well as data protection law, anti-trust law, and trade law). In this light, this chapter will also endeavor to locate possible barriers and challenges to blockchainizing food law at national and international levels and offer recommendations for leveraging such technology in an effective, efficient, and responsible manner.

Section II of this chapter sets the scene of contemporary governance issues in the global agri-food supply chain—namely food safety, authenticity, traceability and transparency, and security and sustainability—and points to information insufficiency, inaccuracy, and asymmetry as some of the most crucial root causes. Section III gives an in-depth discussion on the technical aspects and regulatory benefits of blockchain technologies and looks at three promising pilot programs as examples. Section IV will examine the potentials and challenges of bringing blockchain technologies into the governance endeavors by assessing the benefits of blockchainizing food law and policy, such as a high level of consistency, security, and authenticity of information and unparalleled power of traceability. At the same time, Section IV cautions about the adverse regulatory byproducts that need to be carefully addressed when regulators and businesses try to scale up existing pilot projects. Section V concludes by calling for a more technologically informed policy-making process before rushing into the hype of blockchainizing food law.

II. Regulatory Challenges in the Global Agri-Food Supply Chain

The globalization of food production, distribution, and consumption has—together with trade liberalization, market integration, and technological development in recent decades—generated considerable benefits.[17] At the same time, it has posed significant challenges to the industry, as well as to governments and consumers around the world.[18] Among other issues, food safety, authenticity, traceability, and sustainability are of crucial importance and have serious public health, economic, and social ramifications.[19] Food safety, security, and sustainability are further intertwined in today's multi-level and multi-layered food systems that interact with global environmental change, labor issues, transnational regulatory landscape, scientific development, and other cross-sector interconnectivities.[20] This section provides a quick overview of these issues from a global governance perspective, which will hopefully serve as a premise

17 *See generally* S. F. Halabi (ed), *Food and Drug Regulation in an Era of Globalized Markets* (Boston, Academic Press 2015), at xxvii–xxx.

18 *See* A. B. Marks, "The Risks We Are Willing to Eat: Food Imports and Safety" (2015) 52 Harvard Journal on Legislation 125, 129–35; Y. Motarjemi et al., "Future Challenges in Global Harmonization of Food Safety Legislation" (2001) 12 Food Control 339, 340–41.

19 *See* Lin, *supra* note 1, at 641–64; *see also* A. Alemanno, *Trade in Food: Regulatory and Judicial Approaches in the EU and the WTO* (London, Cameron May 2007), at 73–223.

20 *See* Tai, *supra* note 2, at 112–16.

for subsequent discussions on whether and to what extent disruptive technologies, such as blockchain, can help to address these regulatory challenges.[21]

A. Food Safety and Authenticity

Food safety issues have become globalized, crossing state borders to pose governance challenges to economic development and public health, according to the World Health Organization (WHO).[22] There are more than 3.2 billion cases of foodborne diseases in children above five years of age reported annually in Southeast Asia and 5 billion reported cases worldwide.[23] Because food products can be made in one place with raw materials from multiple regions, processed in another continent, exported into the global supply chain, and delivered to the shelf or the dinner table in distant locations, food safety incidents that occur in a specific node along the supply chain can pose substantial risks globally.

In the United States, for example, documented food safety incidents result in more than 48 million illnesses, 128,000 hospitalizations, and 3,000 deaths annually (based on statistics rather than actual reports).[24] In addition, the Food and Drug Administration (FDA) in the United States has been criticized for its failure to combat "food fraud" in various products such as seafood, fruit juice, and olive oil.[25] To be sure, not all forms of food fraud may directly affect food safety. While some types of economically motivated adulteration (EMA), such as padding, diluting, or substituting certain ingredients of food products, may not threaten food safety, other types of food fraud usually pose serious health risks to consumers.[26] Internationally, cross-border food safety crises are no less problematic: Chinese dumplings tainted with harmful pesticides made

21 While this chapter endeavors to offer a sufficient account of the regulatory challenges on food safety, authenticity, traceability, and sustainability, it cannot and does not intend to exhaust all the problems or examine all the details of these inquiries. This part simply serves to provide for a basic background for the subsequent analysis on using blockchain as a regulatory tool to address these issues.

22 *See* WHO 2015, *supra* note 6, at 76.

23 World Health Organization (WHO), "Regional Food Safety Strategy" (2014) *available at* https://perma.cc/4P7J-USH8, at 2–3.

24 United States Centers for Disease Control and Prevention (U.S. CDC), "Estimates of Foodborne Illness in the United States—Burden of Foodborne Illness: Overview" *available at* https://perma.cc/5DZY-TW85; *see generally* E. Scallan et al., "Foodborne Illness Acquired in the United States—Unspecified Agents" (2011) 17 Emerging Infectious Disease 7. Further, Timothy D. Lytton discusses the methodologies adopted by researchers to estimate the number of foodborne illness cases and economic costs. *See* Lytton, *supra* note 9, at 243–45.

25 L. Layton, "FDA Pressured to Combat Rising 'Food Fraud'", *Washington Post*, Mar. 30, 2010, *available at* https://phe.rockefeller.edu/wp-content/uploads/2010/04/FDA-pressured-to-combat-rising-food-fraud.pdf.

26 *See generally* M. T. Roberts & W. Turk, "The Pursuit of Food Authenticity: Recommended Legal and Policy Strategies to Eradicate Economically Motivated Adulteration (Food Fraud)" (2016) White Paper, Resnick Center for Food Law & Policy, *available at* https://perma.cc/DVA3-BD39, at 5 and 21.

700 people sick in Japan in 2008,[27] bovine spongiform encephalopathy (BSE, commonly known as "mad cow disease") resulted in 180,000 cattle cases in 20 countries and affected human consumption worldwide,[28] and melamine-laced dairy products from China led to over 50,000 cases of infant hospitalization and affected 46 countries.

Coupled with the increase in food trade, the continuing consolidation of agricultural and food companies into large transnational food corporations and the remarkable growth of these resulting companies are essential driving forces behind the sweeping changes in the global food system.[29] With the force of international food trade that ties together companies with different sizes and capabilities in jurisdictions with diverse degrees of oversight, the likelihood, scale, and severity of outbreaks of foodborne diseases and contamination from unsafe foods all have increased exponentially.[30] Food science advances and the modernization of various production methods have also contributed to the ever-growing complexity of the agri-food market globally.[31] Considering the rapid scientific and technological developments in the agri-food sector, eminent scholars have also argued that the establishment of the government's national food strategy "should have the ability to respond to changes in science and technology, as well as new and unexpected challenges that emerge."[32] As a result, information asymmetry abounds along the prolonged supply chain,[33] from farm to fork, further leading to market failures (e.g. consumers do not know the production processes, safety, and quality information behind food products, and suppliers are incentivized to cheat or go easy on safety measures), which, in turn, breed rampant food safety problems worldwide.[34]

In addition to food safety, a related problem concerns the authenticity of food products—food fraud or economic adulteration. As rightly pointed out

27 *See* Andrew Cockburn, "Gyoza Scare Offers Insight into Japan's Culture of Eating", *Japan Today*, Apr. 13, 2008, *available at* https://perma.cc/8TBT-MQFQ.

28 World Health Organization (WHO), "Prion Diseases", *WHO*, Aug. 23, 2010, *available at* https://perma.cc/RY4F-UT3J.

29 *See* D. A. Detomasi, "The Multinational Corporation and Global Governance: Modelling Global Public Policy Networks" (2007) 71 Journal of Business Ethics 321, for a general discussion of globalization and the increasing influence of multinational corporations.

30 *See* WHO, *supra* note 23, at 98.

31 *See* Lin, *supra* note 1, at 641–64.

32 Beyranevand & Leib, *supra* note 2, at 258.

33 *See* Lin, *supra* note 1, at 467–79; *see also* G. K. Hadfield et al., "Information-Based Principles for Rethinking Consumer Protection Policy" (1998) 21 Journal of Consumer Policy 140, 143; M. J. Trebilcock, "Rethinking Consumer Protection Policy" in C. E. F. Rickett & T. G. W. Telfer (eds), *International Perspectives on Consumers' Access to Justice* (Cambridge, CUP 2003), at 68–98.

34 *See* Marks, *supra* note 18, at 125–35.

by the European Union's DG SANTE in its most recent 2018 annual report on the EU Food Fraud Network:[35]

> The complex nature of our globalized food supply chains and the economic motivation to provide cheaper food products have contributed to the prevalence of food fraud. The cost for the global food industry has been estimated at around EUR 30 billion every year, thereby hindering the proper functioning of the internal market. Fraudulent practices in the food sector may also lead to public health risks.[36]

Indeed, food fraud is usually economically driven and emerges when there is a significant price gap between the authentic and substitution products, which incentivizes suppliers to corrupt and adulterate.[37] The increasing globalization and complexity of the agri-food supply chain practically reduces transparency and widens information asymmetry in the marketplace, reducing the risk of being caught, preventing consumers from ascertaining product differentials, and so exacerbating the economic drivers for food fraud.[38] Notable examples include the melamine-tainted infant formula scandal in China in 2008, problems with horsemeat in beef products across Europe in 2013, and the sale of adulterated olive oil in Taiwan in 2013. Given the strong economic incentives for fraud and the weak capability of ensuring transparency (for authenticity verification) in the market, it is unsurprising that even in the European Union, one of the most developed jurisdictions, the number of reported food fraud cases jumped to 234 in 2018, marking a 31% increase compared to reported cases in 2017.[39]

Rampant food fraud—be it dilution, substitution, or mislabeling—can result in economic loss, public distrust, and public health risks, which further weaken the government as well as the industry's credibility and accountability as an effective gatekeeper of food safety and fair trade. While the Food Safety Modernization Act of 2011 (FSMA) incorporates certain rules that aim to cope with intentional adulteration, food fraud (in particular, the European Medical

35 The EU Food Fraud Network was established in 2013 in the wake of the horsemeat scandal to serve as a platform to liaise and exchange information between Member State contact points and to facilitate regulatory work on food fraud cases among EU Member States and some other European countries. *See* European Commission, "The EU Food Fraud Network and the System for Administrative Assistance—Food Fraud Annual Report 2018", *DG SANTE*, Apr. 12, 2019 [hereinafter "EU Food Fraud Network 2018 Report"], *available at* https://perma.cc/2PWE-WUD6, at 5.

36 Ibid., at 4.

37 *See generally* R. Johnson, "Food Fraud and 'Economically Motivated Adulteration' of Food and Food Ingredients", *Congressional Research Services*, Jan. 10, 2014, *available at* https://perma.cc/8P4Z-Q9T8.

38 For more discussion, *see* K. Everstine et al., "Economically Motivated Adulteration (EMA) of Food: Common Characteristics of EMA Incidents" (2013) 76 Journal of Food Protection 723.

39 *See* EU Food Fraud Network 2018 Report, *supra* note 35, at 7.

Association) does not seem to be properly addressed under the law, and the FDA has not devoted adequate resources to alleviate the issue.[40]

At the global level, it becomes more challenging to detect food fraud along the complex and extended supply chain in which a huge number of suppliers, processors, distributors, importers, and retailers are involved. The sheer number of actors taking part in the global supply chain without rigorous cross-border law enforcement means that some can easily remain anonymous or are simply invisible.[41] Commercial practices mean that food products and commodities are often reprocessed, reloaded, and repackaged in different jurisdictions by different factories, increasing the information asymmetry gap and, consequently, the incentives for fraud.[42] Due to the problems of information asymmetry along the global food supply chain, importers and local marketers (except for those that enjoy market power and technical expertise to require third-party auditing and certification) have limited choices other than to rely on the regulatory systems of origin countries.[43]

B. Traceability and Transparency

Traceability generally refers to the "ability to identify and trace the history, distribution, location and application of products, parts, and materials, to ensure the reliability of sustainability claims, in the areas of human rights, labor (including health and safety), the environment and anti-corruption," per the definition provided by the United Nations Global Compact.[44] To be sure, traceability and transparency are not always strictly connected, as the interaction between the two notions is multifold and complex.[45] Yet considering the conceptual and politically and socially constructed nature of transparency and the practical orientation of traceability, this chapter focuses on their mutually reinforcing relationship. In the context of food law, traceability can be

40 *See* J. Spink, "Review: Final Rules for FSMA 'Third-Party Certification,' 'Foreign Supplier Verification,' and 'Produce Rule' Regarding Food Fraud and EMA", *Michigan State University Food Fraud Initiative*, Jan. 28, 2016, *available at* https://perma.cc/EDQ7-3SDE; *see also* Roberts and Turk, *supra* note 26, at 21.

41 *See* Axfoundation, SKL Kommentus, Swedish county councils and regions, Martin & Servera, and Kairos Future, *Blockchain Use Cases for Food Traceability and Control: A Study to Identify the Potential Benefits from Using Blockchain Technology for Food Traceability and Control* (Stockholm, Kairos Future 2017), at 16.

42 *See* ibid, at 18.

43 *See* Marks, *supra* note 18, at 132–38.

44 United Nations Global Compact Office, *A Guide to Traceability: A Practical Approach to Advance Sustainability in Global Supply Chains* (New York, United Nations Global Compact Office 2014), at 6.

45 *See*, for example, N. Wongnum et al., "Systems for Sustainability and Transparency of Food Supply Chains: Current Status and Challenges" (2011) 25 Advanced Engineering Informatics 65, *available at* https://perma.cc/QSW8-TJAJ, at 68; R. R. Pant et al., "A Framework for Traceability and Transparency in the Dairy Supply Chain Networks" (2015) 189 Procedia Social and Behavioral Sciences 385, 385–88; "Understanding Transparency and Traceability in the Supply Chain", *Société Générale de Surveillance (SGS)*, Aug. 2, 2018, *available at* https://perma.cc/A8F8-FHKX.

understood as "the ability to trace and follow a food, feed, food-producing animal or substance intended to be, or expected to be incorporated into a food or feed, through all stages of production, processing and distribution," according to EU General Food Law.[46]

Reading from these texts, we know that traceability is a complete process of knowing each link along the food supply chain and the ability to pinpoint the relationship between different links and activities therein. More specifically, traceability can mean business-to-business documentation of the path of distribution along the supply chain or that of the specific condition (such as microbiological tests, pesticide residues, or quality certifications) of a product at each stage of distribution.[47] The former is a minimal implementation of traceability, while the latter is more robust traceability and requires more technological support. Regardless of the kinds and degrees of traceability possibly required in the supply chain, it has generally remained a costly and demanding endeavor for both the government and industry.[48]

Recent food safety and fraud incidents, as noted previously, have spurred public outcry and consumer demand for the right to know.[49] Traceability is a key element in ensuring food safety because it empowers regulators and companies to facilitate and expedite outbreak response, increases the legal risks of getting caught, and strengthens deterrence effects on potential violators. There have also been serious calls for better governance actions to ensure sufficient traceability to facilitate outbreak response and corruption deterrence.[50] Nevertheless, the globalization and complication of agri-food supply chains, as well as the characteristics mentioned previously (such as weak cross-border law enforcement; information asymmetry in the market; the sheer number of supply chain players with all sizes and abilities; and common commercial practices to reprocess, reload, and repackage) have made traceability a daunting task.[51]

For one, a considerable share of the agri-food industry, especially in less developed jurisdictions, is characterized by labor-intensive manual work and

46 Regulation (EC) No 178/2002 of the European Parliament and of the Council of 28 January 2002 laying down the general principles and requirements of food law, establishing the European Food Safety Authority and laying down procedures in matters of food safety, 2002 OJ L 31, 1 [hereinafter "EU General Food Law"], at art. 3.15.

47 *See generally* T. Pizzuti & G. Mirabelli, "The Global Track and Trace System for Food: General Framework and Functioning Principles" (2015) 159 Journal of Food Engineering 16.

48 *See* Lytton, *supra* note 9, at 193–94.

49 For a recent review and a historical account, *see* Lytton, *supra* note 9, at 24–64.

50 *See* Food and Agriculture Organization of the UN, *Food Traceability Guidance* (2017), *available at* http://perma.cc/WV46-QWQH, at 2.

51 In addition, record keeping costs to firms have also been a big obstacle to the implementation of traceability. *See* C. Mejia et al., "Traceability (Product Tracing) in Food Systems: An IFT Report Submitted to the FDA, Volume 2: Cost Considerations and Implications" (2010) 9 Comprehensive Reviews in Food Science and Food Safety 159.

handwritten paperwork,[52] which are prone to mistakes and vulnerable to fraud. Global food supply chains are not transparent "due to inconsistent or even unavailable data, high proportion of manual (paper) work, lack of interoperability, and limited information on the product's lifecycle or transport history."[53] Indeed, paper-based record keeping tends to be less transparent (not readily sharable among supply chain participants), and handwriting is more error prone and more likely to facilitate fraud. Practically, proper record-keeping and data integrity mean an overhaul of the system that needs the active use of technology to alleviate problems such as human errors in data recording, inconsistent information, and the lack of data standardization and interoperability among systems.[54]

For another, from a supply chain perspective, the world's "[f]ood systems and agricultural practices . . . are diverse and range from modern, large-scale distribution system channels to traditional food chains," rendering the linkages among all players legally and technically difficult.[55] In addition, most transactions along the agri-food supply chain are processed by multiple intermediaries, without a clear, consistent, and efficient set of procedural standards or rigorous implementation. Indeed, contemporary agri-food systems are defined by their "inherently cross-level and cross-scale" complexity.[56] It is, therefore, arduous today for companies—especially those who are small or medium enterprises (SMEs) with less market power and technical expertise—to trace each link in the supply chain of a specific agri-food product back to its origin.[57]

C. Food Security and Sustainability

Because it holds different meanings for different people in different contexts,[58] food security has been defined and redefined by international organizations

52 *See* M. Lierow et al., *Blockchain: The Backbone of Digital Supply Chains* (2017), *available at* http://perma.cc/SQ7G-35UK.

53 Ibid.

54 *See* T. G. Karippacheril et al., "Global Markets, Global Challenges: Improving Food Safety and Traceability While Empowering Smallholders Through ICT" in World Bank (ed), *ICT in Agriculture (Updated Edition): Connecting Smallholders to Knowledge, Networks, and Institutions* (Washington, DC, World Bank 2017), at 298–302.

55 M. Tripoli & J. Schmidhuber, *Emerging Opportunities for the Application of Blockchain in the Agri-Food Industry* (Geneva, Food and Agriculture Organization of the United Nations and International Centre for Trade and Sustainable Development (ICTSD) International Environment House2018), at 6.

56 P. Ericksen et al., "The Value of a Food System Approach" in J. Ingram et al. (eds), *Food Security and Global Environmental Change* (London, Routledge 2010).

57 Ibid, at 1; *see also* Kairos Future, *supra* note 41, at 21.

58 *See generally* M. Gibson, "Food Security—A Commentary: What Is It and Why Is It So Complicated?" (2012) 1 Foods 18; F. Snyder, "Toward an International Law for Adequate Food" in A. Mahiou & F. Snyder (eds), *Food Security and Food Safety* (Leiden, Brill Publishers 2006); K. Mechlem, "Food Security and the Right to Food in the Discourse of the United Nations" (2004) 10 European Law Journal 631; B. Guha-Khasnobis et al. (eds), *Food Security: Indicators, Measurement*

and conferences on many occasions.[59] Among the 200 definitions that can be found in worldwide publications, the most influential redefinition seems to be that of the World Food Summit of 1996:

> Food security, at the individual, household, national, regional and global levels [is achieved] when all people, at all times, have physical and economic access to sufficient, safe and nutritious food to meet their dietary needs and food preferences for an active and healthy life.[60]

There are at least three key elements that form the operational concept of food security in public policy—food stability (an individual's ability to obtain food over time), food access (affordability and distribution of food), and food availability (general supply of food).

The flexible and broad notion of food security incorporates various measures of supply stability, disruption resilience, and equal access, which are closely tied to supply and demand information as well as diverse risk factors (such as climate change, economic instability, wars, and trade measures). For example, one of the biggest disruptions to the stability of the global food market was an incident in which the prices of a few food commodities spiked in 2007 and 2008, seriously impacting global food availability, stability, and access.[61] The adverse consequences of food insecurity were particularly manifest for "developing countries and net food importers, countries that are dependent on the international food market to ensure their domestic food supply."[62]

Determining legal, policy, or technical solutions to ensure productivity and efficiency in the global agri-food supply chain, reducing operational and transaction costs and increasing economic gains for suppliers (especially small and medium entities), and lowering food prices for consumers are of great relevance and importance. Toward such a purpose, market transparency—which can facilitate "greater access to more accurate market information, strengthen the global food system and reduce the incidence and impact of price surges that are a major threat to food security"—is a key element in the promotion of food security and sustainability around the world.[63] This is where blockchain technologies may come in to revolutionize the food supply chain and empower

---

and the Impact of Trade Openness (Oxford, OUP 2007); G. Gruni, *The EU, World Trade Law and the Right to Food: Rethinking Free Trade Agreements with Developing Countries* (Oxford, Hart Publishing 2018).

59 *See* Food and Agriculture Organization of the UN, "Chapter 2—Food Security: Concepts and Measurement" in *Trade Reforms and Food Security* (2003), *available at* http:/perma.cc/GF7F-8SPY.

60 "Rome Declaration on World Food Security and World Food Summit Plan of Action", World Food Summit, Nov. 1996, *available at* http://perma.cc/SY8M-LMC3.

61 *See generally* G. Gruni, "Going from One Extreme to the Other: Food Security and Export Restrictions in the EU—CARIFORUM Economic Partnership Agreement" (2013) 19 European Law Journal 864.

62 Ibid, at 865.

63 Tripoli & Schmidhuber, *supra* note 55, at 18–19.

market players along the agri-food supply chain by increasing transparency, efficiency, and trust among all players. At the same time, applying blockchain technologies to the governance of food safety, traceability, and sustainability, as analyzed in the following, may pose another layer of regulatory questions about technical capacity and infrastructure gap, scalability and implementation costs, global standardization politics, cybersecurity and data protection, and the technologically inherent limits of blockchain. Whether blockchain promises to be a grand "technical fix" calls for a closer examination.

III. Blockchain as a Grand "Technical Fix"—Assessing Existing Pilot Projects

Given the growing consumer demand for transparency from corporations,[64] as well as the need for efficient supply chain management on a business-to-business level,[65] agri-food producers, processors, distributors, and retailers are driven to seek innovative solutions. Due to its unique characteristics, blockchain technology promises to offer transparency, traceability, and security along the food supply chain. Some businesses have addressed traceability challenges by leveraging blockchain technology along the supply chain to ensure product information and data reliability, as well as the consumer's right to know.[66] Notably, there is growing cross-sector collaboration between agri-food and technology companies, which places blockchain at the center of the "technical fix" to regulatory challenges of food safety, traceability, and sustainability. As a result, the total value of blockchain applications in agri-food markets globally is predicted to grow from $41.9 million in 2018 to $195.3 million in 2019 and further jump to $1.4 billion by 2022.[67]

This section examines three prominent examples that shed light on the incremental regulatory shift to "blockchainizing" food law, driven largely by private actors in the agri-food and tech industries. Furthermore, the practical strengths and weaknesses of using blockchain to ensure food safety, traceability, and sustainability will be reviewed. Last but not least, the government's role (or the absence thereof) will be assessed, given the promises and perils of blockchain as it relates to food law in the context of resorting to technology as a regulatory tool.[68]

64 *See* Food and Agriculture Organization of the UN, *supra* note 49, at 1.

65 *See generally* C. F. Lin, "The Emergence and Influence of Transnational Private Regulation of Food Safety" in S. Halabi (ed), *Food and Drug Regulation in an Era of Globalized Markets* (Boston, Academic Press 2015).

66 *See* M. D. Fowler, "Linking the Benefit to the Corporation: Blockchain as a Solution for Certification in an Age of 'Do-Good' Business" (2018) 20 Vanderbilt Journal of Entertainment and Technology Law 881, 913–15.

67 P. Neo & T. Koe, "Trace What Matters: Is Blockchain the Solution to Food Safety, Quality and Brand Reputation?", *Food Navigator Asia*, Mar. 21, 2019, *available at* http://perma.cc/4EB3-MMAY.

68 On technology as a regulatory tool, *see* R. Brownsword & K. Yeung, "Regulating Technologies", in R. Brownsword & K. Yeung (eds), *Regulating Technologies: Legal Futures, Regulatory Frames and Technological Fixes* (Oxford, Hart Publishing 2008), at 7–13.

A. Blockchain as a Potential "Technical Fix"

Blockchain has been called for in various contexts to serve as a "technical fix" of regulatory problems.[69] Regulatory technologies as such may be used to "define and incorporate legal or contractual provisions into code, and to enforce them irrespectively of whether or not there subsists an underlying legal rule."[70] Yet one should be familiar with the technical elements and nature of blockchain as well as the technology's advantages in addressing governance challenges in the global agri-food supply chain. Defined broadly, blockchains (or DLTs) are decentralized databases that are collaboratively stored, maintained, and updated by a distributed network of computing nodes.[71] A combination of technologies—including peer-to-peer networks, cryptographic methods (with public or private key), and consensus mechanisms—constitutes this novel type of database, which is shared among parties who do not otherwise trust each other.[72] Data inserted into the blockchain is simultaneously permanently recorded and updated in each node of the network, and the use of cryptography allows for a mathematical consensus to ensure the consistency and authenticity of such data across the network.[73] Each new transaction is stored as an additional "block" and is cryptographically tied to the "chain" of existing blocks, creating a so-called blockchain.[74] Blockchain information is generally "immutable" because cryptographic methods and networked nodes ensure that only information that is consistent with all earlier versions can be recorded onto the blockchain-based on consensus, while information that conflicts with existing copies of the database would not be accepted.[75] Similarly, information (e.g. transactions) that has been permanently recorded on the blockchain cannot be easily deleted or altered (see additional discussion subsequently).[76]

As a distributed and decentralized system, "[b]lockchain is not controlled by a central authority, person, company, or government" but rather by all network nodes (minders, or participants) based on a predefined algorithm, which keeps "complete information about transactions (and ownership) from the genesis block to the most recently completed block."[77] All of the participants in the network have their own digital signature, which is attached to each of the

69 *See generally* P. De Filippi & S. Hassan, "Blockchain Technology as a Regulatory Technology: From Code is Law to Law is Code" (2016) 21 First Monday 3.

70 Ibid, at 9.

71 P. De Filippi & A. Wright, *Blockchain and the Law: The Rule of Code* (Cambridge, Harvard University Press 2018).

72 Ibid.

73 K. Yeung, "Regulation by Blockchain: The Emerging Battle for Supremacy between the Code of Law and Code as Law" (2019) 82 Modern Law Review 207, 210–11.

74 UK Government Chief Science Adviser, *Distributed Ledger Technology: Beyond Block Chain* (2016), *available at* https://perma.cc/B2PB-87SS, at 5.

75 Yeung, *supra* note 73, at 211.

76 Ibid.

77 P. Ciaian, "Blockchain Technology and Market Transparency", *European Commission*, May 2018, *available at* https://perma.cc/VX8J-4SSS.

transactions added to the blockchain with specific timestamps and details.[78] The history of all of the transactions is, therefore, recorded in the blockchain with great security and accuracy, creating a secure ledger for those who have cryptographic keys (public or private) and can access and manage the shared ledger.[79]

There are many typologies of blockchains based on different benchmarks. The most relevant for the purpose of this chapter is the difference between public (not permissioned) and private (permissioned) blockchains. In a public blockchain, such as the one employed by Bitcoin, all participants in the network can contribute data without being censored or controlled by a single power, and all records are transparent and accessible to them.[80] Public blockchains enjoy a high level of data security, as it is only when all existing ledgers are simultaneously hacked that the data on the blockchain can be tampered with, according to the consensus mechanism.[81] A private blockchain, on the other hand, is owned by one or more entities, and new data is written to the network and verified via a limited consensus procedure by entities with controlling authority over the ledger.[82] Therefore, when we emphasize the critical advantages of the technology as a "distributed, shared, encrypted-database that serves as an irreversible and incorruptible public repository of information,"[83] we are referring to the public (not permissioned) type of blockchains.

All together, a distributed and shared platform, data security and immutability, and transparency and traceability give blockchain technologies the potential to generally ensure accurate and secure records of transactions in the database, generating "trust" for participants in a given market (e.g. supply chain, stock exchange, real estate, or insurance). In this sense, blockchain has the power to "radically disrupt existing political and economic orders by dispensing with the need for conventional third party intermediaries . . . enabling peer-to-peer transactions via the blockchain without the operational inefficiencies."[84] The potential of blockchain is not limited to Bitcoin or the financial sector, although it is regarded as one of the most disrupted issue areas. Rather, the

78 *See* T. Scott et al., "Evaluating Feasibility of Blockchain Application for DSCSA Compliance" (2018) 1 SMU Data Science Review 1, 9–10. Blockchain technologies have "operational resilience" where data is accurate, secure, and accessible, resulting in a situation where "I know who you are. I know who owns this asset. We have a shared record of trusted, validated transactions; no reconciliation required." Ibid.

79 Ibid; *see also* P. Paech, "The Governance of Blockchain Financial Networks" (2017) 80 MLR 1073, 1080–82.

80 UK Government Chief Science Adviser, *supra* note 74, at 17; *see also* P. De Filippi & B. Loveluck, "The Invisible Politics of Bitcoin: Governance Crisis of a Decentralised Infrastructure" (2016) 5 Internet Policy Review 1, 15–19.

81 Ibid.

82 Ibid.

83 A. Wright & P. De Filippi, "Decentralized Blockchain Technology and the Rise of Lex Cryptographia", *SSRN*, Mar. 10, 2015, *available at* https://perma.cc/4LBV-PYDP.

84 Yeung, *supra* note 73, at 212.

technology can be applied in a general manner as a regulatory tool in a myriad of contexts,[85] especially those that value information accuracy, data security, record-keeping, and traceability.

In the area of food law and policy, the previously mentioned governance challenges largely touch upon "information." Specifically, information asymmetry in the supply chain is key to many safety and fraud issues; verifying and sharing information is key to traceability and outbreak response; and sustainability and food security partly depend on accurate information regarding the demand for, and supply of, food. Blockchain technologies can ensure the validity and reliability of the information on the network without relying on a central intermediary and can keep such information cryptographically "tamperproof," as inconsistent or adulterated data are automatically discarded by the network.[86] As such, blockchains can be applied to strengthen digital record-keeping and traceability in the food business, verify transactions and certifications, and increase inventory and management efficiency.[87] A report jointly published by the Food and Agriculture Organization of the United Nations (FAO) and the International Centre for Trade and Sustainable Development (ICTSD) further stresses that

> the potential for DLTs to increase efficiency, transparency[,] and trust throughout agricultural supply chains and empower all market players is real. The technology has the potential to simplify and integrate agricultural supply chains, enhance food safety, reduce risk in trade finance and promote inclusive trade.[88]

Although several governance approaches have been adopted by governments worldwide, blockchain holds great potential and has emerged as a promising regulatory tool (more ambitiously, a "technical fix") for the agri-food industry to strengthen various aspects of supply chain management and deliver strong governance performance.

B. *Examples of Blockchainizing Food Supply Chain Management*

1. *Provenance Seafood Traceability Blockchain*

The first example of blockchainizing food supply chain governance is Provenance, a UK start-up company that incorporates blockchain into its

85 *See generally* M. Finck, "Blockchains: Regulating the Unknown" (2018) 19 German Law Journal 665.

86 Fowler, *supra* note 66, at 881, 898–900.

87 *See* ibid; *see also* J. F. Galvez et al., "Future Challenges on the Use of Blockchain for Food Traceability Analysis" (2018) 107 Trends Analytical Chemistry 222, 222–32; Kairos Future, *supra* note 41, at 24–25.

88 Tripoli & Schmidhuber, *supra* note 55, at 2.

methodology to monitor processes, track products, digitize certifications, and ensure compliance with social and sustainable standards.[89] More specifically, Provenance constructs "a shared and secure platform" based on blockchain technology, which allows for secure transaction audits, supply chain management, and information certainty.[90] As for traceability, Provenance uses blockchain to "enable[] every physical product to come with a digital 'passport' that proves authenticity . . . and origin . . . creating an auditable record of the journey behind."[91] The strengthened traceability and supply chain transparency further help companies in the fishery industry detect and prevent slavery or labor abuse, in line with other social and environmental standards.[92] The company has been working with retailers on a trial of the "from shore to plate" system,[93] requiring local suppliers in source areas (Indonesia) to key in data about their daily catch to a public blockchain with a blockchain ID via text message.[94] Provenance clams that with the successful implementation of this system, the entire history of a seafood product can be recorded online—from catching and processing, to certification, to packaging and distributing, to marketing and selling—and accessed by consumers with a smartphone app.[95]

However, as argued by one commentator, Provenance offers only a partial solution,[96] since the majority of agri-food sustainability issues (e.g. insufficient governance, weak institutions, inferior working conditions, market opacity, and lack of information sharing) happen "at the level of production and first intermediaries/processors," according to the United Nations Environmental Program (UNEP).[97] That is, while blockchain technology can ensure a high level of transparency, traceability, and immutability (security/unchangeable nature), the data initially input by local producers (the first players along the supply chain) remains vulnerable to human mistakes and economic adulteration.[98] Provenance aims to address illegal fishing and fraudulent certification

89 *See* "Blockchain: The Solution for Transparency in Product Supply Chains", *Provenance*, Nov. 21, 2015, *available at* https://perma.cc/5ZPS-HYJB [hereinafter "Provenance White Paper"]; *see also* "How Provenance Uses Blockchain to Digitise Certification", *Provenance*, July 25, 2017, *available at* https://perma.cc/X5U4-CAD6.

90 Provenance White Paper, *supra* note 89.

91 Ibid.

92 *See* T. Levitt, "Blockchain Technology Trialed to Tackle Slavery in the Fishing Industry", *The Guardian*, Sept. 7, 2016, *available at* https://perma.cc/G8QJ-RAUH.

93 For a detailed report on this blockchain pilot system for tracing yellowfin and skipjack tuna fish in Indonesia, *see* "From Shore to Plate: Tracking Tuna on the Blockchain", *Provenance*, July 15, 2016, https://perma.cc/VWW7-R3C6.

94 *See* Luke Parker, "Provenance Tackles Slavery in the Fish Trade, with Blockchain Technology", *Brave New Coin*, Sept. 15, 2016, *available at* https://perma.cc/YF8T-H9PA.

95 Ibid; *see also* Scott et al, *supra* note 78, at 14–16.

96 Fowler, *supra* note 66, at 915.

97 N. Vallejo et al., "The Role of Supply Chains in Addressing the Global Seafood Crisis" (2009), *available at* https://perma.cc/4V27-WAQN.

98 *See* Lytton, *supra* note 9, at 193, 227 for an in-depth discussion on the dependence of "technical fixes" for traceability on human data input.

problems by registering each catch and each sale of fish on the blockchain. Yet the action of registering itself cannot be readily verified by technology without human auditors.

2. *IBM Food Trust Platform*

Another example that demonstrates an infrastructure model for blockchainizing agri-food supply chain management is the cloud- and blockchain-based IBM Food Trust platform service.[99] Following a pilot project between Wal-Mart and IBM that uses blockchain technology to track produce in the United States and pork in China,[100] IBM forged a collaboration with a few other major food producers and retailers, including, inter alia, Dole, Nestlé, Tyson Foods, Kroger, and Unilever in 2017, to leverage blockchain technology to address transparency and traceability challenges along the cross-border food supply chain.[101] Wal-Mart has further required its upstream suppliers of leafy greens to use the IBM Food Trust platform by September 2019.[102] Under this IBM–Wal-Mart cross-sector collaboration, each food item is digitally connected to the data (which can be either merely about the path of movement or detailed records of specific conditions of that item, as discussed in Section II.B) entered into the blockchain system at every step of the process, which makes possible the tracing of a package of mangos in just two seconds, whereas traditionally "it took six days, 18 hours and 26 minutes" from shop to farm.[103] In this case, when an outbreak happens, both the consumer and the retailer can easily retrieve crucial information (such as inspection records) about relevant suppliers, processers, and distributors and swiftly identify what went wrong and where.[104] The government may also incorporate such supply chain management information into a public-private partnership "food cloud" to facilitate evidence-based facility inspection, border control, and outbreak responses.[105] A prominent scholar of food law and policy, therefore, cites the Wal-Mart–IBM collaboration and points out the value of using blockchain technology to

99 *See* Tripoli & Schmidhuber, *supra* note 55, at 2–9.

100 *See* R. Hackett, "Walmart and 9 Food Giants Team Up on IBM Blockchain Plans", *Forbes*, Aug. 22, 2017, *available at* https://perma.cc/R226-PNTC.

101 Roger Aitken, "IBM Forges Blockchain Collaboration with Nestlé & Walmart in Global Food Safety", *Forbes*, Aug. 22, 2017, *available at* https://perma.cc/SU67-7BFA.

102 "Food Traceability Initiative—Fresh Leafy Greens", *Walmart*, Sept. 24, 2018, *available at* https://perma.cc/UF9J-N7HB.

103 S. Wass, "Food Companies Unite to Advance Blockchain for Supply Chain Traceability", *Global Trade Review*, Aug. 22, 2017, *available at* https://perma.cc/5XU4-WC9Q.

104 *See* Galvez et al., *supra* note 87, at 223–25. More specifically, this platform uses IBM and Linux Hyperledger Project architecture to digitally track information that "includes storage temperatures, expiration date, shipping details, origination farm details, batch number and much more relevant data when the food being delivered worldwide." Ibid, at 229.

105 Ibid, at 229.

deliver a more evidence-based food safety governance system with the support of private oversight.[106]

In response to this successful implementation, IBM has expanded its scope of collaboration to work with other players along the agri-food supply chain, such as JD.com, China's second-largest e-commerce company. JD.com has since mid-2017 worked together with "national departments, fresh and consumer goods brands . . . to build anti-counterfeiting and traceability platforms to . . . protect the rights of brands and consumers" based on this blockchain system.[107] This recent development demonstrates how the cross-sectoral "Blockchain Food Safety Alliance"[108] between IBM, JD.com, Wal-Mart, and Tsinghua University in Beijing endeavors to find a technical fix to the traceability challenge in China. IBM has moved to work with Microsoft and the International Article Numbering Association to set international standards for blockchain applications in global supply chains. The Chinese government has yet to intervene and issue standards on this subject matter.[109]

Nevertheless, it should be noted that while the IBM Food Trust Platform is open to agri-food companies, they usually maintain the implementation of blockchain systems in a centralized manner among industry stakeholders (i.e. Wal-Mart itself and its suppliers). Wal-Mart, for instance, while not in a position to easily alter the data stored in the blockchain without being noticed (the system is modifiable or eliminable, yet blockchain makes it more difficult), could "simply, shut down the entire system."[110] As observed by another commentator, "Walmart's system does not solve the information asymmetry between the trades and the consumers; it only solves the information asymmetry between Walmart and its suppliers."[111]

3. *WFP Food Security Initiative*

Similarly, the UN WFP launched the "Building Block" pilot program in 2017.[112] Relying on iris-scanning technologies and blockchains, this program helped refugees verify their identities and directly deduct what they spend from the amount of aid they receive from the WFP.[113] In Jordan's Azraq camp, more than 100,000 refugees can pay for their food by utilizing a private

106 Lytton, *supra* note 9, at 225–28.

107 R. Berti & M. Semprebon, "Food Traceability in China" (2018) 13 European Food and Feed Law Review 522, 530.

108 *See* Roger Aitken, "IBM & Walmart Launching Blockchain Food Safety Alliance in China with Fortune 500's JD.com", *Forbes*, Dec. 14, 2017, *available at* https://perma.cc/3NZ2-P5XZ.

109 Ibid, at 229.

110 Ibid, at 530.

111 Ibid, at 531.

112 *See* United Nations World Food Programme (WFP), "Blockchain Against Hunger: Harnessing Technology in Support of Syrian Refugees", *WFP News*, May 30, 2017, *available at* https://perma.cc/F9UD-GBS5.

113 Ibid.

(permissioned) Ethereum-based blockchain platform "to make cash-based transfers faster, cheaper and more secure"[114] Using biometric registration data from the UN High Commissioner for Refugees (UNHCR) and authentication technologies, refugees can enjoy peer-to-peer financial assistance to purchase food from local supermarkets in the camp instead of cash, vouchers, or e-cards intermediated by local authorities.[115] Refugees can have more control over their identities and money under such an emergency circumstance. At the same time, the WFP can establish a full record of every transaction that occurs on the retailer's end and reduce transaction costs due to market inefficiency, corruption, and logistics. The 2018 annual report of the Regional Refugee and Resilience Plan (3RP, a collaboration between the UNHCR, Member States, and non-governmental organizations in response to the impact of the Syria crisis in Turkey, Lebanon, Jordan, Egypt, and Iraq) cites the success of the Building Blocks pilot project and how blockchain technology has enabled the WFP to assist in a more efficient and economical manner.[116]

Such initiatives have the potential to be generalized to help retailers and consumers pinpoint sources of contamination at times of outbreaks or provide production details and quality certifications (e.g. product origin, farm history, processing and shipping information, and fair trade or safety/sustainability standards). Blockchains can also be combined with smart contract systems or other AI techniques to increase efficiency, simplify transactions, ensure compliance and security, and promote trade facilitation across borders.

IV. Blockchainizing Food Law? A Closer Examination of the "Code as Law" Promise and Its Limits

Blockchain holds the potential to serve as an effective and efficient governance tool in the global agri-food sector. As demonstrated previously, there have been successful cases in which blockchain seems to have provided sufficient solutions to the regulatory problems of food safety, traceability, authenticity, and sustainability, at least in part. In this vein, the promises of blockchainizing food law rest upon the "code as law" ideas in the scholarship of law and regulation, especially in the context of cyberspace.[117] Before we have a closer examination of the promise of "code as law," however, a caveat should be noted: The cases discussed in this chapter are still at an early stage of development and application as industry pilots rather than comprehensive application across the board.

114 Ibid.

115 Ibid.

116 *See* "2018 Annual Report, 3RP—Regional Refugee & Resilience Plan", *available at* https://perma.cc/YHD4-B7FG (last accessed Feb. 29, 2020).

117 *See generally* L. Lessig, *Code and Other Laws of Cyberspace* (New York, Basic Books 1999). Lawrence Lessig was the first legal scholar to articulate these ideas in the areas of law and regulation in the cyberspace and beyond.

Applying blockchain technologies as a regulatory tool to address problems of food safety, traceability, authenticity, and sustainability is premised upon the "code as law" approach, one of the many modalities of regulation including command and control rules, social norms, industry standards, market and architecture, and computer codes.[118] Indeed, technology can be "regulatory" and compliance driven through different mechanisms to make "regulation sustained and focused attempt to alter the behavior of others according to defined standards or purposes to produce a broadly identified outcome or outcomes, which may involve mechanisms of standard-setting, information-gathering[,] and behavior-modification."[119] Just as information and telecommunication technology can force compliance by building in automatic braking at stop signs for self-driving cars,[120] blockchain can de facto shape what is permissive, possible, prohibited, or impossible.[121]

Indeed, blockchain's key features mean that food processes and production information can be recorded in a database that ensures traceability, immutability, and transparency. Agri-food information stored on the blockchain is basically tamperproof, which increases the rate of detection and reduces the incentive to adulterate food or engage in fraud. Data traceability allows for better regulatory control, as competent authorities can trace and identify every registered action from farm to fork (e.g. livestock input, use of fertilizer or pesticide, irrigation, veterinary practices, processing, transportation, storage, etc.),[122] as well as stronger deterrence against food safety violations and fraudulent conduct.[123] The technology's peer-to-peer distributed structure also allows for greater economic and financial inclusion—under certain circumstances, small and medium players can participate without facing formidable financial, technical, and trust-related barriers that prevent them from taking advantage of the market.[124] Further, the disintermediation of data storage and "trustless

118 *See generally* J. Black, "Critical Reflections on Regulation" (2002) 27 Australasian Journal of Legal Philosophy 1.

119 Ibid, at 26.

120 *See* L. B. Moses & M. Zalnieriute, "Law and Technology in the Dimension of Time", in S. Ranchordás & Y. Roznai (eds), *Time, Law and Change: An Interdisciplinary Study* (Oxford, Hart Publishing 2020).

121 Similar approaches (albeit in different conceptual lenses) include "compliance by design," "compliance through design," "design-based regulation," "RegTech," and "privacy by design." *See* id; *see also* M. M. Piri, "The Changing Landscapes of FinTech and RegTech: Why the United States Should Create a Federal Regulatory Sandbox" (2018) 2 Business and Financial Law Review 233, 237–240 (discussing RegTech); D. A. Zetzche et al., "From FinTech to TechFin: The Regulatory Challenges of Data-Driven Finance" (2018) 14 N.Y.U. Journal of Law and Business 393, 399–405.

122 *See* Tripoli & Schmidhuber, *supra* note 55, at 7.

123 Blockchain's immutability potential can ensure that "a digital file, register, certificate of ethical production, photo or video etc. is still the same as it was when it was first registered in the blockchain," as the technology makes agri-food processing and production data "impossible, or at least very hard, to manipulate." Kairos Future, *supra* note 41, at 25–26.

124 However, as argued subsequently, blockchain might price some SMEs out of the market, as have other advances in food safety, which will likely become a difficult tradeoff.

trust" may lower uncertainty between buyers and sellers,[125] reduce transaction costs, and promote sustainable management and development.[126] Information asymmetry can also be alleviated through blockchain systems to foster greater consumer trust. Such trust toward the food supply chain can also be enjoyed by producers and retailers, as there is greater information transparency and credibility in the ecosystem. Some commentators even argue that blockchain holds the potential to "provide[] the agri-food market a trustworthy framework to store every passage of the production and distribution chain."[127]

Despite blockchain's "code as law" promise, there are formidable challenges that may prevent successful implementation of such a technical fix on the ground. As analyzed in the following, while it remains to be seen what problems such pilot projects have encountered as well as what models are likely to be more successful than others and why, a number of challenges such as scaling up, data protection and cybersecurity risks, standardization politics, technical capacity gap, and inherent technological limits are already salient.[128]

A. Capacity Gap Problem: Operational Knowledge and Technical Expertise

First, while blockchain technologies are relatively accessible to business actors due to the high penetration rate of the Internet,[129] stable Internet service is neither available nor affordable in many corners of the developing world,[130] where the primary industry is food and agriculture. It is noted that the future diffusion of blockchain technologies in developing countries may be limited due to the lack of adequate infrastructural support. In particular, network infrastructures for public-key applications pose a formidable obstacle.[131]

125 *See generally* K. Werbach, "Trust, But Verify: Why the Blockchain Needs the Law" (2018) 33 Berkeley Technology Law Journal 487, 498, 549.

126 While the scholarly and practical discourse on how disintermediation may lower uncertainty exceeds the scope of this chapter, it is worth noting that some intermediaries are designed to lower uncertainty and work well too. For a thorough discussion on the advantages and disadvantages of different forms of intermediation, *see* T. D. Lytton, "The Taming of the Stew: Regulatory Intermediaries in Food Safety Governance" (2017) 670 The ANNALS of the American Academy of Political and Social Science 78.

127 Berti & Semprebon, *supra* note 107, at 529.

128 The actual success on the ground depends on the nature of different subsectors with many different kinds of people working in different types of firms. The role of regulatory culture and economic incentives in supporting consistent data collection and entry routines along the supply chain are also relevant factors.

129 *See* C. F. Lin & H. W. Liu, "Disruptive Technologies and Sustainable Development: Implications for Southeast Asia" in *Programme on Inclusive Economic Transformation* (Geneva, International Centre for Trade and Sustainable Development (ICTSD) 2018), at 7–8.

130 International Telecommunication Union (ITU), "ICT Facts and Figures 2017", *ITU*, July 2017, *available at* https://perma.cc/SCY6-FTDT.

131 See R. Zambrano et al., "Unpacking the Disruptive Potential of Blockchain Technology for Human Development" (2017), available at https://idl-bnc-idrc.dspacedirect.org/handle/10625/56662, at 12.

There are also significant barriers to implementation due to deficits of operational knowledge and technical expertise among individual actors, especially for small companies in the food industry that follow conventional practice. It is true that for end-market players, taking advantage of blockchain primarily involves an application on a smartphone, but upstream suppliers will need "digital skills" to access data and navigate applications. Therefore, inadequate operational knowledge and technical expertise will be an obstacle to adoption, especially for small and medium players.[132] Effective use of blockchain in the global agri-food supply chain requires operational knowledge about other technologies, such as network management, smart sensors, biosensors, and the Internet of Things (IoT).

Many businesses in different parts of the agri-food sector have yet to "digitize" supply chain management and record-keeping, not to mention obtaining technical expertise about all of the relevant technologies to link physical food products to various blockchain data. As it is crucial for all participants at all stages to get on the blockchain for the system to ensure comprehensive transparency and traceability,[133] the uneven capacity of different entities (at different nodes of the global supply chain, in different countries, of different sizes, and with different technical backgrounds) underscores just how diverse and fragmented the agri-food industry is. This capacity problem will only become graver as the scope of application expands, especially when "little has so far been done to push this still immature technology."[134] Capacity building and technical assistance at different levels will be of crucial importance.[135] Leaving this capacity challenge unaddressed may lead to greater marginalization among small and medium companies in the agri-food industry.

B. Implementation Burdens and Standardization Costs

Second, the implementation and standardization costs for blockchainizing food law are rather unpredictable and will constitute formidable legal and policy barriers. As we are still at an early and immature phase in terms of applying the blockchain to the global agri-food supply chain, the overall cost of implementing relevant technologies remains difficult to estimate.[136] Further, technically speaking,

> the evolution of DLTs has led to the development of both public and private DLTs, which use different consensus algorithms to validate data

132 Tripoli & Schmidhuber, *supra* note 55, at 22.

133 *See* J. Barnard, "The Missing Link in the Food Chain: Blockchain", *DecisionNext*, 2016, *available at* https://perma.cc/K8S3.

134 Galvez et al., *supra* note 87, at 223.

135 *See generally* Wang & Lin, *supra* note 8.

136 *See generally* T. Makong & T. Ngwira, "Trade Related Capacity Building Measures in African LDCs and the Paradox of the Efficiency-Effectiveness Dichotomy" in J. Pauwelyn & M. Yang (eds),

entries. Current development efforts are implementing a wide range of different consensus mechanisms and types of DLTs.[137]

Existing systems are like silos based on different blockchain technologies, data, and organizations, and companies usually have limited incentive to work together or share confidential information with potential competitors. The participation of new (types of) players, from the tech sector to the broad field of business, will further complicate the dynamics and the structures of interactions. There may be issues regarding conflicts and repetition between different private standards, as well as divergences in existing legal frameworks governing such disruptive innovations, which will, in turn, lead to market barriers or other trade frictions.[138]

From an information management perspective, the promise of blockchain as a technology solution for a governance framework, in particular traceability mechanisms, "requires a well-organized and standardized supply chain between all (internal and external) actors."[139] Practically speaking, the types of blockchain technologies and data structures must be clearly and consistently defined first before automating processes kickstart.[140] At the cross-border level, discussion of whether and how to harmonize rules and standards about the interoperability of blockchain systems across relevant sectors will likely surface and will call for public–private governance dialogues. Some have argued that the agri-food industry should work together with the technology industry to develop best practices and standards for the application of blockchain to the agri-food sector on a global scale.[141] In this regard, the growing use of and reference to the GS1 standards as industry best practices for identifying products, locations, processes, and assets as well as for structuring data and digital infrastructure regarding the global movement of goods may serve as common bases.[142]

Building Legal Capacity for a More Inclusive Globalization: Barriers to and Best Practices for Integrating Developing Countries into Global Economic Regulation (Geneva, The Graduate Institute 2019), at 229–232.

137 Tripoli & Schmidhuber, *supra* note 55, at 21.

138 *See generally* J. Clapp & D. Fuchs (eds), *Corporate Power in Global Agrifood Governance* (Cambridge, MIT Press 2009); Lin, *supra* note 65; D. Prévost, "Private Sector Food-Safety Standards and the SPS Agreement: Challenges and Possibilities" (2008) 33 South African Yearbook of International Law 1 (2008).

139 K. Behnke & M. F. W. H. A. Janssen, "Boundary Conditions for Traceability in Food Supply Chains Using Blockchain Technology" (2020) 52 International Journal of Information Management 1, 9 "Data governance cannot be defined by partners of one Blockchain initiative alone, but requires agreement on sector if not even on industry level. Otherwise, suppliers will have to comply to different interface standards which makes Blockchain technology from an economical point of view inefficient." Ibid.

140 Ibid.

141 M. J. Casey & P. Wong, "Global Supply Chains Are About to Get Better, Thanks to Blockchain", *Harvard Business Review*, Mar. 13, 2017, *available at* https://perma.cc/3CG3-7GJ3.

142 *See* GS1 AISBL, *Bridging Blockchains: Interoperability Is Essential to the Future of Data Sharing* (2018), *available at* https://perma.cc/QL24-72TT.

C. Cybersecurity and Data Protection

Third, many commentators have pointed out the risks to cybersecurity and data protection that are generally applicable to blockchain technologies, and the agri-food sector is not immune from these. As shown by the recent discussion on cyber-attacks and threats to cryptocurrencies,[143] insufficient cybersecurity or weak data protection can lead to huge losses to blockchain users. Indeed, cybersecurity risks must be addressed to ensure data integrity, promote user trust, prevent breaches of private information, and avoid economic losses.

Certainly, market transactions include some types of confidential information that need to be protected, such as personal data and business know-how. There are also other types of information that should be made available for public knowledge to foster consumer confidence and market reliability. A related and more nuanced question, therefore, concerns the proper balance between what types of data should be publicized and what types are best kept private as business secrets. This question "depend[s] on the rules of the DLT that are based on, the purpose of the platform, as well as the preferences of the users."[144] Such choices further call for different plans at different levels to ensure cybersecurity. Currently, what constitutes best practices and methodologies is contingent upon the future development of blockchain technologies, which are still evolving.

D. Inherent Limits of Blockchain

There are a number of inherent limits related to the technological nature of blockchain (and how it works). While ensuring food safety, authenticity, and traceability through blockchain seems promising, the integrity of the system when applied to the agri-food sector (vis-à-vis the case of cryptocurrency) should not be taken for granted. Any data, once input onto the blockchain, is generally immutable, as noted previously. However, there does not exist a verification mechanism to ensure that the process of "inputting" the data itself is free from mistakes, adulteration, or manipulation.[145] For example, if a company or an employee tampers with the production details in the first place or manipulates a sensor, such adulterated information will also be "immutable" on the blockchain without being detected.

For private blockchains, such as the Wal-Mart application, the company that holds authority and control over the entire system can alter raw information (which may be noticed by members of the private blockchain) or simply shut down the system.[146] This concept is noted as the "garbage in, garbage out"

143 *See*, for example, L. Fitzpatrick, "A Hacker's Take on Blockchain Security", *Forbes*, Feb. 4, 2019, *available at* https://perma.cc/JH7T-NEGA; A. Herman, "Why Blockchain Is No Silver Bullet for Cyber Threats", *Forbes*, Oct. 2, 2018, *available at* https://perma.cc/XMD7-ZXKD.

144 Tripoli & Schmidhuber, *supra* note 55, at 21.

145 *See* Galvez et al., *supra* note 87, at 230.

146 Berti & Semprebon, *supra* note 107, at 530.

problem that applies to some DLT systems, as the use of blockchain technology per se does not stop fraudulent data being entered.[147] Therefore, how to ensure accountability in such cases to avoid so-called "second layer information asymmetry"[148] is of crucial importance when we delegate the trust business to machines[149] (or, as argued by Andreas Antonopoulos, a "shift from trusting people to trusting math").[150] Would there still be a need to place auditors on blockchains, and if so, how? Identifying the optimal institutional design to minimize human error (and corruption) in linking physical product details with blockchain digital information constitutes a significant governance challenge.

Last but not least, existing blockchain systems seem to be able to operate only at a relatively low capacity. Indeed, blockchain faces a serious "scalability problem."[151] For instance, systems such as Bitcoin and Ethereum can process around 10 transactions per second, while conventional systems such as Visa or MasterCard can, on average, process around 5,000–8,000 transactions per second.[152] This perhaps explains why the current blockchain systems in the agri-food sector are rather limited to a single product category or raw material. Further, just like other blockchain-based systems, energy and physical space consumption remains a crucial issue for effective and efficient implementation.[153] The move towards "cloud-based" blockchain systems may serve as a solution that reduces the use of energy and physical space, yet it requires considerable time and investment to go forward. How much information can be input, stored, processed, and shared on blockchain systems at a reasonable cost will largely determine its place in the agri-food sector. The capacity and scalability problem would need to be addressed for the broader application of blockchain technologies.

V. Conclusion

As the global agri-food supply chain has been rapidly changing and expanding, there seems to be a need to innovate governance tools by leveraging disruptive technologies. The most recent statements from the FDA Commissioner

147 *See* M. Finck, *Blockchain Regulation and Governance in Europe* (Cambridge, CUP 2018), at 163.

148 *See generally* C. F. Lin, "Challenges to Third-Party Food Safety Audits and Certification", *Harvard Law Bill of Health*, Dec. 5, 2013, *available at* https://perma.cc/QBU9-DZZU.

149 *See* "The Promise of Blockchain: The Trust Machine", *The Economist*, Oct. 31, 2015, *available at* www.economist.com/leaders/2015/10/31/the-trust-machine.

150 A. Antonopoulos, "Bitcoin Security Model: Trust by Computation", *O'Reilly Radar*, Feb. 20, 2014, *available at* https://perma.cc/X8BR-2YAQ.

151 K. Li, "The Blockchain Scalability Problem & the Race for Visa-Like Transaction Speed", *Hackernoon*, Jan. 31, 2019, *available at* https://perma.cc/6DRF-7BDX.

152 Ciaian, *supra* note 77.

153 *See* D. Babayan, "Bitcoin's Energy Consumption Equalled That of Hungary in 2018", *News BTC*, Mar. 14, 2019, *available at* https://perma.cc/J74U-EXHB. But *see* S. Huckle, "Bitcoin's High Energy Consumption Is a Concern—But It May Be a Price Worth Paying", *The Conversation*, Nov. 7, 2018, *available at* https://perma.cc/JVD9-YS8B.

and Deputy Commissioner (who piloted blockchain at Wal-Mart before serving at FDA) also underlined "emerging track and trace technologies that can assist response efforts to allow FDA to intervene in time to alert consumers, implement recalls, and avoid human illnesses . . . includ[ing] blockchain technology."[154] In the area of drug regulation, FDA has successfully launched a pilot program that leverages blockchain technology to execute the agency's duty under the Drug Supply Chain Security Act (DSCSA) to establish a track-and-trace system for medicines by 2023.[155] In the food sector, FDA held a public meeting with a broad range of stakeholders on a new approach—"A New Era of Smarter Food Safety" on October 21, 2019, as part of the agency's ongoing efforts to implement FSMA.[156] This multi-stakeholder deliberation process may help identify legal barriers to the use of this technology (such as concerns over data protection, standardization, and technological limits) and how food law and regulation should be changed in the future. At this moment, FDA aims to adopt this modern approach to addressing issues such as "trac[ing] sources of contaminated foods and using new predictive analytics tools like artificial intelligence to assess risks and prioritize the agency's work and resources" towards a "more digital, traceable, and safer system to help protect consumers from contaminated food."[157] With the support of the president's 2020 budget that brings in resources to modernize FDA's food safety governance efforts, it is possible that blockchain can play an important role in the transparency and traceability mechanisms of the nation's food law.[158] Governments might also embrace such an approach to regulatory technology in other jurisdictions through technical assistance, mutual learning, and trans-governmental cooperation that ease some of the obstacles identified previously.

Although there has been support for the application of blockchain to the global supply chain to deliver enhanced transparency, traceability, safety, and authenticity; to comply with regulatory requirements; and to gain consumer

154 Food and Drug Administration, "Statement from FDA Commissioner Scott Gottlieb, M.D., and Deputy Commissioner Frank Yiannas on New Steps to Strengthen FDA's Food Safety Program for 2020 and Beyond", *FDA.GOV*, Mar. 19, 2019, https://perma.cc/9XB8-SXP6; *see also* Food and Drug Administration, "Statement from Acting FDA Commissioner Ned Sharpless, M.D., and Deputy Commissioner Frank Yiannas on Steps to Usher the U.S. into a New Era of Smarter Food Safety", *FDA.GOV*, Apr. 30, 2019, https://perma.cc/4W8P-FM8F.

155 *See* Food and Drug Administration, "FDA Takes New Steps to Adopt More Modern Technologies for Improving the Security of the Drug Supply Chain through Innovations That Improve Tracking and Tracing of Medicines", *FDA.GOV*, Feb. 7, 2019, *available at* https://perma.cc/5XQW-Z8GU.

156 A New Era of Smarter Food Safety (Docket No. FDA-2019-N-4187), 84 FR 49111 (Sept. 18, 2019).

157 Food and Drug Administration, "FDA Announces Public Meeting to Discuss the New Era of Smarter Food Safety", *FDA.GOV*, Sept. 17, 2019, *available at* https://perma.cc/6C6A-7V5K.

158 While sufficient resources are of significant importance to the FDA's food safety regulation, it should be noted that budgetary allocation is not always tied to effective outcomes, which also depend on many other factors.

trust,[159] the technology does not come without shortcomings. Blockchains can introduce data transparency, traceability, and immutability to help address information-oriented issues in the traditional, manual, and labor-intensive sectors. Yet, as argued previously, there are also problems regarding operational knowledge and technical expertise, implementation and standardization costs, cybersecurity and data protection, and the inherent limits of the technology—which may adversely impact the effectiveness and the efficiency of this new governance tool.

How do we fix the challenges posed by this "technical fix" when we shift toward the new trust machine and blockchainizing food law? Preliminary thoughts include the following. At a certain level, to scale up the existing pilot programs and implement blockchain technologies to make the global agri-food supply chain "smarter," diverse participants must work on a minimal level of digitalization in order to take advantage of blockchain technologies. Governments may also need to provide infrastructural or research and development (R&D) support to reduce implementation costs (particularly in areas with fewer resources) and scalability problems. It is crucial that such infrastructural support and R&D investment address priority areas identified through a public-private, multi-stakeholder decision-making process. The "code as law" promise of blockchainizing food law inevitably relies on an adequate level of data integrity and digital infrastructure in the industry, which allows computer codes to discipline interactions and shape behaviors in cyberspace in a potentially more influential manner than traditional law and regulation.[160] In the long (and perhaps more futuristic) term, as argued by Yochai Benkler, there may be further development of ways in which networked information infrastructure facilitates broad communication and diverse cooperative mechanisms in the agri-food sector and beyond.[161] In this sense, the role that blockchain technologies can play in the regulatory system extends well beyond computer codes and may include other hybrid forms of rules to operate as autonomous normative systems. In the agri-food sector and beyond, law enforcement practices will continue to change alongside rapid technological advancement, and the use of technologies—such as blockchain—as well as the data and digital infrastructure they generate will become an integral part of law enforcement.

In the cross-border context, harmonization and interoperability of standards set by both public and private institutions are of significant importance. Harmonization is likely one of the most daunting tasks (especially in the North-South and South-South context) given the extremely diverse social, economic, political, and culinary underpinnings of different jurisdictions. Institutional and industry culture may also play a role in promoting reliable use

159 *See*, for example, Casey & Wong, *supra* note 141.

160 *See generally* Lessig, *supra* note 117.

161 *See* Y. Benkler, *The Wealth of Networks: How Social Production Transforms Market and Freedom* (New Haven, Yale University Press 2006), at 130, 133, 138–40, 271–72, 385.

of technology to strengthen food safety oversight and consumer trust.[162] Collaborative actions may need to be taken by international organizations and/or other stakeholders, paying due attention to the distributional justice and sustainable development dimensions to ensure that most market players benefit from the productivity gains. At the same time, there are some inherent limits to the technology as a technical fix, and these call for additional governance methods as gatekeepers to ensure accountability. All in all, cooperation and dialogue between public and private institutions at various levels and sectors in the agri-food industry will help to create a better regulatory environment for blockchainizing food law.

162 *See generally* T. D. Lytton, *Kosher: Private Regulation in the Age of Industrial Food* (Cambridge, Harvard University Press 2013); F. Yiannas, *Food Safety Culture: Creating a Behavior-Based Food Safety Management System* (Berlin, Springer 2008).

7 The Legal Definition of Meat

Steph Tai

In August of 2018, Missouri became the first state in the United States to regulate the labeling of artificial meat, with a statute defining meat as something "derived from harvested production livestock or poultry."[1] Mislabeling non-livestock or poultry-derived meats would come with a fine or even jail time.[2] In a statement issued in November of 2018, the US Department of Agriculture (USDA) and the US Food and Drug Administration (FDA) also approached this issue, proposing that "both the USDA and the FDA should jointly oversee the production of cell-cultured food products derived from livestock and poultry."[3]

Both of these actions are still in development. Various organizations filed a lawsuit against Missouri alleging that the law would mislead consumers and stifle competition from plant-based products.[4] Missouri is reportedly in the process of settling this lawsuit, although "details appear scant."[5] The USDA and FDA, in turn, are still "actively refining the technical details of [their] framework."[6] This chapter will examine these legal actions in a broader food studies context. In doing so, it will explore how definitions have shaped and can continue to shape consumer expectations of what constitutes various categories of food themselves.

I. The Legal Meat of This Chapter

What is meat? We use this term in a large number of ways, from literal to more figurative. The Merriam-Webster online dictionary provides several

1 Missouri Meat Advertising Law, MO Rev. Stat. § 265.494(7).

2 MO Rev. Stat. § 265.496.

3 FDA, "Statement from USDA Secretary Perdue and FDA Commissioner Gottlieb on the Regulation of Cell-Cultured Food Products from Cell Lines of Livestock and Poultry" (2018), *available at* www.fda.gov/NewsEvents/Newsroom/PressAnnouncements/ucm626117.htm.

4 *See* G. Balstad & J. Bold-Erdene, "Can You Call It Meat? Lawsuit Takes Issue with Labeling", *Missourian*, Oct. 1, 2018, *available at* www.columbiamissourian.com/news/local/can-you-call-it-meat-lawsuit-takes-issue-with-labeling/article_14d1450e-b13f-11e8-a6ef-c3a0888f96da.html.

5 *See* B. Linnekin, "Arkansas' New Food-Labeling Law Is Veg-on-Veg Crime", *Reason*, Apr. 13, 2019, *available at* https://reason.com/2019/04/13/arkansas-new-food-labeling-law-is-veg-on/.

6 FDA, *supra* note 3.

DOI: 10.4324/9781003271918-9

definitions.[7] First, there is "food: the edible part of something as distinguished from its covering (such as a husk or shell)."[8] Then there is "animal tissue considered especially as food," including "flesh of a mammal as opposed to fowl or fish" and "flesh of domesticated animals."[9] Then the dictionary provides more figurative uses, such as "dinner,"[10] "the core of something,"[11] and "favorite pursuit or interest."[12]

Given these multiple meanings, why might folks be concerned about the precise definition of meat? Because this concern is evident from the recent engagement of states on this issue. That is, a number of states have recently explored "meat labeling" laws that would regulate the use of the word "meat" to characterize various products.

Take Missouri as an example. On August 30, 2018, the Missouri legislature passed a bill known as the "Missouri Meat Advertising Law."[13] The Missouri Department of Agriculture issued a public statement describing the state as "the first state to take steps to prevent misrepresentation of products as meat that are not derived from livestock or poultry."[14] To prevent "misrepresentation," non-livestock-derived products must "must include a prominent statement on the front of the package, immediately before or immediately after the product name, that the product is 'plant-based,' 'veggie,' 'lab-grown,' 'lab-created' or a comparable qualifier."[15] Moreover, "[p]roducts must include a prominent statement on the package that the product is 'made from plants,' 'grown in a lab,' or a comparable disclosure."[16] Various organizations filed a lawsuit against Missouri alleging that the law would mislead consumers and stifle competition from plant-based products.[17] Missouri is reportedly in the process of settling this lawsuit, although "details appear scant."[18]

Despite the current Missouri settlement proceedings, other state legislatures are contemplating similar actions. In Nebraska, State Senator Carol Blood has sponsored a bill restricting insect-based, plant-based, or lab-grown food from

7 Merriam-Webster creates definitions based on usage. *See* Merriam-Webster, "How Does a Word Get into a Merriam-Webster Dictionary?", *available at* www.merriam-webster.com/help/faq-words-into-dictionary (last accessed Apr. 20, 2021) ("To decide which words to include in the dictionary and to determine what they mean, Merriam-Webster editors study the language as it's used. They carefully monitor which words people use most often and how they use them.").

8 Merriam-Webster, Meat (1b), *available at* www.merriam-webster.com/dictionary/meat?src=search-dict-box (last accessed Apr. 20, 2021).

9 Ibid, at (2a) and (2b).

10 Ibid, at (3).

11 Ibid, at (4a).

12 Ibid, at (5).

13 *See* Missouri Meat Advertising Law, *supra* note 1.

14 "Public Statement—Meat Labeling", *Missouri Department of Agriculture*, Aug. 30, 2018, *available at* https://agriculture.mo.gov/animals/meat.php.

15 Ibid.

16 Ibid.

17 *See* Balstad & Bold-Erdene, *supra* note 4.

18 *See* Linnekin, *supra* note 5.

being labeled as "meat."[19] In particular, this proposed bill states that "Meat means any edible portion of any livestock or poultry carcass or part thereof and does not include lab-grown or insect or plant-based food products."[20] Similarly, a bill was introduced in Wyoming by Senator Wyatt Agar that would require all "[c]ell cultured or plant based products" to have labels of "containing cell cultured product" or "vegetarian," "veggie," "vegan," "plant based" or "other similar term indicating that the product is plant based."[21] In Virginia, Delegate Michael Webert moved to amend the state code on misbranded food[22] to require that consumable products marketed as "meat" made from materials other than that "made wholly or in part from any meat or other portion of the carcass of any cattle, sheep, swine, or goats" be labeled as "imitations."[23]

Likewise, the USDA and FDA have announced a proposal to "jointly oversee the production of cell-cultured food products derived from livestock and poultry."[24] Pursuant to this proposal, the USDA and FDA signed a formal agreement on March 7, 2019, to collaborate on the regulation of such products.[25] In particular, the FDA has committed to focusing on the pre-marketing aspects of cultured meats, including the "initial cell collection and the development and maintenance of qualified cell banks,"[26] "proliferation and differentiation of cells through the time of harvest,"[27] and "inspections and follow-up activities, including taking enforcement action if necessary, to ensure that cell bank and cell culturing facilities are in compliance with [FDA's] applicable laws and regulations."[28] The USDA, in turn, would focus on cell harvests, including "[requiring that] each establishment that harvests cells cultured from livestock or poultry subject to the FMIA or PPIA for the purpose of producing human

19 *See* ES. Povich, "'Fake Meat' Battle Spreads to More States", *Pew*, Jan. 25, 2019, *available at* www.pewtrusts.org/en/research-and-analysis/blogs/stateline/2019/01/25/fake-meat-battle-spreads-to-more-states; *see also* Legislature of Nebraska, Legislative Bill 14, *A bill for an act relating to agriculture; to provide for truth in advertising and labeling in the sale of meat and food plans; to define terms; to prohibit misleading or deceptive practices; to provide a penalty; and to provide an operative date* (Jan. 30, 2019), *available at* www.nebraskalegislature.gov/FloorDocs/106/PDF/Intro/LB14.pdf.

20 Legislature of Nebraska, *supra* note 19, at Section 1(3).

21 Legislature of Wyoming, SF0068—*Meat from Harvested Livestock or Poultry* (Feb. 26, 2019), *available at* www.wyoleg.gov/Legislation/2019/SF0068.

22 Va. Code Ann. § 3.2–5123. Misbranded food.

23 Legislature of Virginia, *A Bill to Amend and Reenact § 3.2–5123 of the Code of Virginia, Relating to Meat; Misbranding* (Jan. 9, 2019), *available at* http://lis.virginia.gov/cgi-bin/legp604.exe?191+ful+HB2274; Va. Code Ann. § 3.2–5400. Definitions.

24 FDA, *supra* note 3.

25 "Formal Agreement between the U.S. Department of Health and Human Services Food and Drug Administration and U.S. Department of Agriculture Office of Food Safety" (2019), *available at* www.fsis.usda.gov/wps/wcm/connect/0d2d644a-9a65-43c6-944f-ea598aacdec1/Formal-Agreement-FSIS-FDA.pdf?MOD=AJPERES.

26 Ibid, at 4.A.2.

27 Ibid, at 4.A.3.

28 Ibid, at 4.A.7.

food . . . bear the USDA mark of inspection,"[29] "[conducting] inspection in establishments where cells cultured from livestock and poultry subject to the FMIA and PPIA are harvested, processed, packaged or labeled,"[30] and "[requiring] that the labeling of human food products derived from the cultured cells of livestock and poultry be preapproved and then verified through inspection."[31] Further developments are still proceeding, as the agreement states that the agencies will "develop a more detailed joint framework or standard operating procedure to facilitate coordination of shared regulatory oversight related to the harvest of biological material"[32] and will "undertake a joint process to identify any changes needed to statutory or regulatory authorities to effectuate the framework established pursuant to this agreement, and will work cooperatively to pursue, or to implement, any such changes."[33]

In the meantime, US Senator Cindy Hyde-Smith has introduced a statute that would give the USDA primary authority over the regulation of cell-cultured food products.[34] This bill, known as the Cell-Cultured Meat and Poultry Regulation Act, would further formalize this division of labor between the two agencies, committing the FDA to oversight over "cell collection, cell banks, and cell growth and differentiation"[35] and the USDA to oversight over "the processing, preparation, packaging, and labeling of food products."[36]

This concern over cell-cultured protein has been shared by the Congressional Research Service (CRS), a legislative branch agency which "provid[es] comprehensive and reliable legislative research and analysis that are timely, objective, authoritative and confidential, thereby contributing to an informed national legislature."[37] That is, the CRS has also conducted a review of the statutory basis for the FDA and the USDA Food Safety Inspection Service (FSIS) to exert jurisdiction over cell-cultured meats.[38] To explain the catalyst for its report, the CRS described how, in early 2018, "the livestock industry and the House Appropriations Committee addressed cell-cultured meats"[39] and how the US Cattlemen's Association "submitted a petition to USDA asking [the USDA Food Safety and Inspection Service] to establish meat labeling requirements that exclude product not derived directly from animals raised and

29 Ibid, at 4.B.2.
30 Ibid, at 4.B.3.
31 Ibid, at 4.B.4.
32 Ibid, at 4.C.1.
33 Ibid, at 4.C.2.
34 Cell-Cultured Meat & Poultry Regulation Act of 2019 (S. 1056).
35 Ibid, § 3(a)(1).
36 Ibid, § 3(a)(2).
37 Library of Congress, "History and Mission [of CRS]", *available at* www.loc.gov/crsinfo/about/history.html (last accessed Apr. 20, 2021).
38 Congressional Research Service, "Regulation of Cell-Cultured Meat" (2018), *available at* https://fas.org/sgp/crs/misc/IF10947.pdf
39 Ibid, at 1.

slaughtered."[40] As the CRS noted, "[f]ood labeling is often contentious. The dairy industry has long argued that the term milk as applied to plant-based products (e.g. almond and soy milk) is misleading and violates FDA standards of identity for milk."[41]

II. A Brief History of Meat in the United States

So why is meat in particular such a contentious issue in the United States? To better understand this, we must look at the history of "meat" in this country. As Maureen Ogle, a historian, writes in *In Meat We Trust: An Unexpected History of Carnivore America*, "[t]o the men and women who settled North America, the idea of a world without livestock was as peculiar, and dangerous, as the notion of a world without God. Therein lay the road to savagery."[42] To the European settlers, meat represented dominance[43] and civilization.[44]

Meat also provided a relatively stable source of nutrition, as more plant-based diets required more labor to produce, while meat could be dried, preserved, or slaughtered at appropriate periods of time.[45] Indeed, as Ogle chronicles, meat played an especially prominent role in the American diet. "Across Europe, a non-royal was lucky to see meat once or twice a week. A typical [colonial] American adult male, in contrast, put away two hundred pounds a year."[46]

Eventually, what began as a more homesteading enterprise transformed into its own economy. Ogle traces the development of the cattle-grazing, feeding, and driving enterprise of the Ohio River Valley area of the United States,[47] as well as the 1840 center of pork production in Cincinnati, then sometimes referred to as Porktopolis,[48] a term later "stolen" by Chicago.[49]

Indeed, by the late 1800s, the "American[] prodigious appetite for meat" had become "world-renowned."[50] This led to the development of vast additional

40 Ibid, at 2.

41 Ibid, at 2 (also noting how in July 2018, the FDA "announced it would review the labeling of plant-based 'milk' and 'yogurt' products.")

42 M. Ogle, *In Meat We Trust: An Unexpected History of Carnivore America* (Boston, Houghton Mifflin Harcourt 2013), at 2.

43 Ibid, at 2 (contrasting the ways in which early settlers described the distinction between themselves and Native Americans in part through the European method of "settl[ing] their cattle").

44 Ibid, at 3 (describing settlers as "priz[ing] livestock as evidence of civilization and sources of wealth").

45 Ibid, at 3.

46 Ibid, at 4.

47 Ibid, at 10.

48 Ibid, at 11; *see also* G. Hand, "Remember, Cincinnati: "Porkopolis" Was Not a Compliment", *Cincinnati Magazine*, Nov. 14, 2016, *available at* www.cincinnatimagazine.com/citywiseblog/remember-cincinnati-porkopolis-not-compliment/?fbclid=IwAR3k_ihgN4bEJyIAikBdrtG6gl-WzyXFpFYs3lv_RlS-Rz60A-dfgB4anYW0 (describing the pervasiveness of swine and their excrement in the streets of Cincinnati in the 1840s).

49 *See* Ogle, *supra* note 42, at 21.

50 Ibid, at 11.

grazing areas out West,[51] which in turn transformed the American landscape not only through the movement of livestock production geographies but in terms of the US transportation industry.[52] That is, the livestock

> stockyard at Chicago was funded primarily by railroad companies, which recognized that livestock represented one of their more lucrative and important categories of freight. . . . Investors, nearly all of them connected to the railroads, built duplicate stockyards at the other end of the line.[53]

But that transformation also shaped American consumers' relationship to meat. The more that consumers, especially in cities, became isolated from meat production, the more they came to value their isolation from the sights and smells of livestock slaughter. "[I]n the 1870s and after[,] Americans wanted cities. They wanted meat, too. But they no longer wanted the one in the other. In modern America, the making of meat would increasingly be out of sight and out of mind."[54]

Ogle also traces the growth of the meat industry in America through the triumph of the meatpacking sector over the American beef market.[55] But while she details the various legal and economic mechanisms used to solidify this dominance, she also recognizes consumers' roles.

> The rising standard of living [in the last thirty years of the nineteenth century] shaped shoppers' demands, and people in every economic class developed an insatiable appetite for fresh beef. But not just any cuts. Families satisfied with tongue or cheek twenty years earlier now demanded finer cuts.[56]

Adding to the desire to reach a perceived better standard of living was also the belief in the late nineteenth century that "linked food to national power and racial superiority."[57] She describes essays published during that period that linked European and American geopolitical dominance to their meat-rich diets and Asian "inoffensive"ness to their more grain and plant-based diets.[58] This combination of institutional disconnect, desire for a particular standard of

51 *See* ibid, at 18.
52 *See* ibid, at 22.
53 Ibid, at 22.
54 Ibid, at 25.
55 *See* ibid, at 46–49.
56 Ibid, at 49.
57 Ibid, at 50.
58 Ibid, at 50; *see also* W. J. Warren, *Meat Makes People Powerful: A Global History of the Modern Era* (Iowa City, University of Iowa Press 2018), at 49–102.

living, and connection with national status led to a sense of entitlement to meat. During this period of time,

> [u]rban Americans didn't care that meat comes from animals, or that food for those animals, like its human counterpart, depends on weather. As far as consumers were concerned, the price of meat was connected only to their own pocketbooks, to an intangible price defined not in dollars or relative to rainfall, but simply as "affordable."[59]

But eventually the American consumer became more circumspect regarding its approach towards meat. First, Upton Sinclair's exposé on the unfair labor practices and negligible food safety standards of the livestock industry captured the public imagination.[60] Then, the Federal Trade Commission's series of investigations regarding the anticompetitive practices of the packer industry highlighted the suspect economic practices.[61] Finally, various popular nutritionists arose touting the additional benefits of "vitamins" contained in "once-lowly foodstuffs" over meats.[62]

In response, "The Meat Institute, a packers' trade Association, and the American National Livestock Association mounted a pro-meat publicity campaign."[63] They ended up, in the 1920s, persuading the USDA to promote and protect the entire US meat production system, integrating meat promotion with the federal government.[64]

Much of the remainder of Ogle's comprehensive history explores the ways in which livestock market interests, food safety and food security interests, nutritional interests, and environmental/sustainability interests sparred throughout in the twentieth century.[65] What does Ogle ultimately conclude about the American consumer's relationship to meat? That

> [we're] a complicated group, we Americans, and we struggle to reconcile our conflicting desires and passions. On one hand, many of us want meat, lots of it, and we don't care how it's made as long as it doesn't cost much. On the other, some of us are determined to break the chains that bind livestock production and meatpacking to assembly-line processes.[66]

Ogle, consistent with her perspective as a historian, leaves few detailed recommendations for the future, but her recounting of the American history with

59 *See* Ogle, *supra* note 42, at 67.
60 *See* ibid, at 75–79.
61 *See* ibid, at 81–84.
62 *See* ibid, at 85–89.
63 Ibid, at 88.
64 *See* ibid, at 89.
65 *See* ibid, at 90–262.
66 Ibid, at 263.

meat is still relevant in framing how we might approach what foodstuffs we choose to call "meat." First, her historical account suggests that meat presents a particular signifier in the traditional American diet: one of "necessity" in terms of political, power, and cultural identity.[67] Next, it demonstrates that the American consumer's expectations of "meat" are interwoven with various market dynamics. Finally, it highlights how these expectations and desires can be shaped by other concerns, such as food safety, nutritional impacts, and even sustainability issues.

III. Non-Livestock "Meat"

But livestock-based "meat" has also not been the only way in which eaters—both American and otherwise—have approached this category of food. This section will first provide a brief history of meats in the context of vegetarian and other limited-meat cultures (both generally and within the United States). Then this section will explore the more recent phenomenon of cultured meats.

A. Vegetarian Meats/Meat Analogues

Vegetarian and other limited-meat cultures have developed around the world for a number of reasons. Some of these are spiritual, others are based on ethics of non-violence, and even others are founded on nutritional/environmental concerns.[68] These philosophical foundations are not the focus of this chapter. However, the presence of these cultures for centuries—whether plant-based proxies or fully alternative diets—means that humans have been exploring things described as alternative meats for quite some time. This section bypasses any full discussion of the philosophical grounding for vegetarian diets, as well as the development of fully alternative diets, and instead focuses on historical uses of foods used to replace livestock-based meats in traditional cuisines.

1. Generally

Modern historical accounts of vegetarian analogues[69] for livestock-based meats tend to be sharply divided between Eastern and Western histories. But the short summary is that modern historical accounts of Eastern plant-based analogues tend to reach further back in time than modern historical accounts of

67 And perhaps, more problematically, in terms of racial identity.

68 *See* T. Stuart, *The Bloodless Revolution: A Cultural History of Vegetarianism from 1600 to Modern Times* (London, W. W. Norton 2006), at xvii–xxvi; *see also* K. Iacobbo & M. Iacobbo, *Vegetarian America: A History* (London, Praeger 2004), AT 104–105 (describing a number of foundations for vegetarianism, from religious to scientific to ethical to esthetic to economical to necessity).

69 By "substitutes," I mean food matters that could be used in place of livestock-based meats in traditional cuisines of particular cultures.

Western plant-based analogues (although this history of vegetarianism in both areas are quite histories).

Much of the modern historical account of Eastern plant-based analogues focuses on soy, a plant that has a "long history in Asia."[70] That is, "tofu and its value as an animal-protein substitute were clearly known in China by the time of the Tang Dynasty (618–907 CE), when the people called it 'small mutton'."[71]

But vegetarian meat analogues in the East were not limited to soy.[72] As one food expert, Fuschia Dunlop, has explained, "There are records from the Tang dynasty, which is 618 to 907, of an official hosting a banquet serving imitation pork and mutton dishes made from vegetables."[73] Other analogues include gluten-based analogues[74] and jackfruit-based analogues.[75] Indeed, the names of these analogues themselves include the term "meat" in other languages. For example, "[i]n Mandarin, mianjin, or wheat gluten, means literally 'wheat meat'."[76] Similarly, the Bengali word for jackfruit translates as "tree mutton."[77]

These analogues were not uniformly eaten by all Asians, however. While Chinese Buddhists often relied heavily on analogues in "temple cuisine," Japanese Buddhists and Indian vegetarians did not.[78] But when they were consumed, their consumption was related to virtue and frugality. For example,

> The earliest known reference to tofu (worldwide) appears in China in the Anecdotes, Simple and Exotic (Qing yilu) [in 965] by Tao Ku. It states: When Shi Ji was the magistrate of Qing Yang, he emphasized the virtue of frugality among the people, and discouraged the consumption of meat. Instead he promoted the sale of tofu. But rather than calling it doufu (the

70 C. M. Du Bois, *The Story of Soy* (London, Reaktion Books 2018), at 26.

71 Ibid, at 30.

72 *See* R. Lott-Lavigna, "The Origins of Fake Meat Are Rooted in Chinese Cooking", *Vice*, Feb. 5, 2019, *available at* https://munchies.vice.com/en_uk/article/8xyqqz/the-origins-of-fake-meat-are-rooted-in-chinese-cooking.

73 Ibid.

74 *See* L. Braman, "Seitan: The Other Fake Meat", *Smithsonian*, Aug. 25, 2010, *available at* www.smithsonianmag.com/arts-culture/seitan-the-other-fake-meat-97622092/ (describing seitan, or wheat gluten, as having "been used as a meat substitute for centuries in China and Japan, where it was developed by vegetarian Buddhist monks.").

75 *See* E. Stephenson, "Behind Jackfruit's Rise from South Asian Staple to Vegan Trend", *Eater*, May 17, 2016, *available at* www.eater.com/2016/5/17/11683930/jackfruit-vegan-pulled-pork ("Jackfruit is grown in many countries, but India—with a vegetarian population in the hundreds of millions—is the only one with a history of using the young fruit as a stand-in for meat, most often in stir-fries, curries, and a popular rice dish called *kathal ki biryani*. The Bengal word for the fruit translates as 'tree mutton' or 'the meat which grows on a tree.'")

76 C. Erway, "The Buddhist Mock-Meats Paradox", *Taste*, Apr. 25, 2018, *available at* www.tastecooking.com/buddhist-mock-meats-paradox/.

77 Stephenson, *supra* note 73.

78 Erway, *supra* note 76.

> Chinese name for tofu), he referred to it as "mock lamb chops" or "the vice mayor's mutton."[79]

Similarly, in the 1620s, "[a]t a banquet in Ming-dynasty China, a group of Buddhist nuns is reassured: 'This is vegetarian food made to look like meat. It has come from the temple, and there can't possibly be any harm in eating it.'"[80]

In the Western world, at least according to William Shurtleff and Akiko Aoyagi, the compilers of a comprehensive history of meat alternatives, the first mention of such alternatives was made in 1852.[81] It was a vegetarian sausage, "composed mainly of red flannel and turnip tops, chopped fine."[82] This is not to say that vegetarian diets did not exist in the West prior to that; such diets were promoted for similar reasons as in the East. As Tristram Stuart recounts in his history of vegetarian philosophies:

> Meat-eating came under fire from a spectacular array of viewpoints in the seventeenth and eighteenth centuries. Revolutionaries attacked the bloodthirsty luxury of mainstream culture; demographers accused the meat industry of wasting resources which could otherwise be used to feed people; anatomists claimed that human intestines were not equipped to digest meat; and travellers to the East presented India as a peaceful alternative to the rapacity of the West. . . . The luxury of *choosing* to abstain from meat may have been restricted to small sectors of European society, but these often drew their inspiration from the underfed poor who seemed to live, and labour, without needing vast quantities of meat.[83]

During World War II, Westerners also began to adopt vegetarian meat analogues for another reason: disruption in traditional food supplies due to the war.[84] To replace the imported meats and livestock whose supply was disrupted by the Germans, the British began to include soy protein in their wartime sausages.[85] But they did not plant their own soybeans. Instead, "they cultivated an extraordinarily close relationship with the emerging soy sovereign, the USA. Winston Churchill assiduously courted the Americans, realizing that they would be an indispensable source of both war material and food."[86]

The United States supported this effort. While soy had been primarily used as a rotation crop before World War II, farmers were encouraged to use the

79 W. Shurtleff & A. Aoyagi, "History of Meat Alternatives" (2014), *available at* www.soyinfocenter.com/pdf/179/MAL.pdf, at 5.

80 Ibid.

81 Ibid.

82 Ibid.

83 Stuart, *supra* note 68, at xix (emphasis in original).

84 *See* Du Bois, *supra* note 70, at 79–81.

85 *See* ibid, at 80.

86 Ibid.

crops to produce soybeans.[87] Indeed, one American World War II pamphlet stated "Remember—when you grow more soybeans, you are helping America to destroy the enemies of freedom."[88] What we see in this extremely brief history of vegetarian meat substitutes is that very similar values have historically been used to valorize both livestock-based meats and vegetarian meat analogues.

2. *In the United States*

Vegetarianism in the United States began with more Christian religious underpinnings.[89] But from early Americans like Benjamin Franklin to Johann Conrad Beissel, a German immigrant who founded the Seventh-Day Baptists in Pennsylvania, vegetarians were present during the foundations of the United States.[90]

But they did not always seek to create meat analogues. In one documented meal by Benjamin Franklin (hosting George Washington, Benjamin Rush, and John Hancock), "Franklin served cucumber, a pot of butter, a jug of spring water, a loaf of bread, lettuces, leeks, a cheese, and foaming beer 'more brisk than strong.'"[91] Even in the earlier 1800s, when books like William Andrus Alcott's *Vegetable Diet*[92] were read by the public, the dietary focus appeared more on eating a variety of grains and vegetables versus providing suggestions for meat analogues.[93] Even a prominent vegetarian meal covered by the New York Daily Times in 1853 seemed to provide few direct meat analogues:

> [v]egetable soup, tomato soup, rice soup, farinacea, Graham bread, mixed-fruit cake, fruitbread, apple biscuit, wheat-meal cakes, moulded rice, corn blanc mange, moulded wheaten grits, vegetables, baked sweet potatoes, stewed cream squash, pastry, mixed-fruit pie, pumpkin pie, fruits, melons, apples, peaches, pears, grapes, pineapples, cooked fruits including plum jelly and baked apples, relishes consisting of coconut custard and fruited ice cream, and a beverage of pure cold water.[94]

87 *See* ibid, at 82–83.

88 Ibid, at 83.

89 *See* Iacobbo & Iacobbo, *supra* note 68, at 1 ("The seeds of the modern vegetarian movement were firmly planted in the nineteenth century by Christians. Vegetarianism in the United States dates to even before it was a nation.").

90 *See* ibid, at 2–3.

91 Ibid, at 2.

92 W. A. Alcott, *Vegetable Diet as Sanctioned by Medical Men, and by Experience in All Ages Including a System of Vegetable Cookery* (1838).

93 *See* ibid, at 42–43.

94 Ibid, at 84–85.

It was John Harvey Kellogg who most advanced the marketing of vegetarian meat analogues in America.[95] "After developing additional meat substitutes, Kellogg formed the Sanitas Nut Food Company in 1889."[96] The Sanitas products were described in relation to livestock-based meats. Nuttose, for example, was "largely made from nuts, and it had the consistency of cream cheese. The food, according to company literature, 'exhibited none of the objectionable qualities of flesh meat' with 'no toxins.'"[97] Similarly, Nuttelene—also nut-based—"was billed as a delicate white meat as dainty and juicy as the breast of a spring chicken."[98]

Kellogg's motivation for developing these plant-based analogues was this:

> In dropping meats from the diet it was difficult at first to find a satisfactory substitute because for so many generations meals had been built around meats and to most people a meal without meat as its center was unthinkable. . . . In biologic living we left out the meat, left out all the condiments, coffee and tea, and what was finally left was very plain and tasteless for those who were accustomed to high flavors.[99]

Since then, others in the United States have promoted vegetarian meat analogues. The counterculture of the 1960s and 1970s looked to vegetarianism as a counterweight against traditional values it deemed harmful.[100] During this period, Stephen Gaskin, founder of a prominent vegetarian commune, worked to purchase 1,000 acres of woods eventually known as "The Farm."[101] In 1976, commune members used soybeans grown on The Farm to produce "soy products such as soy burgers, soy loaf, and soy sausage. The community built a soy dairy that churned out soy milk, soy yogurt, and soy ice cream."[102]

Since then, vegetarian meat substitutes have grown exponentially. A short timeline in *Mother Jones* documents this progress.[103] Vegetarian burger substitutes abounded, and producers explored innovations such as "mushroom in origin" meats.[104]

95 *See* Iacobbo & Iacobbio, *supra* note 68, at 128–33; *see also* Shurtleff and Aoyagi, *supra* note 79, at 6 ("1895–1899—Charles Dabney interests Dr. John Harvey Kellogg in developing substitutes for meat.").

96 Iacobbo & Iacobbo, *supra* note 68, at 128.

97 Ibid, at 128.

98 Ibid.

99 Ibid, at 129 (citing Publisher's Department, 33 *Good Health* 522 (Aug. 1898).

100 *See* ibid, at 169–93.

101 Ibid, at 174.

102 Ibid, at 175.

103 M. Connolly, "Timeline: A Short and Sweet History of Fake Meat", *Mother Jones*, Nov./Dec. 2013, *available at* www.motherjones.com/environment/2013/12/history-fake-meat/.

104 Ibid; *see also* Pacific Standard Staff, "A Brief History of Fake Meat", *Pacific Standard*, June 14, 2017, *available at* https://psmag.com/news/a-brief-history-of-fake-meat.

B. Cell-Cultured Meats

Cell-cultured meats are a more recent phenomenon than the plant-based livestock meat analogues outlined previously. That is, it wasn't until the last few years that lab-grown meats began to appear viable as a commercial product.[105] Unlike plant-based meat analogues, they are developed through the collection of stem cells from animal muscle and multiplied through processes that allow those cells to differentiate into fibers that can form a sort of muscle tissue.[106] One pioneer in this industry, Mosa Meat, "says that one tissue sample from a cow can yield enough muscle tissue to make 80,000 quarter-pounders."[107]

Proponents of such lab-grown meat cite potentials for lowering environmental impacts,[108] raising nutritional profiles,[109] and even promoting more ethical consumption from an animal rights framework.[110] This is not to say that such products are economically viable just yet. "Getting to a price consumers would be willing to pay at a restaurant is still at least five to 10 years away, according to several CEOs of the leading cultured meat companies."[111]

The production methods for such lab-grown livestock-meat analogues can vary. But in general, they start with creating what is known as a bio-reactor (basically a sterile vat that provides controllable conditions for cell growth) to grow the cultured meats.[112] Then the lab-grown meat enterprise must acquire livestock stem cells, taken from living animal muscle, with satellite cells—which are "responsible for muscle regeneration after injury"[113]—being the most promising type of stem cells for this use. After that, the producer must proliferate those cells by basically attaching the cells to a three-dimensional scaffold that—when the cells are grown—can mimic the structure of

105 *See* G. O. Schaefer, "Lab-Grown Meat: Meat Produced without Killing Animals Is Heading to Your Dinner Table", *Scientific American*, Sept. 14, 2018, *available at* www.scientificamerican.com/article/lab-grown-meat/.

106 *See* ibid.

107 Ibid.

108 *See* T. A. Mayhall, "The Meat of the Matter: Regulating a Laboratory-Grown Alternative" (2019) 74 Food and Drug Law Journal 151, 153–154, 160–61; D. Carrington, "World's First Lab-Grown Steak Revealed—But the Taste Needs Work", *The Guardian*, Dec. 14, 2018, *available at* www.theguardian.com/environment/2018/dec/14/worlds-first-lab-grown-beef-steak-revealed-but-the-taste-needs-work; D. Parry, "Cultured Meat Seems Gross? It's Much Better Than Animal Agriculture", *The Conversation*, Feb. 27, 2019, *available at* http://theconversation.com/cultured-meat-seems-gross-its-much-better-than-animal-agriculture-109706.

109 *See* Mayhall, *supra* note 83, at 155–56, 161.

110 *See* ibid, at 161; Carrington, *supra* note 83, at 157–58 (describing sponsorship of animal rights activist groups such as the People for the Ethical Treatment of Animals); Parry, *supra* note 83; O. Khazan, "The Coming Obsolescence of Animal Meat", *The Atlantic*, Apr. 16, 2019, *available at* www.theatlantic.com/health/archive/2019/04/just-finless-foods-lab-grown-meat/587227/.

111 *See* E. Brodwin & K. Canales, "We Tried the First Lab-Grown Sausage Made without Killing Animals. It Was Smoky, Savory, and Tasted Like Breakfast", *Business Insider*, Sept. 22, 2018, *available at* www.businessinsider.com/lab-grown-clean-cell-meat-photos-taste-review-2018-9.

112 *See* Mayhall, *supra* note 83, at 159.

113 Ibid, at 159.

livestock-harvested meats.[114] Finally, the cells must be stretched and further grown so that they can be harvested as commercial viable products.[115]

But readers who think of food categories in terms of taste and mouthfeel might ask, what does this food taste like? At least according to two reviewers of New Age Meats's[116] sausage, during a tasting in which photographs of Jessie the pig, from whom the cell biopsies were extracted, were displayed, "The flavor was smoky and savory. The texture was distinctly sausage-like. It tasted like meat."[117] More significantly, the reviewers added, "Then again, it is meat."[118]

In a different tasting, this time of a lab-grown steak (a more difficult product to create as a livestock-meat analogue, since producers cannot rely upon physical food processing to replicate textures) by Aleph Farms of Israel, reviewers stated that " 'It's close and it tastes good, but we have a bit more work to make sure the taste is 100% similar to conventional meat,' he said, 'But when you cook it, you really can smell the same smell of meat cooking.' "[119]

IV. How Labels Shape "Meat"

The very compacted history of meat presented in this chapter demonstrates the complicated role that "meat" as a concept has in the lives of Americans as well as eaters in general. Meat can represent a unique place in our diets, signifying achievements of culture, standards of living, and even political power. At the same time, "meat" can represent a concept that eaters might consider problematic, due to traditional livestock's impact on animal welfare, the economy, human health, and even the environment. Moreover, it can present troublesome histories involving concerns of colonialism and disregard for cultural autonomy.

The development of plant-based meat analogues has also reflected this complicated understanding of the term. As seen in the brief history presented through this chapter, the development of such livestock-meat analogues were an attempt to synergize plant-based diets with existing cuisines while complying with external religious, ethical, health-based, or environmental considerations. Especially in the modern era, plant-based meat analogues have been marketed as ways for those identified as vegetarians to incorporate those analogues into their pre-existing diets with minimal disruption and even for those not identified as vegetarians to reduce their livestock meat consumption.

Cell-cultured meat analogues further these complications by introducing technological developments into the picture. While many livestock meats and

114 Ibid, at 159.

115 Ibid, at 160.

116 *See* New Age Meats, "About", *available at* www.newagemeats.com/ (last accessed Apr. 20, 2021).

117 Brodwin & Canales, *supra* note 86.

118 Ibid.

119 Carrington, *supra* note 83.

plant-based meats were promoted as "natural" or "clean"—with positive values associated with those words—cell-cultured meats may not invoke such connotations (of "naturalness" or even "cleanliness," depending on eaters' associations with those terms). Yet they may still be associated with positive values as well, along similar lines of ethical, health-based, or environmental considerations. Indeed, given the "high tech" nature of these products, they might even be associated with some form of wealth-based prestige, similar to some of the earlier associations with livestock-based meats.

What does this all mean for how food labels can shape our perception of meat? If cell-cultured, or even plant-based, meat analogues are excluded from our legal definitions of meat, or are at least required to provide some sort of disclaimer, it may mean that these products have less access to the historical values of prestige and standard of living associated with livestock-based meats. Indeed, that appears to be reflected in some of the concerns raised by both the National Cattlemen's Beef Association regarding the use of the term "meat" by non-livestock-based meats,[120] as well as some of the concerns raised by plant-based meat producers in their legal challenges.[121] The converse may be the case if cell-cultured or plant-based meats are allowed access to the same term—"meat"—used by livestock-based meats.

But the complicated history of our cultural understandings of meat suggests that the values associated with the term are not static. That is, even were states or the US federal government to exclude or limit plant-based or cell-cultured meat analogues from accessing the term "meat," such foods may still develop other associational values that appeal to different desires of eaters.[122] Moreover, promoters of both livestock and plant/cell-based meats appear to gesture towards similar values of virtue, healthfulness, and patriotism.

V. Conclusion

This current debate in the United States over what foods to label as meat is just the latest part of a longer history of constructing eaters' approach to meat through social, economic, and legal processes. During this longer history, plant-based meat analogues were also consistently in use and promoted in various communities through their own sets of social, economic, and legal processes. Participants in the current debates would do well to recognize this

120 Wyatt Bechtel, *Cattlemen's Groups Voice Concerns with Lab-Grown Meat to USDA, FDA*, Ag Web (Oct. 24, 2018), *available at* www.agweb.com/article/cattlemens-groups-voice-concerns-with-lab-grown-meat-to-usda-fda/.

121 *See* Balstad & Bold-Erdene, *supra* note 4.

122 *See* Deena Prichep, *The Rise of Mock Meat: How Its Story Reflects America's Ever-Changing Values*, NPR (Sept. 2, 2017), *available at* www.npr.org/sections/thesalt/2017/09/02/547899191/the-rise-of-mock-meat-how-its-story-reflects-americas-ever-changing-values.

broader history and understand that legal recognition may not be the only way to access positive values associated with particular sets of foods. Moreover, participants in these debates should tackle this broader history when addressing other labeling debates about other food categories, such as "milk," "rice," and "cheese."

Part III

Regulatory Options for Foods Derived From Genome-Editing Technology and Novel Materials

8 Regulation of Gene-Edited Products

Wen-Shen Chu and Pei-kan Yang

I. Introduction

Genetically modified crops on the market have gained a history of use as food for more than 20 years since the genetically modified tomato was first approved for commercialization. While large-scale planting is currently carried out in major countries such as the United States, Brazil, Argentina, India, and Canada, most countries do not allow commercial cultivation of genetically modified crops because of the concern that foreign gene(s) inserted in such crops may have uncertain effects on the safety of the environment and/or human health. Therefore, genetically modified crops must pass strict safety risk assessments before being approved for marketing in various countries to ensure that they are safe and sound. With the continuous advancement of science, some emerging biotechnology can modify and improve crop characteristics without foreign gene insertion. Among them, gene-editing (genome editing) technology is one of the booming technologies in recent years.

Gene-editing technology can be divided into two categories (Table 8.1): site-directed nucleases (SDNs), and the other is oligonucleotide-directed mutagenesis (ODM). Site-directed nucleases can further be divided into different types of techniques: meganuclease (MN), zinc finger nuclease (ZFN), transcription activator-like effector nuclease (TALEN), and clustered regularly interspaced short palindromic repeat (CRISPR)-associated nuclease Cas9 (CRISPR-Cas9).[1]

Site-directed nuclease technology can be divided into three categories depending on the cell's gene repair mechanism and whether a template sequence is delivered: (1) SDN-1 produces a DNA double-stranded break, which is repaired via the cell non-homologous end joining (NHEJ) repair mechanism, resulting in deletion or insertion of one or a few base pairs. (2) SDN-2 produces a DNA double-stranded break, and at the same time, a homologous repair

1 M. Lusser, C. Parisi, D. Plan & E. Rodríguez-Cerezo, *New Plant Breeding Techniques, State-of-the-Art and Prospects for Commercial Development* (Luxembourg, Belgium, Publications Office of the European Union 2011), at 18–20. M. Lusser, C. Parisi, D. Plan & E. Rodríguez-Cerezo, "Deployment of New Biotechnology in Plant Breeding" (2012) 30(3) Nat. Biotechnol 231, at 232.

DOI: 10.4324/9781003271918-11

Table 8.1 List of current gene-editing technology[2]

Categories	*Gene-editing techniques*	*Material used*
SDN	MN	Nuclease with nucleic acid binding region
	ZFN	Nuclease with nucleic acid binding region
	TALEN	Nuclease with nucleic acid binding region
	CRISPR-Cas9	1. Nuclease 2. RNA
ODM	ODM	DNA or RNA

template is added. The break is repaired via a cellular homologous recombination (homology-directed repair; HDR) repair mechanism using the template, where precise and small genetic modifications are generated. (3) SDN-3 produces a DNA double-stranded break. A DNA fragment with homologous ends in combination with non-homologous sequences is used as a template. The break is repaired using the template via a cellular HDR repair mechanism, resulting in the insertion of an exogenous gene at a specific location.

Given that the debate over whether the gene-editing technology is equivalent to genetic modification technology and whether it can deviate from the regulatory mode of genetic modification technology, the regulatory approach to gene-edited food has not settled into a specific mode among various countries. Some countries regulate in accordance with the original regulatory model as GMOs, while others are still discussing possible different approaches.

II. Regulation of Gene-Edited Products in Selected Countries

A. European Union

The European Food Safety Authority (EFSA) Panel on Genetically Modified Organisms (GMO Panel) delivered a scientific opinion related to risk assessment of plants developed using the SDN-3 technique, in which major considerations include: (1) the source of the inserted gene and the safety of the gene product. If the inserted gene is a homologous gene (i.e. cisgene), the product is essentially similar to that of traditional breeding techniques. If the inserted gene is a non-homologous gene, the requirement of risk assessment should be the same as that of genetically modified crops. (2) The alterations to the host genome at the insertion site and elsewhere, that is, whether the position of the gene inserted will change the host genome.[3] Since SDN-3 can accurately insert DNA fragments into the target position, the risk caused by random insertion will be

2 J. D. Wolt, Wang, K., and Yang, B., "The regulatory status of genome-edited crops" (2015) 14(2) *Plant Biotechnol. Journal* 14, 510–518.

3 European Food Safety Authority (EFSA), "Scientific opinion addressing the safety assessment of plants developed using zinc finger nuclease 3 and other site-directed nucleases with similar function" (2012) 10 *EFSA Journal*. 2943.

greatly reduced, and at the same time, the SDN-3 technique can optimize the genomic environment for gene expression and minimize hazards associated with the disruption of genes and/or regulatory elements in the recipient genome.

The use of the NHEJ repair mechanism may involve the risk of duplicated insertions, partial deletion or insertion, and reversion of the inserted DNA sequence. Site-directed nucleases may cut DNA at unintended locations, which are called "off-target effects"; therefore, the alternations to the host genome must be considered. While the EFSA panel on GMO believes that the off-target effects caused by using the SDN-3 technique are similar to those using traditional mutagenesis techniques, products using SDN-3 still require risk assessment since they are considered GMOs due to the same technique as that for GMOs being used to produce the products.

Advocate General Michal Bobek of the Court of Justice of the European Union delivered an opinion on January 18, 2018[4] addressing an inquiry about whether products obtained by mutagenesis are regarded as GMOs, an issue that must be answered depending on whether they are covered under the scope of GMOs or whether the method of altering the gene is natural. Mr. Bobek holds the view that since GMOs do not necessarily have to be embedded with foreign transgenic genes, products using mutagenesis techniques can be excluded from the scope of GMOs if recombinant nucleic acid is not used or the method used to generate mutation is within the list of GMO exemptions. However, the European Court of Justice later ruled on July 25, 2018, that organisms obtained by means of mutagenesis techniques are within the scope of GMOs, and only organisms obtained by means of mutagenesis that have conventionally been used in a number of applications and have a long safety record are excluded from the scope of GMOs. Given that the newly invented gene-editing technology does not have a long history of safety, it is still subject to the regulation of GMOs, requiring the assessment of possible risks to human health and the environment. Verification of traceability must also be confirmed. Product labeling and post-market monitoring should be conducted.[5]

B. United States

From January 2017 to June 2017, the US Food and Drug Administration (FDA) publicly solicited public comments on the management methods of gene-edited plant-derived food or feed,[6] with four points for soliciting comments on gene-edited plants, as follows. (1) In what ways are the food safety risks associated

4 Court of Justice of the European Union, According to Advocate General Bobek, organisms obtained by mutagenesis are, in principle, exempted from the obligations in the Genetically Modified Organisms Directive, No. 04(18) Luxembourg, 18 January 2018.

5 E. Gelinsky & Hilbeck, "European Court of Justice Ruling Regarding New Genetic Engineering Methods Scientifically Justified: A Commentary on the Biased Reporting about the Recent Ruling" (2018) 30(1) Environ. Sci. Eur. 52.

6 Genome Editing in New Plant Varieties Used for Foods; Request for Comments, FDA-2016-N-4389, 82 FR 6564, 6564–6566 (2017).

with human and animal foods from genome-edited plants the same as or different from those associated with other plant development methods (e.g. hybridization, chemical- or radiation-induced mutagenesis, and non-targeted genetic modifications using *in vitro* recombinant DNA technologies)? (2) Are there categories of genome-edited plant varieties for which there are scientific bases to conclude that foods from such categories are unlikely to present food safety risks different from or greater than those for traditional plant breeding? Similarly, are there categories of genome-edited plant varieties for which the regulatory status of the food derived from such plant varieties can be said to be no different from that of traditionally bred plants so that there is no need to seek advice from the FDA before marketing? (3) Are there categories of genome-edited plant varieties for which there are scientific bases to conclude that foods from these categories are more likely than traditionally bred plants to present food safety risks? (4) What steps can we take to help small firms, including those who may be considering using genome editing to produce new plant varieties for use in human or animal food, to engage with FDA about any questions related to food safety or the regulatory status of foods from their new plant varieties?[7]

As for genetically engineered crops, the United States Department of Agriculture/Animal and Plant Health Inspection Service (USDA/APHIS) is the agency in charge of regulatory oversight over genetically modified or edited crops in reviewing potential risks of harmful plants in certain genetically engineered corps according to the Plant Protection Act (PPA). In 2012, APHIS issued an official statement stating that if crops are produced by the use of zinc finger nuclease technology and the NHEJ mechanism to repair DNA breaks, and they do not contain exogenous genes that are harmful to plants, they will not be regulated. The developers can request a confirmation from APHIS that a modified plant qualifies for an exemption and is not subject to the regulations. Therefore, the USDA has established an inquiry process called "Am I regulated?" in accordance with 7 CFR part 340. In applying for the confirmation letter, the applicant must include following information with the request: a description of a plant's genus and species, a description of the intended or actual traits of the plant, expected activity (relating to movement or release), genetic modifications in the final product, the vector or vector reagent used, the name and description of the recombinant DNA (including operon, promoter, origin of replication, terminator, ribosome binding site, etc.), and experimental methodologies used for confirming genetic modifications.[8]

The USDA has completed the hearing of a total of 24 applications for gene-editing technology (Table 8.2). The species developed include corn, soybean, rice, wheat, potatoes, mushrooms, tomatoes, *Setaria viridis*, flax mustard

7 Food and Drug Administration, FDA, "Genome Editing in New Plant Varieties Used for Foods" (2017); Request for Comments, *available at* www.federal register.gov/documents/2017/01/19/2017–00840/genome-editing-in-new-plant-varieties-used-for-foods-request-for-comments (last accessed July 24, 2020).

8 USDA, "Am I Regulated Under 7 CFR part 340?" (2019), *available at* www.aphis.usda.gov/aphis/ourfocus/biotechnology/am-i-regulated (last accessed July 24, 2020).

(camelina), alfalfa, tobacco, lettuce, pennycress, and others. According to the Plant Protection Act, developing crops using genetically engineered organisms as a donor or carrier won't subject they to USDA regulation as long as the product itself is not a harmful or a weedy plant and the product does not contain exogenous genes, or the exogenous genes are removed after screening. Nonetheless, USDA's reply letter to every confirmation request always emphasizes that the products still need to be regulated by the FDA and the Environmental Protection Agency (EPA).

In 2018, the USDA announced a statement on plants derived from new plant breeding techniques (NPBTs), which also include gene-editing technologies. The statement indicated that the USDA regulates those plants in accordance with the original biotechnology regulations. The USDA will not regulate plants that are indistinguishable from traditional breeding plants and will not propose any regulatory plans in the future either as long as those plants are developed without using harmful organisms or weedy plants as donors or carriers. Such new biotechnology simply creates plants modified with the deletion of any small fragments of genes, replacement of single base pairs, insertion of sequences from compatible plants, and offspring that no longer contain transgenic gene(s).

US Secretary of Agriculture Sonny Perdue announced the SECURE rule (the Sustainable, Ecological, Consistent, Uniform, Responsible, Efficient rule) on May 14, 2020, which is based on the Plant Protection Act. The Plant Protection Act has aimed to update and modernize the USDA's biotechnology regulations. The SECURE rules will eliminate repetitive and outdated processes, thereby bringing USDA's plant biotechnology regulations into the twenty-first century, so as to promote the development and availability of these technologies through a transparent, consistent, scientific, and risk-proportional regulatory system. This new regulation will help American farmers obtain key tools to increase agricultural productivity and sustainability, increase the nutritional value and quality of crops, prevent pests and diseases, and enhance food safety. The SECURE rule regulates the import, interstate transfer, and environmental release of organisms developed using genetic engineering technology that may become harmful plants. According to the revised regulations, certain types of genetically engineered plants are not subject to regulations. On August 17, 2020, the exemption and confirmation process will replace the existing "Am I regulated (AIR)?" process. For specific requesters and specific plants, organisms that were previously confirmed as unregulated by AIR reply are still considered valid and exempt from the new regulations.[9]

Developers can check the regulations to assess whether a plant belongs to one of the exempt categories. The following three categories of plants are not regulated: (1) a change resulting from cellular repair of a targeted DNA break in the absence of an externally provided repair template, (2) a targeted single base pair substitution, (3) introduction of a gene known to occur in the plant's gene

9 USDA, "USDA SECURE Rule Paves Way for Agricultural Innovation" (2020a), *available at* www.aphis.usda.gov/aphis/newsroom/news/sa_by_date/sa-2020/secure (last accessed July 24, 2020).

Table 8.2 US Department of Agriculture's inquiry list for gene-edited crops

Date	*Institution*	*Technology*	*Product*	*Feature*
2012.3.8	Dow AgroScience	ZFN	Corn	Reduce production of acid
2015.5.5	Cellectis Plant Sciences	TALEN	Soybean	Remove FAD2 gene
2015.5.20	Cellectis Plant Sciences	TALEN	Soybean	Remove FAD3 gene
2015.5.22	Iowa State University	TALEN	Rice	Disease resistance
2016.2.11	Calyxt, Inc.	TALEN	Wheat	Powdery mildew resistance
2016.4.13	Penn State	CRISPR/Cas	Mushroom	Anti-browning
2016.4.18	DuPont Pioneer	CRISPR/Cas	Waxy corn	Change sugar composition
2016.9.15	Calyxt, Inc.	TALEN	Potato	Improve processing characteristics
2016.12.2	Simplot Plant Sciences	TALEN	Potato	Reduce browning
2017.4.7	Donald Danforth Plant Science Center	CRISPR/Cas	*Setaria viridis*	Delay flowering
2017.8.29	Yield10 Bioscience	CRISPR/Cas	Camelina	-
2017.9.25	Calyxt, Inc.	TALEN	Alfalfa	Improve nutritional quality
2017.10.16	USDA ARS	CRISPR/Cas	Soybean	Drought and salt tolerance
2017.12.29	North Carolina State University	MN	Tobacco	Low level nicotine
2018.1.16	DuPont Pioneer	CRISPR/Cas	Corn	Resistance to northern leaf blight
2018.3.20	Calyxt, Inc.	TALEN	Wheat	Nutritionally enhanced
2018.5.14	University of Florida	CRISPR/Cas	Tomato	Easy to harvest
2018.7.12	Iowa State University	CRISPR/Cas	Corn	-
2019.2.8	Intrexon Corporation	Genome-edited	Lettuce	Prolong storage
2019.2.25	Max Planck Institute for Chemical Ecology	CRISPR/Cas9	Tobacco	Remove Nectarine protein expression
2019.4.19	Illinois State University	CRISPR	Pennycress	-
2019.6.17	University of Minnesota	CRISPR/Cas	Soybean	Changes in petiole length
2019.6.17	University of Minnesota	CRISPR/Cas	Soybean	Changes in seed composition
2019.7.2	Nexgen Plants Pty Ltd	Genome-edited	Tomato	Virus resistance

pool or a change in a targeted sequence to correspond to a known allele of such a gene or to a known structural variation present in the gene pool. In addition to these categories, modified plants will not be subject to the regulations if they have plant-trait mechanism of action (MOA) combinations that are the same as those of modified plants for which USDA has conducted a regulatory status review and found not to be subject to regulation. The USDA can expand the scope of exemptions related to modification that can be achieved through traditional breeding to ensure that regulations are consistent with technological and scientific development. Stakeholders can also request extensions of such scope through the process of public notifications and comments. Developers can seek confirmation from the USDA whether the plant meets the exemption requirements and is not subject to the regulations of 7 CFR Part 340. The regulatory exemption process takes effect on August 17, 2020.[10]

C. Canada

The Canadian Food Inspection Agency (CFIA) and the Ministry of Health (Health Canada, HC) are jointly responsible for the regulation of plants with novel traits in accordance with the Novel Food Regulation. The new traits may be produced by traditional breeding, mutation, or genetic engineering, and such plants will be reviewed on a case-by-case basis. Given that gene-edited products derived from CRISPR/CAS9 technology or products derived from other new technologies are novel products, that is, plants with new traits, it is not necessary to modify the regulations for reviewing products using these new technologies in Canada.

Health Canada conducts safety assessments on novel plant foods based on the principle of substantial equivalence with the aim to confirm that their composition and nutrition are equivalent to those of traditional foods and that novel foods do not contain toxins or cause allergic reactions. As for the review of environmental safety and animal feed, the Canada Food Inspection Agency conducts an assessment to confirm that the novel plant does not have the potential for weedization after hybridization with other plants, the possibility of the novel plant affecting biodiversity, and the safety of the novel plant for animal feed and the equivalent value of nutrition to the traditional plant. Moreover, it assesses whether exposure to such novel plants will cause harm to human beings and animals.[11] Currently, the only gene-edited crops approved in Canada are rapeseed developed by Cibus using oligonucleotide-directed mutagenesis technology, which was approved for marketing in 2013.

10 USDA, "About the SECURE Rule" (2020b), *available at* www.aphis. usda.gov/aphis/ourfocus/biotechnology/biotech-rule-revision/secure-rule/secure-about/340_2017_perdue_biotechreg (last accessed July 24, 2020).

11 Canadian Food Inspection Agency, "Plants with Novel Traits", *available at* www.inspection.gc.ca/plants/plants-with-novel-traits/eng/1300137887237/1300137939635 (last accessed July 24, 2020).

D. Argentina

Argentina is the first country in the world to promulgate regulations for emerging plant breeding technologies. The National Advisory Commission on Agricultural Biotechnology (CONABIA) of the Directorate of Biotechnology and the Biosafety Commission jointly discussed zinc finger nuclease technology in 2014 and preliminarily concluded that SDN-1 products of zinc finger nuclease technology are not genetically modified organisms, since they cannot be distinguished from the products of traditional mutation technology and have little probability of increasing the risks regarding food safety. As for SDN-2 products of zinc finger nuclease technology, whether they are products of GMOs needs to be determined on a case-by-case basis, whereas SDN-3 products of zinc finger nuclease technology are considered GMOs because transgenic gene(s) are inserted into the host genome. With respect to the products of oligonucleotide-directed mutagenesis technology, the Argentine regulatory authority does not consider them GMOs because such technology will not increase or create new risks, and it is difficult to distinguish such derived foods from those with traditional mutations or naturally occurring mutations.[12]

In 2015, in accordance with Resolution No. 763/11[13] of Genetically Modified Organisms[14] of the Ministry of Agriculture, Livestock and Fisheries (Ministerio de Agricultura, Ganadería y Pesca, MAGyP), Argentina issued Resolution No. 173/15 adopting product-based regulation of GMOs and establishing a set of consultation procedures for determining whether the products of emerging plant breeding technologies are GMOs in order to determine if such products will be subject to GMO regulation. The standard of the decision is mainly based on whether the product of emerging plant breeding technology possesses a novel combination of genetic material and whether the final product of the emerging plant breeding technology contains foreign transgenic genes or DNA sequences.[15]

Developers of products of emerging plant breeding technologies must provide background information about the process of breeding and screening crops, techniques and methods used for introducing new traits, evidence of the introduced genetic modification in the final product, and evidence of the possible transient use of transgenic gene(s) during the development process. Through the consultation process, after 60 days of review time, the applicant

12 Schuttelaar and Partners, "The Regulatory Status of New Breeding Techniques in Countries Outside the European Union", The Hague, The Netherlands: Author, 6–10 (2015), *available at* www.nbtplatform.org/background-documents/rep-regulatory-status-of-nbts-oustide-the-eu-june2015.pdf (last accessed July 24, 2020).

13 Ministerio de Agricultura, Ganadería y Pesca (MAGP), Resolución 763/11 – Organismos Genéticamente Modificados (OGM), 2011, http://argentinambiental.com/legislacion/nacional/resolucion-76311-organismos-geneticamente-modificados-ogm.

14 Ibid.

15 MAGP, Resolucion 173/2015. Ministry of Agriculture, Forestry and Fisheries (MAFF), 新たな育種技術研究会 (2015), http://www.affrc.maff.go.jp/docs/commitee/nbt/ top.htm.

can receive a reply from the authorities on whether the products of emerging plant breeding technologies are subject to regulation. According to this process, the end products of specific DNA sequence changes in crops by applying the SDN-1and SDN-2 and ODM technologies will not be subject to existing GMOs regulation as long as they do not contain foreign gene(s).[16]

E. Japan

The Ministry of Agriculture, Forestry and Fisheries (MAFF) of Japan convened experts and scholars to establish a research committee on emerging breeding technologies on October 4, 2013. Seven meetings had been held as of July 22, 2015. The Committee discussed issues ranging from the definition and scope of emerging breeding technologies to the impact of research and development and practical applications of such technologies on biodiversity. Since GMOs in Japan are governed by the Cartagena Protocol on Biosafety, GMOs are defined as organisms that possess nucleic acids, or a replicated product thereof, obtained through the use of genetic engineering technology. The committee suggested that for emerging breeding crops, (1) it should be considered whether there are foreign gene(s) in plants, and (2) it should adopt the same regulatory principles as the current ones; that is, organisms obtained by self-cloning and natural occurrence are not subject to regulation.[17]

The Ministry of the Environment (MOE) is the agency in charge of the assessment of the impact of GMOs on environmental risks. On May 28, 2018, the Natural Environment Subcommittee of the MOE established a research group on gene editing technology to discuss whether gene-edited crops are within the scope of GMOs under the Cartagena Protocol on Biosafety and, if not, whether gene-edited crops can be regarded as general crops and it can be ensured that they do not affect biodiversity. The Natural Environment Subcommittee concluded in March 2019 that gene-edited products are not considered GMOs under the Cartagena Biosafety Protocol as long as the process of development does not involve foreign nucleic acids, such as SDN-1 technology using protein or ribonucleoprotein (RNP), or transient expression. If foreign DNA is used and inserted into the genome, such as those in SDN-2 and SDN-3 technologies, the products should be regarded as GMOs. However, SDN-2 and SDN-3 products obtained by self-cloning and natural occurrence are not regarded as GMOs according to the Cartagena Biosafety Protocol. Developers are encouraged to submit a report to the regulatory agency before marketing, explaining the process and method of gene editing.

16 A. I. Whelan & A. Lema, "Regulatory Framework for Gene Editing and other New Breeding Techniques (NBTs) in Argentina" (2015) 6 GM Crops Food 253–265, doi:10.1080/21645698.2015.1114698

17 Ministry of Agriculture, Forestry and Fisheries, MAFF, 新たな育種技術研究会 (2015), *available at* www.affrc.maff.go.jp/docs/commitee/nbt/top.htm (last accessed July 24, 2020).

If such products are determined to be products with no foreign nucleic acids or obtained by self-cloning and natural occurrence, they are not considered GMOs.[18]

The Ministry of Health, Labour and Welfare (MHLW) also adopted regulatory measures for gene-edited foods in March 2019, stating that gene-edited foods are different from genetically modified foods and do not involve the genes of other organisms in the process. Such products simply edit the gene of the species itself and cannot be distinguished from the products obtained by traditional breeding methods. Therefore, they cannot be regarded as GMOs, such as SDN-1 and SDN-2 products. So the focus should be on whether the final product has foreign DNA to determine if it is a GMO. According to this test, SDN-3 products are regarded as GMOs. Developers of gene-edited foods are also encouraged to provide five pieces of relevant information before marketing: (1) the name and end use of the food, (2) the method and process of the gene-editing technology used, (3) confirmation of DNA changes and off-target effects, (4) residual status of foreign gene(s), and (5) changes in metabolites or nutrients. The MHLW will also publish relevant information on its website.[19]

F. Australia and New Zealand

The Ministry of Health and Ageing of Australia, in accordance with the Gene Technology Act of 2000 and the Gene Technology Regulations of 2001, is responsible for approving and regulating genetically modified crops and emerging crops in Australia. In 2014, Food Standards Australia New Zealand (FSANZ) issued relevant opinions on emerging breeding technologies based on the scientific advice of the expert working group. When new genes are introduced into crops, this type of technology is equivalent to genetic modification, so the derived food should be regarded as genetically modified food. As for foods derived from SDN-1 and SDN-2 types of zinc finger nuclease technology and oligonucleotide site-directed mutagenesis technology, they should not be regarded as genetically modified foods since such technologies are similar to traditional mutations used in traditional plant breeding, and it is difficult to distinguish the products of ODM technology from those of traditional mutations or naturally occurring mutations.[20]

The Australian government launched the National Gene Technology Scheme (NGTS) in July 2017 and established a professional advisory group for gene technology review to collect opinions from multiple parties through a

18 Ministry of the Environment, MOE, ゲノム編集の概念の整理について (2019), *available at* www.env.go.jp/council/12nature/y120-35/mat03_4.pdf (last accessed July 24, 2020).

19 Ministry of Health, Labour and Welfare, 薬事・食品衛生審議会 食品衛生分科会 新開発食品調査部会 資料 (2019), *available at* www.mhlw. go.jp/stf/shingi2/0000203059_00011.html (last accessed July 24, 2020).

20 Schuttelaar and Partners, *supra* note 9, 11–15; 30–32.

three-stage consultation process. The first stage was to collect written opinions, and the second stage was to discuss possible policy solutions. In the third stage, the investigation results were presented followed by conducting two webinars. The NGTS separately discussed different aspects of issues surrounding technology, regulations, government, and social ethics. The results were announced in October 2018. It is recommended that the definition of the Gene Technology Act enacted in 2000 should be revised up to date, and consideration must be given to whether current emerging technology products are included in the scope of regulation.[21]

Food Standards Australia New Zealand established an expert advisory group for emerging breeding technologies in 2017 to discuss regulatory methods for emerging plant breeding technologies,[22] including gene editing technologies that do not have foreign gene(s). The public opinion consultation was conducted from February to August 2018, and it is expected that the final results and the proposal to amend the current laws and regulations will be announced at the end of 2019.[23]

The Office of the Gene Technology Regulator (OGTR) discussed the definition of genetic modification in the current Gene Technology Act in October 2016 and proposed three principles: (1) all new technologies must be regulated, so both zinc finger nuclease technology and oligonucleotide-directed mutagenesis technology-derived crops must be regulated. (2) On the "technology-based" regulation, products derived from the SDN-2 and SDN-3 types of zinc finger nuclease and ODM technologies are subject to regulation because they have nucleic acid templates inserted into the genomes of organisms, while SDN-1 products of zinc finger nuclease technology can be exempted from regulation. (3) On "product-based" regulation, crops derived from the SDN-1 and SDN-2 types of zinc finger nuclease technology and ODM technology can be excluded, whereas products of the SDN-3 type of zinc finger nuclease technology are regulated as GMOs and subject to public consultation procedure.[24] In April 2019, the Australian government announced that as long as no new genetic material was introduced, the Australian Gene Technology Authority would not regulate the use of gene-editing technology in plant, animal, and human cells.[25]

21 Department of Health, DOH, "Third Review of the National Gene Technology Scheme" (2019), *available at* www.health.gov.au/internet/main/publishing.nsf/Content/gene-technology-review (last accessed July 24, 2020).

22 This Standard is Australia New Zealand Food Standards Code – Standard 1.5.2 – Food Produced Using Gene Technology (2016).

23 Food Standards Australia New Zealand, FSANZ, "Food Derived Using New Breeding Techniques—Review" (2019), *available at* www.food standards.gov.au/consumer/gmfood/Pages/Review-of-new-breeding-technologies-.aspx. (last accessed July 24, 2020).

24 Office of the Gene Technology Regulator (OGTR), *Options for regulating new technologies*. Australian Government (Department of Health Discussion paper, 2016).

25 S. Mallapaty, "Australian Gene-editing Rules Adopt 'Middle Ground'" (2019) Nature, doi:10.1038/d41586-019-01282-8.

G. *Taiwan*

Gene editing technology has become a popular gene manipulation technique for the next generation, especially the booming system of CRISPR/Cas9. Manufacturers have begun to develop gene-edited foods and even have products ready to go on the market, so how to regulate such products should be a top priority. When making the regulatory policy for gene-editing technology, the authority should refer to the international trends of gene-editing regulation and take into account the legislative definition of genetic modification technology in order to adopt regulatory principles that can avoid creating barriers to international trade and support the development of domestic biotechnology industry while minimizing consumers' health risks at the same time. In 2018, the Food and Drug Administration commissioned the Food Industry Research and Development Institute to develop various regulatory plans for policy making regarding foods derived from gene-editing technology. Based on the suggestion of consulting experts, the most supportive option, among various plans, is the early consultation system. Under the proposed early consultation system, applicants must provide relevant information of the gene-edited foods, including the process of gene editing, molecular characteristics, test data on whether foreign DNA or RNA fragments are present in the derived food, and related data or analysis regarding off-target effects. The competent authority shall determine whether the food is a genetically modified food and its corresponding regulatory approach.

III. Concluding Remarks

Emerging biotechnology brings more new breeding plants to mankind. At present, many gene-editing technology-derived crops that do not contain foreign gene(s) are about to go on the market, which not only poses challenges to the competent authorities of various countries but also has difficulties concerning being compatible with existing GMO regulations. The competent authorities of various countries need to immediately review the current regulatory approaches and make necessary adjustments to the scope of regulation. So far, only a few countries have put forward clear regulations for crops derived from gene editing technology (Table 8.3). Canada clearly adopts an approach of novel plant varieties, whereas the European Union follows an original route with its GMO regulatory approach. The USDA and Argentina take a case-by-case approach requiring the submission of relevant information in early consultation or a confirmation letter to decide if gene-edited crops are regulated. However, most countries' food regulators, including the United States, South Korea, and Taiwan, have not yet announced their regulatory approaches or policy.

In spite of unclear regulatory status toward gene-edited products globally, small and medium-sized R&D companies and academic research institutes have invested a lot of funds and manpower in the development of gene-edited

Table 8.3 Countries' regulatory approaches on products derived from gene editing

Countries		*Gene-editing technologies*			
		SDN-1	*SDN-2*	*SDN-3*	*ODM*
US	**USDA**	Exemption	Case-by-case	Regarded as GMOs	Exemption
		End product cannot contain foreign gene			
	FDA	Not yet promulgated			
Argentina		Exemption	Case-by-case	Regarded as GMOs	Exemption
		Need to conduct consultation to decide if subjected to regulation			
Japan	**MHLW**	Exemption	Exemption	Regarded as GMOs	-
		End-product cannot contain foreign genes			
	MOE	Exemption	Regarded as GMOs	Regarded as GMOs	-
		Insertion of foreign nucleic acid is regarded as GMO, while SDN-2 and SDN-3 using self-cloning as a template can be exempted			
Australia	**OGTR**	Exemption	Regarded as GMOs	Regarded as GMOs	Regarded as GMOs
Canada		**Regulate as novel crops**			
EU		**Regulate as GMOs**			
Taiwan		**Under draft**			

products. Excessive and stringent regulations will stifle the development of innovative biotechnology and the potential of commercialization of gene-edited products. Such innovative and emerging technologies need to be accompanied by effective regulations, rule-making, and substantive application in order to maximize the innovation and transformation of the biotechnology industry in Taiwan.

9 The Regulation of "Novel Food" in China

The Tendency of De-Regulation

*Juanjuan Sun**

As put by P.B. Hutt, the history of progress in food and drug regulation over the past century is largely the history of the development of science, not the enactment of statutory provisions.[1] Indeed, the development of science not only changes the way food is produced and consumed but also the regulatory response, especially the application of risk assessment to reinforce a science-based risk regulation in a preventive way. Taking the cultured meat that is currently highly relevant as an example, developments in the business of cultured meat go fast, and both American and European regulators have reacted to deal with this novel food in line with their own exiting legislative arrangements.[2] Among the others, the system in the EU is specifically designed to handle food developed from newly emerged science and technology, namely novel food regulation. Historically speaking, the European regulation of novel foods[3] emerged as a reaction to the application of new technologies in the food domain, in particular the use of genetic modification in food.[4] Accordingly, foods and food ingredients are considered novel if they have not been used for human consumption to a significant degree prior to May 15, 1997, within the EU. This concept of novel foods not only includes tech-foods, as mentioned previously, but also exotic foods, which may be traditional food with a long history of use outside the EU.[5] However, six years after the implementation of the so-called Novel Foods Regulation, the regulation of GM foods has been separated and transferred to a series of specific

* This chapter is an update of a previous paper; *see* "The Regulation of 'Novel Food' in China: The Tendency of Deregulation" (2015) 10(6) European Food and Feed Law Review 442, 442–448.

1 R. I. Field, *Health Care Regulation in America: Complexity, Confrontation, and Compromise* (Oxford, OUP 2007), at 114.

2 K. Verzijden & J. Buijs, "Meat 3.0—How Cultured Meat Is Making Its Way to the Market" (2020) 15(2) European Food and Feed Law Review 96.

3 Regulation (EC) No 258/97 of the European Parliament and of the Council of 27 January 1997 concerning novel foods and novel food ingredients, 1997 OJ L 43, 1.

4 C. Ballke, "The New Novel Food Regulation" (2014) 5 European Food and Feed Law Review 285.

5 M. Hermann, "The Impact of the European Novel Food Regulation on Trade and Food Innovation Based on Traditional Plant Foods from Developing Countries" (2009) 34 Food Policy 500.

DOI: 10.4324/9781003271918-12

regulations, which address requirements for authorization,[6] traceability, and labeling.[7] Now, revised regulation on novel food[8] has introduced a centralized assessment and authorization process that makes the overall process more efficient.

Comparatively, the regulation of "novel food" in China resembles the EU model. For example, cultured meat also became a hot topic for the representatives at the two sessions[9] this year. To facilitate business development and protect public health, a representative from the Chinese People's Political Consultative Conference (CPPCC) has proposed regulating cultured meat like the EU, since the Measures on the Safety Review of Novel Food Material in China is like the Novel Food Regulation in the EU.[10] Yet such regulation in China can be traced back in 1990. Generally speaking, the specific rule targeting "novel food" was Measures on the Hygiene of Food from Novel Sources, implemented in 1990. Accordingly, hygiene assessment and pre-market approval were required if the food were legally classified as novel, such as newly invented food or newly imported food without a history of use in China. As a new invented food from biotechnology, GM food should be subject to the requirements provided by this general rule. What is more, to reinforce the regulation of GM food and protect consumers' health and right to know, a specific rule, the Measures on Hygiene of Genetically Modified Food, was established in 2002. In addition to safety assessment and pre-market approval, this rule also required the food producer to keep records and perform labeling.[11]

In comparison to the EU, the specifics of regulating "novel food" in China can be outlined and illustrated as follows. First, while the so-called Novel Foods Regulation targets food and food ingredients in the EU, the regulated targets in China have evolved from novel sources towards novel food and finally focused on novel material (as shown in Table 9.1). That is to say,

6 Regulation (EC) No 1829/2003 of the European Parliament and of the Council of 22 September 2003 on genetically modified food and feed, 2003 OJ L 268, 1.

7 Regulation (EC) No 1830/2003 of the European Parliament and of the Council of 22 September 2003 concerning the traceability and labelling of genetically modified organisms and the traceability of food and feed products produced from genetically modified organisms and amending Directive 2001/18/EC, 2003 OJ L 268, 24.

8 Regulation (EU) 2015/2283 of the European Parliament and of the Council of 25 November 2015 on novel foods, amending Regulation (EU) No 1169/2011 of the European Parliament and of the Council and repealing Regulation (EC) No 258/97 of the European Parliament and of the Council and Commission Regulation (EC) No 1852/2001, 2015 OJ L 327, 1.

9 From early to mid-March, the National People's Congress, the top legislature, and the PPCC National Committee, China's top political advisory body, convene their annual sessions.

10 "政协委员孙宝国：建议加大人造肉的研发投入 建立健全法律法规 [Representative Baoguo SUN from the CPPCC: Suggest to Increase Investment in Research and Development of Cultured Meat While Establish and Update Legal Rules]", *CE*, May 25, 2020, *available at* www.ce.cn/cysc/sp/info/202005/25/t20200525_34974117.shtml.

11 Notably, this rule had been cancelled. As far as the regulation of genetically modified food in China is concerned, *see* J. Sun, "Genetically Modified Foods in China: Regulation, Deregulation, or Governance" in K-C. Liu & R. Uday (eds), *Innovation, Economic Development, and Intellectual Property in India and China* (Singapore, Springer 2019), at 347–366.

Table 9.1 Successful authorization of domestic produced or imported novel food/material

Year	2008	2009	2010	2011	2012	2013	2014	2015	2016	2017	2018	2019	2020
Domestic	27	48	24	50	25	44	1	11	12	8	0	6	2
Imported	14	22	5	11	14	27	1	9	3	1	0	0	0

Time	*Rule*	*Target*
1987	Measures on Hygiene of Novel Sources for Food	Novel sources
1990	Measures on Hygiene of Food from New Sources	Novel food
2007	Measures on Food from New Sources	Novel food/material
2013	Measures on the Safety Review of Novel Food Material	Novel food material

Figure 9.1 The evolution of rules concerning "novel food" in China

currently, "novel food material regulation" is a more precise label for the approach in China. Second, while the safety assessment constitutes a prerequisite administrative approval, the procedure has been streamlined to provide deregulation to a certain degree, in particular by introduction of a substantial equivalence principle. Third, the traditional custom that the same raw materials such as plants can be used for both food and medicine because of their beneficial health effects is taken into consideration.[12] As a result, traditional materials like herbals can be further exploited as novel food material to promote health food.[13] In view of this, not only the definition of food in the Chinese *Food Safety Law* but also the regulation of novel food material has taken into account such Chinese characteristics. Last but not least, there is the relation to patent law. Food safety is a highly sensitive issue. The competent authority responsible for granting patents has been blamed in the case of "poisonous gelatin" made from leather due to their failure to guarantee safety by granting a patent to such artificial gelatin.[14] Consequently, while investment in the development of novel materials can be encouraged by patent protection, the competent authority is under pressure to consider safety during the review of applications.

12 Q. Chen et al., "药食同源食品起源与行业现状分析 [Origin and Industry Status Analysis of Medicinal and Edible Food]" (2011) 7 黑龙江农业科学 [Heilongjiang Agricultural Sciences] 114, 114–115.

13 H. Pu & S. Zhang, "新资源食品的研究与发展[The Research and Development of Novel Food]" (1995) 3 浙江预防医学 [Zhejiang Journal of Preventive Medicine] 54, 54–55.

14 Y. Zhao, "解读"毒明胶食品"事件中的专利问题[The Analysis of Patent in the Case of Food Made from Poisonous Gelatin]" (2012) 5 中国发明与专利[China Invention & Patent] 22, 22–23.

I. The Evolution of Rules Concerning "Novel Food" in China

The basic law regulating food safety regulation in general, and "novel food" regulation in particular, from 1983 to May 31, 2009, was the Food Hygiene Law. From June 1, 2009, the Food Safety Law has provided the legal foundation for regulating novel food/material. For the former, the Food Hygiene Law on trial in 1983 had required a hygiene and nutrition assessment for producing food and food additives from novel sources, while approval would be granted if legally required food hygiene standards were satisfied. Also, even food-related products like food containers, packaging material, and tools produced from novel sources had to go through a hygiene assessment and obtain approval at that time. For the latter, the Food Safety Law has confirmed that businesses engaging in food production using novel food material shall submit a safety assessment document, while an approval will be granted if the food safety requirements are satisfied. Against this background, the following will further illustrate the evolution of the definition and scope of "novel food" in China.

Although the Measures on Hygiene of Novel Sources for Food was established in 1987 as one of the implementing acts for the Food Hygiene Law of 1983, the definition of novelty had not been clarified until the arrival of the Measures on Hygiene of Food from Novel Sources in 1990. According to this rule, four categories of new sources for food had been clarified, including newly invented sources, newly discovered sources, newly imported sources without history of consumption in China, and existing sources in China with history of consumption only in certain local places. Then, novel food meant the food produced from these novel sources, including food material as well as the final product. It was in line with this definition that genetically modified (GM) food was regarded as novel food. As a transition from the novel food orientation towards the novel food material orientation,[15] the Measures on Food from New Sources in 2007 further clarified the definition and scope. For one thing, this rule re-grouped the novel foods into four categories: animals, plants, and microorganisms without custom of use; food materials extracted from animals, plants, and microorganisms without custom of use; new varieties of microorganisms used in food processing; and food materials leading to changes of original ingredients or structure as a result of adoption of a new process in production. With such categories, it can be said that the regulation of novel food in China has taken a process-based criterion for safety assessment.[16] Another striking change in the regulation of novel food is to exclude GM

15 "中国药房 [China Pharmacy], 卫生部发布《新资源食品管理办法》The Establishment of Measures on Food from New Resources by Ministry of Health" (2007) 21 中国药房 [China Pharmacy] [-], 1627.

16 D. L. Pelletier, "FDA's Regulation of Genetically Engineered Foods: Scientific, Legal and Political Dimensions" (2006) 31(6) Food Policy 570, 575.

food from the scope of novel food. As a result, the regulation of GM food has been placed under a separate regulatory framework of GM organisms operated by the agriculture department, such as the Regulations on Administration of Agricultural Genetically Modified Organism Safety. For this reason, it is said that there are legislative gaps regarding the regulation of GM food, while the existing regulation or rules rather than law are at relatively lower levels of legal hierarchy. Thus, the attitude of the government in the regulation of GM food is quite ambiguous.[17]

With the establishment of the Food Safety Law to replace the Food Hygiene Law in 2009, the new basic law has employed the terms of novel food material instead of food from novel sources and confirmed the requirement concerning pre-market approval. Therefore, the updated Measures on the Safety Review of Novel Food Material in 2013 has further simplified the definition of its target, namely what can be regarded as novel food material. Accordingly, the first general requirement is the lack of traditional consumption habits in China. A traditional habit of consumption means that a certain type of food has been produced or traded as standard-packaged food or non-standard-packaged food in a province for over 30 years and has not been listed in the Pharmacopoeia of the People's Republic of China. Second, the qualified articles include the categories of animals, plants, and microorganisms; ingredients extracted from animals, plants, and microorganisms; food ingredients the original composition of which has been changed; and other newly developed food raw materials. Third, the rule excludes GM food, health food, and food additives as its regulated targets.

In a nutshell, there are three stages with regard to what is focused on by the so-called "novel food regulation." They are stage I for novel sources, stage II for novel food, and stage III for novel food material. The evolution is first closely linked to the modernization of food safety regulation as a background. As mentioned, the progress of the Food Safety Law replacing the Food Hygiene Law has re-structured the safety guarantee in the interest of public health. As far as the legal framework is concerned, vertical legislation has been completed on the basis of the Food Safety Law to cover different food or food-related categories like health food and food additives. This is why the initial scope of novel sources has been narrowed down to exclude products like food additives. Second, experience has indicated that the material-focused rules rather than product-focused ones can reduce the administrative workload and promote the application of novel food material because once a kind of food material is classified as safe raw material, food operators can use it in a variety of food products as long as they respect the requirements regarding the usage quantity and labeling.[18] That is to say, a food product produced with approved novel food material is regarded as

17 X. Li, "The Predicament and Outlet of Genetically Modified Foods Regulation in China" (2015) 1 Journal of South China Normal University [-], 140–141.

18 Y. Wang, "我国新资源食品管理现状与分析 [The Status-Quo of Novel Food Regulation in China and Its Analysis]" (2011) 1 中国卫生监督杂志[Chinese Journal of Health Inspection] [-], 20–23.

conventional food rather than novel food. Third, taking the latest definition of novel food material as reference, on the one hand, the final catch-all clause in the form of all other newly developed food raw materials provides flexibility to allow applying for a material resulting from newly advanced science and technology in food production.[19] On the other hand, the precision of what can be perceived as traditional consumption habits is measured by 30 years at the provincial level. Notably, while novel food from the perspective of traditional food refers to exotic food outside the EU under the European novel food regulation, the different opinion on this aspect in China also includes local food with no history of consumption at the national level. Actually, as a country of diversity in food and food material, such a provision will provide chances to exploit local traditional food and ethnic food while taking account of modernized safety requirements. In this aspect, local food safety standards can be further established if national food safety standards are lacking, which are the mandatory measures to make sure that food entering into the market will not cause hazards to public health.

II. Current Safety Assessment and Administrative Approval

The introduction of the risk assessment principle and substantial equivalence principle by Measures on Food from New Sources of 2007 was a turning point in the transition from hygiene assessment to safety assessment. To apply for approval for novel food material, the applicant needs to submit a safety assessment document that clearly indicates the involved chemical substances like food additives and processing aids, the composition, labeling, and so on.[20] Whether these statements comply with the mandatory national food safety standards will be further reviewed by the scientific experts. Notably, when an approval is granted, a follow-up assessment may be conducted in light of newly emerged scientific information or safety issues related to the approved food material in question in order to avoid health risk. Both for review at the stage of application and the follow-up review, risk assessment has become an essential tool that shall be conducted in line with the Measures on Food Safety Risk Assessment.

As far as the substantial equivalence principle is concerned, if a certain new food raw material regarding which an application has been filed and a food or a new food raw material that has been approved are equivalent in terms of species, source, biological property, main ingredients, edible parts, usage quantity, scope of use, potential consumers, and other aspects, and they adopt basically the same techniques and quality requirements, they may be deemed equally

19 C. Sun & G. Zhao, "从新资源食品到新食品原料的制度变迁与应对 [The Systematic Changes from Novel Food towards Novel Food Material and Respond]" (2014) 1 食品工业科技 [Science and Technology of Food Industry] [-], 19.

20 Ministry of Health, Specification on the Safety Review regarding Novel Food Material.

safe and substantively equivalent. With this provision, it is the responsibility of the experts, who are selected from an expert database consisting of professionals from the domain of food, nutrition, and medicine, to carry out the review. If the reviewer finds that the applied novel food material is substantively equivalent to conventional food or announced novel food material during the review, he or she can close the review. And then, with this scientific opinion, the competent authority can put the food material in the catalogue. As a positive list, food operators can use all foods included in the catalogue directly without additional application. In practice, however, guidelines for food operators for how to carry out a comparison in line with the substantial equivalence principle on their own are still lacking. So, businesses usually depend on administrative assistance to apply this principle.[21]

Following the expert opinion, pre-marketing approval issued by the responsible health department constitutes the basic legal mechanism for using novel material in food production. Along with the evolution of legal requirements, there are the following changes regarding the approval procedures. First, before 2007, the approved new sources could be used in production and marketing only within a given location for a trial period of two years. During this period, the composition and production method would not be allowed to change and the involved technique could not be transferred to others, either. Second, the catalogue of approved novel food and food material has been established since 2007 and announced to the public. Accordingly, food operators can directly use the listed food materials as long as they respect the requirements provided in the announcement, such as the usage quantity and labeling. Notably, the health department also has the power to exclude an approved food material from the catalogue in two situations. One case is when the concerned food material is deemed as safe as conventional material on the ground of a period of safe use, and the other case is that the food material at issue is not safe anymore given new scientific opinion issued from a re-review. Third, with the development of administrative law, the rule of law in the approval procedure for novel food material has also been strengthened. As accompanying rule to the Measures on the Safety Review of Novel Food Material, the Rule on Application and Review of Novel Food Material has reinforced the competent authorities' responsibility in paperwork like in-time notification in receiving the application, demanding additional documents, or refusing an application.

III. The Use of Novel Food Material in Health Food

When it comes to food, the definition in the Chinese Food Safety Law refers to both raw materials and finished products for human consumption. It is worth

21 Y. Yang, "国内外新资源食品实质等同的判断及依据 [The Judgment and Criteria of Substantial Equivalence Regarding Novel Food Inside and Outside China]" (2011) 1 中国卫生监督杂志 [Chinese Journal of Health Inspection] [-], 18–19.

mentioning that the legal definition of food also includes articles that are traditionally used in food and medicine due to the fact that food therapy and dietary regime are important elements in Chinese traditional medicine, under which the former is for curing diagnosed diseases with functional food like certain herbals and the latter for promoting health and longevity.[22] Therefore, to keep up this tradition for promoting health, a list of the materials that can commonly be used in food and medicine has been established by the health department.[23] In China, food that has the function to promote health, like dietary supplements in the United States or functional food in Japan, is called "health food." According to the Measure on Heath Food in 1996,[24] health food should be approved on the basis of safety assessment and evidence of its effectiveness, while follow-up review is possible if monitoring shows changes in the function regarding an approved health food. With the revision of the Food Safety Law, a list of food material used in health food and a list of legally permitted health claims are required to be established by the China Food and Drug Administration (China FDA) in the near future. As a result, if a non-listed food material is used to produce health food as well as in an imported a health food, it must be registered first. However, imported health food consisting of only vitamin or mineral supplements is exempted from registration and filing to the China FDA.

As far as the linkage between novel food material and health food is concerned, it is allowed to use new food material in health food if it has the function to offer a beneficial health effect. Actually, before introducing the Measure for Health Food in 1996, food operators who developed food from novel sources to promote health had to apply for approval on the ground of such novel food. The troublesome issue at that time was exaggerated health claims, while no rules could be applied to fight against misbranding. Fortunately, with the introduction of the Measure on Health Food, the requirement on safety assessment as well as health claims for health food have been provided. Since novel food is forbidden to claim a function, food operators changed the strategy under which they preferred registering a product using novel food material as health food rather than applying for approval as novel food.[25] Therefore, it

22 T. Shi, "中国饮食文化民族性特征概说 [The General Introduction of the National Characteristics of Chinese Food Culture] (1993) 5 商业研究 [Commercial Research] [-], 16–17.

23 "卫生部关于进一步规范保健食品原料管理的通知 [Notice on the Further Regulation of Material Used in Health Food]" (中国卫生健康委员会[Ministry of Health], Mar. 11, 2002, *available at* www.nhc.gov.cn/sps/s3593/200810/bc239ea3d226449b86379f645dfd881d.shtml.

24 With the revision of Chinese Food Safety Law in 2015, this rule has also been under update in order to introduce a new regulatory approach in the form of a catalogue for both approved material and approved health claims.

25 L. Wang et al., "我国新资源食品管理的现状及对策探讨 [Current Situation and Strategy for Novel Food Regulation in China]" (2006) 4 中国卫生监督杂志 [Chinese Journal of Health Inspection] [-], 263–264.

can be said that labeling in the form of a health claim was an important tool at that time to tell the difference between novel food and health food.

In view of this, it is important to figure out the difference between and linkage of the following lists regarding what can or cannot be used in food products, including:

- List of the materials that can be commonly used in food and medicine
- List of the materials that can be used in health food
- List of the materials that cannot be used in health food
- List/catalogue of novel food material

These lists can be updated to include new materials according to the application. Among them, the first, second, and fourth lists are set up in the form of positive lists, while the third one is a negative list. Accordingly, the materials from the first list can be used in conventional food, but materials only used in medicine may not be used in any kinds of food. As indicated by the name, the materials from the second list are only for health food, while the third one includes materials that are forbidden for health food. Notably, if the materials from the second one are intended to be used in conventional food, first approval as novel food material is required. For the fourth list, the approval for this kind of material only considers the safety, not the effectiveness. Therefore, to avoid duplication of administrative work, the health department has confirmed that the regulation of novel food material is to exclude the review of material that is only used for health food. That is to say, even if the material can be regarded as novel according to the Measures on the Safety Review of Novel Food Material, the use only in health food can exempt it from approval required by this rule.

IV. Safety Considerations in the Application of Patents Regarding Novel Food Material

Generally speaking, to be patentable in China under the Patent Law, a food material shall be characterized as being novel, inventive, and practically applicable, while it does not fall into categories like scientific discovery or animal and plant varieties. Accordingly, the invention of novel food material with new science and technology can be patented, but it cannot be patented if it is only a new discovery of a local plant for promoting its use at national level.[26] Although novelty is the focus of both the Measures on the Safety Review of Novel Food Material and the Patent Law, safety of the concerned food material is of paramount importance to obtain an approval under the former rule, yet safety will only be considered if the patent application contravenes any law or social moral

26 C. Sun, "新资源食品的公众认知与认同 [The Public Perception and Recognition of Novel Food]" (2013) 2 食品工业科技 [Food Industry Technology] [-].

or public interest according to the Patent Law.[27] Admittedly, a material that is patentable does not suggest that it is also safe, since in some cases it is not the invention itself but the methods of its application that violates the legal requirements. Nevertheless, when it comes to a patent application for a food material or a material intended to be used in food production, the review for granting a patent is also expected to play the role of "safety valve" to ensure food safety.

First, given that no patent shall be granted for an invention that contravenes any law, the reviewer is supposed to consider the Food Safety Law if the applicant applies for a patent for novel material used in a food product. That is to say, he/she is obliged to refuse the application if the novel material does not comply with the food safety requirement. As a matter of fact, the current most disturbing food safety issue in China is the abuse of chemical substances in comparison to biological contamination in western countries. Therefore, it is not surprising that the Food Safety Law clearly prohibits producing food with non-edible material or non-food-additive chemical substances or other substances potentially hazardous to human health.

Second, for a novel food material, whether the applicant is obliged to present the safety assessment for applying patent is still a disputed subject.[28] A strict opinion argues that to apply a patent for a food material, it is necessary to present the safety assessment issued by the health department. This means the applicant shall apply an approval for food material according to Measures on the Safety Review of Novel Food Material and then apply for patent on the basis of officially assured safety. As argued by opponents, such a requirement is too burdensome for the applicant since the two administrative procedures are time consuming and thus discourage innovation. Therefore, it relies on the applicant to claim the safety in the description. Otherwise, there will be a negative review if the description lacks a safety statement. Comparatively, the second opinion is more practically applicable and closer to the purpose of the Patent Law, namely to encouraging inventions.

Third, as a remedy, it is also essential to mention the possibility of invalidating a patent in the case that the patented food material is regarded as unsafe with newly proved evidence. As required in the Measures on the Safety Review of Novel Food Material, a novel food material shall be re-reviewed if a doubt is raised about its safety as science and technology develop or there is existing evidence that shows that its safety is questionable. If the follow-up review confirms the safety issue with the patented food material, anyone can ask to invalidate the patent. Interestingly, the revised Food Safety Law has provided a co-governance principle to encourage all stakeholders and the public to take part in food safety assurance. Within this context, not only the reviewer for

27 According to the Patent Law, no patent shall be granted for an invention that contravenes any law or social moral or that is detrimental to public interests, Article 5.

28 J. Wang, "专利审查如何为食品安全把关 [The Safety Guarantee in the Review for Patent Application" (2011) 6 中国发明与专利 [China Invention & Patent] [-], 27.

granting patent rights but also anyone else can take advantage of invalidation to make sure of the safety of novel food material.

V. Conclusion

From the historical evolution of the "novel food" regulation in China, a promising tendency of deregulation is apparent in this field, for example, the cancellation of the two-year trial period after granting approval, the introduction of the substantial equivalence principle, and the final target for the novel food material to promote its application in food production, in particular health food. At this point, regulation in China is supposed to balance safety protection and invention promotion, because the Measures on Food from New Sources in 2007 has indicated the intention to encourage the research and development of novel food (material). Based on this, a total of 365 applications have been received during the period of January 2008–April 2020. The successful authorizations of domestic produced or imported novel food or material can be summarized as follows.[29]

Interestingly, the low number of applications for 2018 indicates that the reform of administrative regulation did have an impact on businesses' expectations and thus their application choice. As a specialty in China, organizational arrangements for food safety regulation always change with biannual administrative reform, in 1998, 2003, 2008, 2013, and 2018, in order to solve the problems of regulatory gaps and overlaps. As far as the latest one is concerned, the long-standing reform of food and drug regulation has been replaced by market regulation in a comprehensive way. That is to say, most food regulatory functions have been integrated into the newly established market regulation department, as the State Administration for Market Regulation at a central level.[30] Despite this, the regulation of novel food material before its entrance into the market is still the responsibility of health department, which has been changed from the Ministry of Health into the National Health Commission. An organizational arrangement like this can be explained by the efforts to separate risk assessment and risk management as well as administrative decision-making and enforcement. For example, there is scientific authority under the National Health Commission to assist its risk assessment and monitoring, namely the China National Center for Food Safety Risk Assessment. When it comes to novel food material application, it has issued guidelines to facilitate applicant preparation work.

29 Y. Gu, "中国新食品原料申报与审批现状及分析 [The Status Quo and Analysis of Application of Novel Food Material in China]", *CIRS*, Apr. 10, 2020, *available at* www.cirs-group.com/foodcn/news/11584.html.

30 For more information about the reform in 2018, *see* J. Sun, "Update on Food Safety Governance in China After Organizational Reform in 2018" (2019) 2 Rivista di dirittoalimentare [-], 47–53.

When it comes to enforcement, the use of non-approved novel food material in food can be sanctioned administratively, including the revocation of production permission in serious cases. Also, the current Chinese practice in the food domain is characterized by governance.[31] Therefore, the participation of different stakeholders also contributes to food safety in general and novel food material in particular. Taking punitive damage as an example, the Food Safety Law enables consumers to demand a seller pay ten times the price paid for a food that failed to satisfy a national mandatory food safety standard. So-called professional consumers have engaged aggressively to claim such punitive payments by targeting mistakes in labeling. In this context, the labeling of food containing novel food material without the alert required by corresponding administrative announcements has also been targeted by those professional consumers. For example, imported food may contain aloe as an ingredient. In China, only aloe vera gel has been approved to use as novel food material. Also, food products with this kind of aloe should be labeled with an alert to use with caution in pregnant women and infants. Therefore, imported food products which inform the consumer of aloe rather than aloe vera gel may be regarded as damaging consumers' rights and subject to compensation. In view of this, the application of novel food material in China shall pay attention not only to the safety assessment for chemical substances but also labeling if an alert for consumption is required.

31 For more information about food safety governance in China, *see* J. Lepeintre & J. Sun (eds), *Building Food Safety Governance in China* (Luxembourg, Publications Office of the European Union 2018).

10 Revisiting Novel Food Regulation

Yuan Hung Tseng

I. Introduction

If the European Union, since the signing of the Maastricht Treaty in 1992 and the ensuing consolidating of a unified economic community, has attempted to further strengthen the common governance of the European Union under a legal umbrella[1] while attempting to define the identity of "food" within the EU by way of promulgation of the Novel Food Regulation (NFR) in 1997, it is undoubtedly a concrete manifestation of the EU's intention to strengthen its "soft border" through intervening with Member States via administrative rules.

However, the NFR seems to be full of controversy since it was enacted, or even at the first date its idea was proposed. On the one hand, externally, the NFR caused harsh conflicts with international economic and trade agreements, such as the World Trade Organization (WTO) or General Agreement on Tariffs and Trade (GATT), and caused trouble between the EU and other economic communities in the world on the issue of fairness related to trade; on the other, the European Parliament, which has always been a supplementary institution under the skepticism of the democratic deficit,[2] was also disappointed with the final version of the NFR that was agreed on in 1997, believing that the NFR provides no protection to EU citizens through its neglecting "the right to know"[3] of the public.

The formulation of the NFR was originally set by the EU in response to both foods imported from outside the borders of the EU and all new foods

1 J. Henderson, "Michel Foucault: Governmentality, Health Policy and the Governance of Childhood Obesity" in F. Collyer (ed.), *The Palgrave Handbook of Social Theory in Health, Illness and Medicine* (New York, Palgrave Macmillan 2015), pp. 324–39.

2 A. Follesdal & S. Hix, "Why There Is a Democratic Deficit in the EU: A Response to Majone and Moravcsik" (2006) 44(3) JCMS. 533–62.

3 C. W. Kirkham, "Legislative Developments: Novel Foods and Food Ingredients" (1997) 3(2) CJEL. 317–19, *available at* http://cjel.law.columbia.edu/print/1997/leg-dev-novel-foods-and-food-ingredients/ (last accessed July 22, 2020).

DOI: 10.4324/9781003271918-13

developed from new technologies, such as genetic modification and nanotechnology.[4] The primary purpose is not only to regulate the commercial operations of food but also to ensure people in the EU won't suffer health damage from eating foods that have not been used in the EU traditionally.

Historically, the formulation of the NFR was the most time-consuming one of the EU's various food-related regulations. Moreover, the attributes of the regulated subjects, apart from its arbitrary design by taking time and geographical boundaries as the watershed, have repeatedly changed over the years. The most obvious example is the removal of genetically modified food (GMF), which was once included but then exclusively regulated by the tailor-made Regulation (EC) 1829/2003; as for food provided by cloned animals, which has been continuously mentioned in the debate through the legislative process ever since 1992, it stands as another candidate for would-be exclusion. While observing even further, the NFR, just like the transitional border control established through customs, is to provide the EU institutional means for the identification of food passing through.

II. History of the NFR

Novel food is nothing new. Since the 1960s and 70s scientists have focused on plants and microorganisms instead of traditional crops as alternative sources of protein for human beings to counter the worldwide food shortage problem,[5] while in the 1990s, the improvement of food production through biotechnology became the new pet of scientists. Among these innovations in food producing, crops "manufactured" by genetic modification are upheld as the emerging savior of a stable food supply. Further, at the turn of the new century, "functional" food ingredients that provide specific health benefits[6] by innovative food processing technologies, within which nanotechnology is an important driving force for the development, have been intensively reviewed

4 European Commission, "Regulation (EC) No 258/97 of the European Parliament and of the Council of Jan. 27, Concerning Novel Foods and Novel Food Ingredients" (1991) Official Journal of the European Communities (OJ). L43/1.

5 D. Jonas, "Safety Evaluation of Novel Foods: A European and International Perspective" (2000) EUFIC Review 04/2000, *available at* www.eufic.org/en/food-production/article/safety-evaluation-of-novel-foods-a-european-and-international-perspective (last accessed July 22, 2020). Also *see* D. Wilson, "Marketing Mycoprotein, The Quorn Foods Story" (2001) 55(7) Food Technology Magazine. 48–50, *available at* www.ift.org/news-and-publications/food-technology-magazine/issues/2001/july/features/developing-food-market (last accessed July 22, 2020).

6 N. Binns & J. Howlett, "Functional Foods in Europe: International Developments in Science and Health Claims" (2009) 48(1) European Journal of Nutrition. 3–13.

by administrative agencies[7] and the media.[8] Besides, aided by breakthroughs in animal reproducing technology, meat produced by cloned animals attracted the spotlight from the public in the debate regarding the moral standards of EU citizens on animal welfare.

These advanced developments, whether involving the appearance or attributes of foods brought about by technological achievements, exceeded the coverage of contemporary food-related safety-assessing measures of the EU and resulted in a vacuum in management.[9] What made the situation complicated was that the different policies adopted by varied Member States[10] threatened the practical operation of the EU single market. This situation prompted the institutions of the EU to address these challenges with generalized and unified administrative governance through legitimate instruments.

Throughout the legislating process, in line with the principle of "substantial equivalence" that "new technologies will not cause food to be inherently less safe than those produced by traditional methods,"[11] which has been the core logic of the global regulatory framework for a long time, the European Union's food control authorities began to evaluate and develop new regulation based on the characteristics of so-called "novelty" food. However, compared to the definition of novel types of food proposed by the United Nations, that is, "food that was not originally eaten by humans" (Protein Advisory Group of the United Nations System, 1983), the definition adopted by the EU obviously added some administrative considerations, while it is just these considerations that have triggered endless disputes in the formulation, implementation, and revision of the NFR.

In July 1992, the EU proposed the first NFR.[12] Historically, the lengthy process of discussion, deliberation, and negotiation was known as the most difficult and time-consuming of the EU's food-related laws at the time. Among the

7 European Food Safety Authority, "Scientific Opinion of the Scientific Committee, The Potential Risks Arising from Nanoscience and Nanotechnologies on Food and Feed Safety (2009) 958 EFSA Journal. 1.

8 F. Macrae, "'Grey Goo' Food Laced with Nanoparticles Could Swamp Britain" (2000) *Daily Mail*, Jan. 8, 2010, *available at* www.dailymail.co.uk/news/article-1241506/Britain-maybe-swamped-nanoparticle-grey-food.html (last accessed July 22, 2020).

9 J.H. Maryanski, "Special Challenges of Novel Foods (Biotechnology)" (1990) 45(5) Food, Drug, Cosmetic Law Journal. 545–50.

10 S. Waters, "The Regulation of Herbicide Resistant Crops in Europe" in S. Duke (ed.), Herbicide Resistant Crops: Agricultural, Economic, Environmental, Regulatory, & Technological Aspects (Cleveland, CRC Press 1995), pp. 347–62.

11 World Health Organization, 'Strategies for Assessing the Safety of Foods Produced by Bio-Technology: Report of a Joint FAO/WHO Consultation' (1991) 24. *See also* D. Jonas, "Safety Evaluation of Novel Foods: A European and International Perspective" (2000) EUFIC Review Apr. 2000, *available at* www.eufic.org/en/food-production/article/safety-evaluation-of-novel-foods-a-european-and-international-perspective (last accessed July 22, 2020).

12 European Commission, Proposal for a Council Regulation (EEC) on Novel Foods and Novel Food Ingredients (1992), Official Journal of the European Communities (OJ), C190/4.

reasons that complicated the situation, the innermost epistemological problem encountered was how to define whether a food is "novel."[13]

According to the promulgated texts in Regulation 258/97, novel foods are defined as those foods and ingredients which have not been circulated in the market, that is, commercialized, at a significant scale for human consumption in any of the EU Member States prior to May 15, 1997. Based on this, the relevant EU administrative agencies, initially both the EU institutions and the governments of various Member States, have the right to determine whether a food meets the two conditions listed subsequently and should be regarded as "novel" in the EU "market."

First, under the EU's governance, the NFR stipulated the legitimized time and space conditions of novelty. On the one hand, it took May 15, 1997, the day the NFR was enforced, as an arbitrary boundary, while, on the other, it drew on the right to review food that "is not obviously consumed by the people in the EU or not." The administrations of the Member States and the EU are empowered to judge the condition of "inside vs. outside" the governing territory. These two elements provide a subjective basis for determining whether any food, under the governance of the EU, meets "novel" status. Second, according to the NFR, a food should also be categorized as "novel" if it belongs to one of the following four categories: food with modified main molecular structure; food derived from microorganisms; food derived from plants, food ingredients, and animals; and food manufactured through innovative production processes.

Under the EU's jurisdiction, when an "exotic food" is first introduced into the EU "territory," once it is judged novel, the importer must file an application to the government of the member country where the food is intended to be sold first with relevant scientific safety certifications before it is marketed; correspondingly, the relevant authority of the Member State will conduct a preliminary evaluation of the food and decide whether it can be legally introduced into the market or further evaluation is needed. The European Commission or any Member State can express reasonable objections to the application, while in the latter case, or when further evaluation by the European Food Safety Authority (EFSA) is required, the relevant EU administrative agencies, including experts from member States, will be consulted. In other words, under the NFR, novel foods can only be commercialized and marketed through the companies that enjoy the approval issued by the Executive Committee. As for certain products that can be proven "substantially equivalent" to existing foods in the EU market, in accordance with article 5 of the NFR, they are detoured through simplified procedures and can be marketed more efficiently.

However, as mentioned, it is essentially an administrative consideration other than a scientific one to determine which items should be included. For example, since the very beginning, the European Parliament has expressed objections

13 Ibid.

to juxtaposing GMOs with other novel foods[14] under the NFR. Besides, for meat produced from cloned animals, although its identity of "novel" makes it a potential candidate, the design of the regulatory provisions that allowed these products to be sold without clear labeling is deemed totally against the EU citizens' moral values and violated the consumers' "right to know" in choosing.[15] Some people argued that the simplified prior notification procedure is too rough to provide any protection for the consumers.

Therefore, in response to these concerns, the EU agencies revised the original proposal that did not mention consumer protection but only included it in the second legislative reason of the NFR and adopted more stringent texts on procedures and labeling.[16] As for the controversial GMF, it was finally removed from the regulated subjects in 2003 and placed under the management of another deliberately formulated regulation, Regulation 1829/2003. The issue of meat produced from cloned animals, for which is difficult to define its "novel" identity, has a pending status and is still attracting the spotlight as a hot topic.

However, after its promulgation in 1997, the NFR encountered challenges that were never touched on in the initial negotiation, namely the continuous changing of the territory of the EU, on which the original time and geographical delineation of the "novel" identity are based. On the other hand, countries outsides the EU that are eager to export traditional domestic crops, such as Peru,[17] protested that the formulation and implementation of the NFR create a needless obstacle to international trade, especially the lengthy and complicated license application process, and interfere with the international flow of goods and economic development under globalization[18] because traditional food in their country is regarded by the EU as "novel" and treated unfairly.

III. Regulation No. 2015/2283

In view of these difficulties and obstacles encountered after the promulgation of the NFR for nearly two decades, the EU legislature proposed a revised version of the NFR (Regulation No. 2015/2283, nNFR) on January 1, 2015, and suspended Regulations No. 258/97 and No. 1852/2001. Through this revision,

14 "MEPs Vote to Amend Novel Foods Proposal" Europe Environment, Nov. 9, 1993.

15 C. W. Kirkham, "Legislative Developments: Novel Foods and Food Ingredients" (1997) 3(2) Columbia Journal of European Law. 317–19. http://cjel.law.columbia.edu/print/1997/leg-dev-novel-foods-and-food-ingredients/ (last accessed July 22, 2020).

16 Regulation (EC) 258/97 of the European Parliament and of the Council Concerning Novel Foods and Novel Food Ingredients (1997) L43 Official Journal of the European Communities (OJ), 40, 1.

17 WTO, "Statement by Peru on Regulation No. 258/97 of the European Communities" G/SPS/GEN/713, July 12, 2006.

18 A. Lähteenmäki-Uutela, "European Novel Food Legislation as a Restriction to Trade" 2007 106th Seminar, Oct. 25–27, 2007, Montpellier, France 7909, European Association of Agricultural Economists, *available at* https://ideas.repec.org/p/ags/eaa106/7909.html (last accessed July 20, 2020).

the nNFR is expected to improve the conditions under which food enterprises are allowed to efficiently distribute new and innovative foods, provided that the high-quality food safety standard set by the EU agencies is met. Besides, it's worth noting that, within the nNFR, issues related to the interests of EU citizens are formally juxtaposed with business operations and incorporated into the text of the provisions[19] in response to previous criticism.

As for other significant amendments, they can be summarized as follows:

- Expanded categories: The definition of novel foods includes more different items of foods that originated from plants, animals, microorganisms, cellular breeding, minerals, and so on and specific food categories such as whole insects, while foods resulting from novel production processes and practices and those resulting from advanced technologies which could not be produced before 1997 may be also classified as novel food.
- Improved efficiency and transparency.
- Another simplified and faster notification system for third-world traditional foods based on historical records of food usage.
- Generalized authorizations: Under the nNFR, all authorizations (new or old) are general. This means that any enterprise is qualified to place a certified novel food on the European market legally, provided that the conditions of use, labeling requirements, and authorized specifications are met.
- Simplified procedure for authorization: The procedure is managed by the European Commission and can be applied for online.
- Centralized safety assessment: The European Food & Safety Authority will be responsible for a centralized safety assessment.
- Establishment of a union list of authorized novel food: The Commission of Rule Implementation holds the duty to update this list. Once an item is added to the list, it is legal to commercialize it within the EU market.
- Encouragement to innovation: By granting a five-year individual authorization in the protection of confidential data, this aim is expected.

However, even with these endeavors, there are some obstacles yet to be overcome.

IV. Persistent Arguments and Conflicts

Judging from the past, the nNFR involved lots of legal and social issues that cover a wide range of levels within and outside the EU. Whether the amendments can really make the nNFR attain the goals of effectively ensuring food safety for people in the EU, improving and lowering trade barriers, and promoting the development of emerging food technology industries remains to be confirmed by the implementation experience after 2018. But how has the

19 EC Regulation 2015/2283, article 1.2.

NFR, both the original and revised version, caused so many formidable sociolegal problems? Perhaps, taking food neophobia as an observed benchmark can make the consideration of sociolegal issues clearer and provide a direction for further revision of the nNFR in the future.

According to the definition, the food neophobia is defined as the unwillingness or refusal to eat or the tendency to avoid new foods[20] based on three reasons, danger, aversion, and disgust.[21] In other words, "one of the major sources of resistance to novelty lies in the attitude of the consumer, who in many cases may be suspicious or hostile as a result of specific ideologies, overly attached to tradition, or affected by neophobia."[22] Under this understanding, whether the content of the nNFR is feasible, a clearer image can be obtained.

From the perspective of social needs, except basic functions to manage business affairs, the formulation of regulation must take the will and compliance of various actors into account at the level of enforceability.[23] Therefore, within the multi-level governance of the EU,[24] the implementation of the nNFR will inevitably touch on other issues outside the commercial considerations that the public is highly concerned about.

The causes of rejection of new foods are extremely complex.[25] Research suggests, compared with other areas, the EU public's acceptance of new foods, such as whole insects as food,[26] is inherently low. Moreover, the degree of rejection is also inconsistent due to geographical,[27] age,[28] and gender[29] factors.

20 P. Pliner & K. Hobden, "Development of a Scale to Measure the Trait of Food Neophobia in Humans" (1992) 19(2) Appetite. 105–120.

21 P. Rozin & A. Fallon, "The Psychological Categorization of Foods and Non-Foods: A Preliminary Taxonomy of Food Rejections" (1980) 1 Appetite. 193–201; A. E. Fallon, P. Rozin & P. Pliner, "The Child's Conception of Food: The Development of Food Rejections with Special Reference to Disgust and Contamination Sensitivity" (1984) 55 Child Development. 566–75; P. Rozin, J. Haidt & C. R. McCauley, "Disgust" in L. F. Barrett, M. Lewis & J. M. Haviland (eds.), *Handbook of Emotions* (New York, The Guilford Press 2016), 4th ed., pp. 815–34.

22 E. Faccio & L. Guiotto Nai Fovino, "Food Neophobia or Distrust of Novelties? Exploring Consumers' Attitudes toward GMOs, Insects and Cultured Meat" (2019) 9 Appl. Sci. 4440.

23 R. Baldwin & M. Cave, *Understanding Regulation: Theory, Strategy and Practice* (Oxford, Oxford University Press 1999).

24 Y.-C. Lan, "Multi-Level Governance of the European Union: Theoretical and Empirical Research" (2005) 24 Taiwanese Journal of Political Science. 49–76.

25 T.R. Alley, "Conceptualization and Measurement of Human Food Neophobia" in S. Reilly (ed.), *Food Neophobia: Behavioural and Biological Influences* (Amsterdam, Elsevier B.V 2018), pp. 169–92.

26 F. La Barbera, F. Verneau, M. Amato & K. Grunert, "Understanding Westerners' Disgust for the Eating of Insects: The Role of Food Neophobia and Implicit Associations" (2018) 64 Food Quality and Preference. 120–25.

27 C. Proserpio, V. L. Almli, P. Sandvik, M. Sandell, L. Methven, M. Wallner, H. Jilani, G. G. Zeinstra, B. Alfaro & M. Laureati, "Cross-National Differences in Child Food Neophobia: A Comparison of Five European Countries" (2020) 81 Food Quality and Preference. 103861.

28 U.-K. K. Hursti & P.-O. Sjödén, "Food and General Neophobia and their Relationship with Self-Reported Food Choice: Familial Resemblance in Swedish Families with Children of Ages 7–17 Years" (1997) 29(1) Appetite. 89–103.

29 S. Nordin, D. Broman, J. Garvill & M. Nyroos, "Gender Differences in Factors Affecting Rejection of Food in Healthy Young Swedish Adults" (2005) 43(3) Appetite. 295–301.

In other words, even if, based on existing scientific proof, the new food is safe and sound, whether it makes consumers feel disgust or involves personal unacceptable moral violations are still important determinants. Does the design of the NFR, even the nNFR, really consider the interests and rights of the people in the EU? Apart from security, how much influence do the other two considerations have on the persistence and compromise of legislative considerations? It is the social and legal issues triggered by the nNFR that must be addressed and discussed.

A. *Traditional Foods Outside the EU: The Paramount Battlefield in the Name of Security*

Since the purpose of NFR is mainly to regulate new technologies, traditional exotic foods, such as foreign fruits, have not been registered as an issue in its drafting provisions. For a long time, third countries outside the EU have firmly determined that this type of traditional food does not belong to so-called novel food by definition[30] and should be regarded as part of the abolished provisions of Article 1.2(e), "for foods and food ingredients obtained by traditional propagating or breeding practices and having a history of safe food use."

It seems reasonable, because if there is any product that could be spared the burden of proof of authorization, then traditional foreign foods that have been used by the local people for centuries, especially crops, are legitimate candidates. However, since there is not a formal expression of the legal basis for its position provided by third world countries, the European Commission and Member States still tend to place these products under the jurisdiction of the NFR.[31] Besides, due to political considerations, the EU arbitrarily restricts the "history of safe usage" to within the EU market.[32] In the impact assessment report, the EU legislature also pointed out that traditional food should be resolutely treated as a new type of food to ensure the safety of people in the EU.[33]

This approach, on the one hand, is undoubtedly strengthened by the previous unfavorable experience of dealing with foreign products,[34] and, more

30 WTO, "Statement by Peru on Regulation No. 258/97 of the European Communities" G/SPS/GEN/713, July 12, 2006.

31 European Commission, "Evaluation Report on the Novel Food Regulation 258/97" (2004) Concerning Novel Foods and Novel Food Ingredients. 5.

32 C. Larramendi, J. García-Abujeta, S. Vicario, A. García-Endrino, M. López-Matas, M. García-Sedeño & J. Carnés, "Goji Berries (Lycium barbarum): Risk of Allergic Reactions in Individuals with Food Allergy" (2012) 22(5) Journal of Investigational Allergology & Clinical Immunology. 345–50.

33 European Commission (2007), Draft report on Impact Assessment for a Regulation Replacing Regulation (EC) No 258/97 on Novel Foods and Novel Food Ingredients, COM (2007) 872 final (Commission nNFR Impact Assessment), 3. https://op.europa.eu/en/publication-detail/-/publication/ca2af1dd-e99d-4239-bbc7-07af6b7a0a98/language-en (last accessed July 20, 2020).

34 Regulation (EC) No 258/97 of the European Parliament and of the Council (2000). OJ L61, 14.

importantly, on the other hand, it reflects the cautious attitude of the EU people toward foreign foods in the name of safety.

Correspondingly, in view of the expanded interpretation of the definition of novel food by the EU agencies and the impact of the overwhelming import trade procedures accompanying this "novel" categorization, proving a food's identity as "novel," rather than proving its safety, has become the utmost commercializing strategy. However, in practice, this behavior, although nearly 20 years have passed since the NFR was promulgated and implemented, is not easy for most foreign food because of the absence of available data that would quantitatively[35] support it in meeting the ill-defined criteria "consumption by the people within the EU prior to 1997 to some extent" to prove its legitimacy.[36] Therefore, how to attain the requirements of EU regulators in the name of safety is not only a source of confusion for businessmen raised in foreign cultures but also a special burden of proof for third world countries and therefore, becomes an excuse for appeals in the WTO.

In addition, whether to define "novel' identities based on a politically assumed date is another matter at issue in international trade. For a long time, the recorded names of these foreign traditional products registered in EU customs have been vague, and after entering the border, they are often transported to specific immigrant communities. Even the importers cannot accurately locate them, let alone the local administrative agencies. In other words, for importing merchants, the expedient process in the past has now become a nightmare.[37] Furthermore, the requirement that the information provided must be traced back to May 1997 empowers any Member State to doubt and challenge the claimed "non-novel" status of these exotic foods. What further causes trouble is that Member States differ in their reviews of the same food due to different local epistemology.

Simply put, the fate of any individual product varies in different Member States and communities,[38] while a common and consistent operating procedure is inaccessible. Therefore, the review process, which involves data requirements, makes third world countries believe that the NFR poses a redundant

35 European Commission (2007). Proposal for a Regulation of the European Parliament and of the Council on novel foods and amending Regulation (EU) No XXX/XXXX COM (2007) 872 final (nNFR), Art 3.2(a) i.

36 M. Hermann, "The Impact of the European Novel Food Regulation on Trade and Food Innovation Based on Traditional Plant Foods from Developing Countries" (2009) 34(6) Food Policy. 499–507.

37 N. Craddock, "The EU Novel Food Regulation: Impact on the Potential Export of Exotic Traditional Foods to the EU: Suggestions for Revision" Discussion paper prepared for UNCTAD and CBI, in Cooperation with GTZ, GFU and IPGRI, Nov. 6, 2005 (2006), *available at* https://green.4ento.com/wp-content/uploads/2017/06/the-novel-food-regulation.pdf (last accessed July 15, 2020).

38 European Commission, "Evaluation Report on the Novel Food Regulation 258/97" (2004) Concerning Novel Foods and Novel Food Ingredients. 5.

and insurmountable obstacle for their products to be imported into the EU market.[39]

Regarding these difficulties, although the content of the nNFR 2015/2283 can be technically improved to speed up the efficiency of reviews and reduce the risk of international trade disputes, from the perspective of sociology of law, the EU legislature, after this revision, still failed to fully realize the right to define the novel identity of "food" imported under EU governance. Instead, it continues, through a centralized and dedicated review mechanism, to hold the power firmly in hand to strengthen the EU's legal borders while simultaneously weakening the sovereignty of the Member States. Therefore, how much can such an amendment led by the promotion of commercial interests really protect the well-being of the people in the EU? Will the relatively wealthier countries in the EU really become more interested in the traditional foods of the third world because it is easier to enter the EU market? This is still left to be observed.

B. Cloned Animals as Food: An Issue Haunted by Moral Considerations

Although animal cloning is obviously a new technology, the food it produces is equivalent to traditional food. Scientifically, it doesn't fit squarely into a classification as a typical novel food. According to Grahame Bulfield, the former director of the Roslin Institute who was responsible for the production of the first replicated animal, Dolly the Sheep, using the concept of "new" to treat meats manufactured from cloned animal is meaningless.[40] Furthermore, whether food produced with the offspring of cloned animals is "novel" brings the issue into endless disputes.

Based on scientific evidence, meat produced from cloned animals and their progeny does not show any difference from the counterparts bred by traditional natural techniques.[41] Moreover, with existing scientific development, in terms of practical operation, there is no generally recognized reliable bio-tagging tool that can be used to distinguish between cloned and non-cloned animals.[42] However, in terms of public opinion, taking cloned animals as food has encountered great difficulties in the EU.

39 Hermann, *supra* note 36, at 499–507.

40 J. Meikle & R. Smithers, "Cloning-Derived Milk Claim Prompts Food Agency Enquiry" *The Guardian*, Aug. 3, 2010, *available at* www.theguardian.com/uk/2010/aug/02/fsa-investigating-gm-milk-claims (last accessed July 5, 2020).

41 S. Pang, "A Review of Potential Analytical Approaches for Detecting Cloned Animals and their Offspring in the Food Chain: Government Chemist Programme 1 May 2011–31 May 2012 Project RF1/3.1" (2012) (Report number: LGC/P/2012/130). https://assets.publishing.service.gov.uk/government/uploads/system/uploads/attachment_data/file/332618/Cloned_animal_report.pdf (last accessed July 22, 2020).

42 Ibid.

According to a public opinion survey,[43] due to ethical considerations, people in the European Union generally oppose the application of clone technology to produce meat for human consumption. In a proposal submitted at the end of 2013,[44] more than 80% of EU citizens showed a wide range of negative perceptions about cloning animals for food production. However, against the spectrum from the political considerations of administrative agencies to the moral adherence of public opinion, the support for cloned animals as food is randomly distributed in a space between the technic rhetoric of what the USFDA calls "as an assisted reproductive technology"[45] in overall food production process to the demon of endless moral persistence.[46]

Viewed in terms of practical benefits, meat manufactured directly from cloned animals show no advantage in the food supply chain.[47] Therefore, for consumers, the focus of controversy is shifted to the identity of the offspring of cloned animals. This generation-skipping means the relevant administration encounters the dilemma of whether to intensively control the manufacturing process or allow the market to decide their fate.[48] Furthermore, within the global arena, the situation is even more harsh because five major agricultural and husbandry countries, led by the United States, held a seminar for grazing animals in Buenos Aires in March 2011 and gave a statement that clearly intends to exclude meat produced by the offspring of cloned animals from the definition of the "novel" type.[49]

In terms of legislative design, it is obvious that the NFR was not originally intended to provide a platform for the debate on the issue of cloned animals.

43 *See* both the Flash Eurobarometer, "Europeans' Attitudes Towards Animal Cloning: Analytical Report", *available at* https://ec.europa.eu/commfrontoffice/publicopinion/flash/fl_238_en.pdf (last accessed July 29, 2020), and the Special Eurobarometer, "Biotechnology: Report", *available at* https://ec.europa.eu/commfrontoffice/publicopinion/archives/ebs/ebs_341_en.pdf (last accessed July 30, 2020).

44 European Commission, "Proposal for a Directive of the European Parliament and of the Council: On the Cloning of Animals of the Bovine, Porcine, Ovine, Caprine and Equine Species Kept and Reproduced for Farming Purposes, Brussels, Dec. 18, 2013. SWD (2013) 519 final", *available at* https://eur-lex.europa.eu/legal-content/EN/TXT/PDF/?uri=CELEX:52013PC0892&from=EN (last accessed July 22, 2020).

45 L. Rudenko, J. Matheson & S. Sundlof, "Animal Cloning and the FDA-the Risk Assessment Paradigm Under Public Scrutiny" (2007) 25(1) Nature Biotechnology. 39–43.

46 S. Poulter, "Cloning Opens Door to 'Farmyard Freaks'" *Daily Mail*, Jan. 11, 2007, *available at* www.dailymail.co.uk/news/article-427963/Cloning-opens-door-farmyard-freaks.html (last accessed July 20, 2020).

47 G. S. Becker & T. Cowan, "Biotechnology in Animal Agriculture: Status and Current Issues" (2009) Congressional Research Service Reports. 32, *available at* https://digitalcommons.unl.edu/crsdocs/32 (last accessed July 22, 2020).

48 D. A. Kysar, "Preferences for Processes: The Process/Product Distinction and the Regulation of Consumer Choice" (2004) Cornell Law Faculty Publications. Paper 8, *available at* https://scholarship.law.cornell.edu/cgi/viewcontent.cgi?referer=www.google.com/&httpsredir=1&article=1007&context=lsrp_papers;Preferences (last accessed July 22, 2020).

49 Joint Statement on Animal Cloning for Livestock Production, Mar. 16, 2011, *available at* www.fas.usda.gov/joint-statement-animal-cloning-livestock-production (last accessed July 22, 2020).

Hence, when cloned animals are included in the regulated subjects, everything seems out of place and full of controversy. Although this issue was indeed mentioned during the consultation meeting before the proposal, the Executive Committee neither included cloned animals as food in the impact assessment of the proposal nor mentioned this technology in the original legal text. However, based on the tendency and pressure of public opinion, the European Parliament requires comprehensive labeling of cloned animal meat sold in the EU to ensure the rights of people in choosing food.

It is inevitable that the differences originating from people located in various countries may cause trade conflicts once the regulation is deliberated under varied moral values. The gradually more stringent labeling requirements for food in the EU, especially those related to animal welfare based on the moral values of the global north,[50] is very likely to lead to conflicts between the nNFR and the content of GATT or WTO because, regarding the welfare of animals, there is no firm and consistent universal value among the WTO members on which level should be considered "rational."

According to the nNFR, the EU grants the "novel" status to cloned animals and further requires importing merchants to fully label the products produced from them. Obviously, it must be a meaningless and formidable trading barrier for some husbandry countries that export animal meat as their economic support. Meanwhile, practically, the concept of the "consumer's right to know," which is commonly cited by the European Parliament, even if is explained in terms of absolutes, should still be given limitations.[51] In other words, it is debatable whether the right to know can extend its boundaries endlessly until a trade barrier is formed. For example, regarding the issue of cloned animals or their offspring as meat, Hungarian Prime Minister Sándor Fazekas once pointed out sarcastically that it is impossible to pursue practically unless you "draw a family tree for each slice of cheese or salami" and expressed dissatisfaction toward the European Parliament's making use of public opinion as an excuse in the process of revising the law.[52]

So, when the debate is still focusing on labeling requirements, how can the EU hold a sturdy stance of such insistence? Obviously, the difficulty still exists because it will eventually increase the cost of goods, whether for importers or uncaring consumers, which in turn will create a heavy burden on international trade. Moreover, even if the EU can clarify its moral values, there is

50 F. Santeramo, D. Carlucci, B. De Devitiis, A. Seccia, A. Stasi, R. Viscecchia & G. Nardone, "Emerging Trends in European Food, Diets and Food Industry" (2019) 104 Food Research International. 39–47.

51 I. Cheyne, "Proportionality, Proximity and Environmental Labelling in WTO Law" (2009) 12(4) Journal of International Economic Law. 927–52.

52 Statement of the Hungarian Presidency, 'Cloned Foods Unleashed', HunPR/22/2011, Mar. 29, 2011.

no guarantee that WTO's arbitration committee would accept these morally oriented legal definitions.[53]

If the right to know is absolute, then one pragmatic approach that might deviate from free trade is comprehensive labeling requirements. But this will inevitably impact the primary goal of the economic community for which the EU was initially established. On the contrary, if the purpose of labeling is just to give those consumers who pay special attention to technology the right to choose, then a universal voluntary labeling approach outside the legal requirements, which symbolizes the governing right, may be a viable alternative.[54] However, this approach will inevitably lead the function of the nNFR to degrade into a commercial handbook of promoting economic development. As for the moral persistence and preference of the people in the EU, it will no longer be a topic of concern.

C. *Yuck Factor: Insects as Food*

Although insects were considered a delicacy in ancient Roman times, they are not part of typical European eating habits,[55] even though around 2.5 billion people around the world eat insects currently. Although research suggests edible insect species are surely candidates to rescue people from food shortages, containing higher levels of some polyunsaturated essential fatty acids and minerals than traditional meats and comparable protein levels,[56] insects are still unlikely to elicit appetite among EU citizens.[57]

According to the definition, the cause of food neophobia stems from safety considerations; moral values; and whether the food causes unpleasant emotion, that is, the "yuck" factor. As food, whole insects at least inevitably involve two. Although, on the one hand, safety considerations can be resolved by scientific endorsements issued from recognized authorities, such as United Nations Food and Agricultural Organization[58] and EFSA, and this provides excellent support for the importers, on the other, the "yuck" factor, which results from innermost psychological rejection, remains a determinant for whether whole

53 B. McGrady, "Necessity Exceptions in WTO Law: Retreaded Tyres, Regulatory Purpose and Cumulative Regulatory Measures" (2009) 12(1) Journal of International Economic Law. 153–73.

54 S. Keane, "Can a Consumer's Right to Know Survive the WTO? The Case of Food Labeling" (2006) 16 Transnational L. & Contemporary Problems. 291–332.

55 "Are Europeans Ready for an Insect-Based Diet?", *available at* www.euractiv.com/section/agriculture-food/news/are-europeans-ready-for-an-insect-based-diet/ (last accessed July 21, 2020).

56 A. Van Huis, J. V. Itterbeeck, H. Klunder, E. Mertens, A. Halloran, G. Muir & P. Vantomme, "Nutritional Value of Insects for Human Consumption" in Van Huis et al. (eds.), *Edible Insects: Future Prospects for Food and Feed Security* (Rome, Food and Agriculture Organization of the United Nations, 2013), 67–88.

57 C. Hartmann & M. Siegrist, "Insects as Food: Perception and Acceptance. Findings from Current Research" (2017) 64(3) Ernahrungs Umschau. 44–50.

58 Van Huis et al., *supra* note 56.

insects would be accepted as food (the author believes that very few people are currently reluctant to eat insects for moral reasons).

Broadly taking insects as a human food may be a plausible option to relieve the food shortage, though[59] this trend could be jeopardized by the aversion that people show, especially in western countries, towards insects as food.[60] According to media reports, the acceptance and legitimacy of this "new" type of food vary greatly among EU Member States.[61] For example, though compared to other countries outside Europe, it is not considerable, the acceptance of whole insects as food in the United Kingdom, Netherlands,[62] and Belgium[63] is relatively high and has a promising future,[64] while the Nordic countries also show great variance. Finland is the forerunner in promoting insects as food,[65] but the Swedish have relatively lower acceptance, and the relevant domestic administration has made contradictory moves toward the issue through simultaneously strictly reviewing the "novel" status of whole insects as foods[66] while encouraging enterprises to develop their potential.[67] As for Italy, the limits are set at only accepting insects as food supplements,[68] while countries in the central European region show the least acceptance.[69]

Of course, legally the EU can consolidate its sovereignty further by drawing on administrative power to concretize the boundaries of its centralized and generalized governance. However, the foreseeable implementation might ultimately be varied among the Member States in compliance with local public opinion, even though the law, that is, the nNFR, provides a unified legitimate basis within the EU. Different from the situations in which foreign traditional

59 Van Huis et al., *supra* note 56.

60 La Barbera, *supra* note 26.

61 "Edible Insect Status in Europe 2018", *available at* https://entonation.com/1888-2/ (last accessed July 25, 2020).

62 J. House, "Insects as Food in the Netherlands: Production Networks and the Geographies of Edibility" (2018) 94 Geoforum. 82–93.

63 R. C. Megido, L. Sablon, M. Geuens, Y. Brostaux, T. Alabi, C. Blecker, D. Drugmand, E. Haubruge & F. Francis, "Edible Insect Acceptance by Belgian Consumers: Promising Attitude for Entomophagy Development" (2014) 29 Journal of Sensory Studies. 14–20.

64 Ibid. *See also* "Sweden: The Most Anti-Edible-Insect Country in Europe?' *Bugburger*, www.bugburger.se/politik/sweden-anti-edible-insect-country-europe/ (last accessed July 24, 2020).

65 "Five Reasons Why Finland Is Leading the Edible Insect Revolution" *Bugburger*, *available at* www.bugburger.se/foretag/five-reasons-why-finland-is-leading-the-edible-insect-revolution/ (last accessed Aug. 5, 2020).

66 "Sweden: The Most Anti-Edible-Insect Country in Europe?" *supra* note 64.

67 "Swedish Govt Spends Millions Telling Citizens to Eat Insects to End Global Warming", *Breitbart*, Apr. 28, 2020, *available at* www.breitbart.com/europe/2016/04/28/swedish-government-spend-millions-encourage-citizens-trade-meat-insects-end-global-warming/ (last accessed July 25, 2020).

68 R. Roma, G. Ottomano Palmisano & A. De Boni, "Insects as Novel Food: A Consumer Attitude Analysis Through the Dominance-Based Rough Set Approach" (2020) 9(4) Foods. 387.

69 S. Piha, T. Pohjanheimo, A. Lähteenmäki-Uutela, Z. Křečková & T. Otterbring, "The Effects of Consumer Knowledge on the Willingness to Buy Insect Food: An Exploratory Cross-Regional Study in Northern and Central Europe" (2016) 70 Food Quality and Preference. 1–10.

food will cause trade barrier arbitration within the WTO institutions and the debate surrounding whether abandoning mandatory labeling of cloned animals will collide with public moral values, the introduction of whole insects to the EU market through the nNFR would inevitably challenge the administrative capacity of various countries. No matter if the nNFR paves a broad road for emerging innovative industries to commercialize whole insects as food, it seems that there is still a long way to go before meeting the interests of the people in the EU.

V. Conclusion

While revisiting the nNFR, something beyond the provisions emerged. As aforementioned, the NFR was ill fated since the very beginning. In the original text proposed in 1992, the European Parliament's focus for this regulation was not mainly about people's safety but to attempt to provide and strengthen the legality of the EU's governance. However, this attempt has caused continuous controversy since its implementation due to epistemological differences regarding "novelty," and its content has repeatedly undergone major revisions.

Technically, the nNFR had indeed made efforts to reduce trade conflicts between the EU and its international trading partners to satisfy practical needs, such as the unique application procedure for the third world's "traditional food," while, viewed in terms of legal implicitness, through unified and centralized, but complicated, administrative procedures, the EU has indeed externally contributed to its sovereignty by re-iterating the right to define "novelty" while internally moving in the direction of common governance, that is, a common food policy.[70] But the dilemma haunting the nNFR is still growing.

On the one hand, for a long time, continuing disputes about the "democratic deficit"[71] related to the EU's governance and legislative procedures have not subsided. The nNFR, like other regulations, has indeed brought criticisms from within. How and to what extent to care for people's psychological comfort given different preferences due to geographical locality under the unified and centralized nNFR seems to be an almost irresolvable problem. Moreover, the practice of arbitrarily defining the novel status of food with boundaries and time to consolidate the EU's governance is continuing to face challenges from third-world trading partners and create unnecessary trade obstacles, though lots of effort has been made already. Perhaps the nNFR will reduce the barriers of international trade, and we can hold optimistic expectations about that. But, for people living in the relatively economically prosperous EU, not only do

70 "Towards a Common Food Policy for the EU", Framing Paper for the EU Food and Farming Forum 2018, *available at* www.ipes-food.org/_img/upload/files/Towards-a-Common-Food-Policy-for-the-EU.pdf (last accessed July 22, 2020).

71 Follesdal & Hix, *supra* note 2.

the acceptance and circulation of exotic and novel foods still have a pessimistic future, but so do the psychological and moral feelings of the EU people.

From a practical view, with the implementation of generalized authorization, foods defined as novel will eventually be removed from the pending list one by one as time goes by. Does this mean that in the future, the function of the nNFR will be eventually replaced by other deliberated regulations, like the one for GMOs, that is, GMF, and left to no practical purpose anymore? This needs further observation.

But one thing for sure is that, with the establishment of the legal basis for the centralization of EU governance, the functions of the nNFR seem to go back to the very basics—that is, an extremely elementary design destined just for commercial operations. In other words, for the special multi-level governance of the EU, the function of the nNFR is limited to the minimum demand of politics "in the name of safety" or at the service of international trade. As for the psychological satisfaction of the public, both inside and outside the EU, it still dwells in a twilight zone where the sun is yet to shine.

11 Regulatory Responses to the Use of Nanoscale Substances in Food in ASEAN

Muhammad Nizam Awang and Sharifudin Md Shaarani

I. Introduction

Nanotechnologies have been valorized as one of the platform technologies of the twentieth century, where their resulting applications and products span converging scientific disciplines, industries, and markets. The growth of nanotechnology as a niche market segment is dynamically receptive of more innovation into the base industries, mainly electronic and electric products, energy and environment, automotive, and food and agriculture. The segment of food nanotechnology in the global market is forecast to grow more than 24% between 2020 and 2023.[1] Over 180 applications in diverse products have already entered the market, with more than 200 products coming from the food and agriculture sector.[2] In the food market, the scale of nano-based products is likely to witness an exponential climb and reach more than 50% of the current world population.

Concerns over the safety of nanomaterials have progressively grown with the volume of commercialized nanofood products in the market. This has called food safety authorities around the world to review the adequacy of existing regulatory frameworks to manage the risk and safety concerns posed by food cultivated, produced, processed, and packaged using nanotechnology and nanomaterials. Food safety authorities in the the Association of Southeast Asian Nations (ASEAN) region maintain the regulatory status quo that the current food laws are elastic enough to accommodate nanotechnology applications and products in food. This position is consistent with the findings of various scientific and regulatory reports that nanotechnology itself is not being viewed as "new" from a policy and regulatory perspective unless there is safety assessment

1 "Global Food Nanotechnology Market 2019–2023", *Business Wire*, *available at* www.businesswire.com/news/home/20190610005263/en/Global-Food-Nanotechnology-Market-2019-2023-Growing-Applications (last accessed Aug. 15, 2020).

2 *See*, for instance, Nanodatabase, *available at* https://nanodb.dk (last accessed Oct. 30, 2020); Nanotechnology Consumer Product Inventory, *available at* https://nanotechproject.org (last accessed Oct. 30, 2020).

DOI: 10.4324/9781003271918-14

data showing a new risk to human health.[3] Despite the insufficiency of safety data, food safety authorities are conscious of the gaps they might encounter in utilizing legal authority under the food law and the limitations of the current risk assessment methodologies on nanofood products.

This chapter will discuss the role of law in controlling and creating (new) regulatory space for the use of nanomaterials under the food law. The discussion is divided into three sections. Section II begins by providing context around the applications of nanotechnologies and potential safety issues associated with them. Section III elaborates on the regulatory practices of food safety law in the European Union (EU) and the United States (US) context relating to products and specified conditions of use in food incorporating nanomaterials such as additives, flavorings, and enzymes. Regulatory responses among ASEAN member countries on the safe use of nanoscale substances in food are deliberated on in Section IV. The deliberation looks at how food regulations have evolved in making substantive changes and responses on the market authorization procedures involving nanofood, particularly the intended condition of use of pre-market requirements and the appropriateness of conventional safety assessments to nanofood. It concludes that the principles and practices of food safety law in the ASEAN region are robust enough to cover nanofood in wide product classes and for any newly developed novel food materials, including nanofood. While there are some differences in national food legislation regarding product classification and the need for pre-market authorization, it would not be likely to cause any discriminatory barrier to the free movement of products within the region or the importation of nanofood products from a third country.

3 *See*, for instance, Diana Bowman and Graeme Hodge, "A Small Matter of Regulation: An International Review of Nanotechnology Regulation" (2007) 8 Columbia Science and Technology Law Review. 1–36; Elen Stokes, "Nanotechnology and the Products of Inherited Regulation" (2012) 39(1) Journal of Law and Society. 93–112; Linda Breggin et al., *Securing the Promise of Nanotechnologies: Towards Transatlantic Regulatory Cooperation* (London, Chatham House 2009); Geert van Calster, "Risk Regulation, EU Law and Emerging Technologies: Smother or Smooth?" (2008) 2(1) Nanoethics. 61–71; Robert Falkner and Nico Jaspers, "Regulating Nanotechnologies: Risk, Uncertainty and the Global Governance Gap" (2012) 12(1) Global Environmental Politics. 30–43. In the food sector, the need for comprehensive regulatory review has also been examined in several legal treatises; *see* Anna Gergely et al., "Regulatory Perspectives on Nanotechnologies in Food and Food Contact Materials" in *International Handbook on Regulating Nanotechnologies* (Cheltenham, Edward Elgar 2010), 321–41; Ksenia Takhistova, "Note & Comment, Food Nanotechnology—In Search of a Regulatory Framework" (2009) 35 Rutgers Computer and Technology Law Journal. 255; Geert van Calster, "Simply Swallow?—The Application of Nanotechnologies in European Food Law" (2009) 4(3) European Food and Feed Law Review. 167; Bernd Haber & Sieglinde Stähle, "Nanotechnology in Foods—Fact or Fiction?" (2008) 3(6) European Food and Feed Law Review. 400–6.

II. Overview of Nanotechnologies

The main goal of food law is to protect consumers against unreasonable risk to human health and irresponsible manufacture and consumption of food. Food is basically regulated by product class, such as food and food ingredients (flavoring, additives, enzymes, contaminants). Regulatory layers in production (upstream activity) and consumption (downstream activity) of food mainly cover market authorization requirements, including the condition of intended use of ingredients in food, pre-market review, post-market surveillance, and labeling.[4]

A. Application of Nanotechnologies in Food

Nanotechnology has emerged as an enabling technology that has opened new horizons in its applications for various industries, including the agriculture and food industry. It has been regarded to have revolutionized the whole agri-food sector from farm to table.[5] Once known as the "science of the small," nanotechnology has proved itself superior to conventional food processing technologies in areas such as increased shelf-life, preventing contamination, and enhanced food quality.[6] This is a technology that deals with manufacturing and utilizing materials on a nanometer scale (1–100 nm), which results in nanomaterials that have novel properties.

Based on the dimension of their structural elements, nanostructured materials can be categorized into nanofilms and coatings (one dimension), nanotubes and nanorods (two dimensions), and nanoparticles (three dimensions).[7] Due to their unique features, like a high surface to volume ratio, nanomaterials have been utilized to improve sensory characteristics (i.e. texture, color, and flavor) of food and in food packaging, food processing, dietary supplements, antimicrobial agents, and nanosensors.[8] The fundamental drivers for most nanotechnology applications are the potential improvement in material properties, development of new functionalities, and/or reduction in amount of chemicals used for a function.[9]

4 Breggin et al., *supra* note 3 at 57–73.

5 Ladan Rashidi & Kianoush Khosravi-Darani, "The Applications of Nanotechnology in Food Industry" (2011) 51 Critical Reviews in Food Science and Nutrition. 723.

6 Shivrahj Hariram Nile et al., "Nanotechnologies in Food Science: Applications, Recent Trends, and Future Perspectives" (2020) 12(1) Nano-Micro Letters. 2–11.

7 Micheal F. Hochella Jr, "Nanoscience and Technology the Next Revolution in the Earth Sciences" (2002) 203 Earth Planet Science Letters. 593.

8 Hyunjong Yu et al., "An Overview of Nanotechnology in Food Science: Preparative Methods, Practical Applications, and Safety" (2019) 6–7 Journal of Chemistry. 1–10; Trepti Singh et al., "Application of Nanotechnology in Food Science: Perception and Overview" (2017) 8 Frontiers in Microbiology. Art 1501, 2–4.

9 Qasim Chaudhry et al., "Nanotechnologies in Food: What, Why and How?" in Qasim Chaudhry et al. (eds.), *Nanotechnologies in Food* (London, Royal Society Chemistry 2017), 1–19.

The application of nanotechnology in the food industry captures the whole production chain (Figure 11.1). Food processing is a process of transforming raw materials into value-added products that depends very much on the original quality of the raw materials. Quality and safe raw materials are desired by any food producer, and they are a prerequisite to produce a good finished product. Hence, the advancement of nanotechnology in agriculture has helped to ensure, for example, a low amount of fertilizers and pesticides used in farming through controlled delivery mechanisms. This ensures plants will get fertilizer in the desired amount and rate. Hence the presence of heavy metals in vegetables and fruits is no longer an issue.

The raw materials will be transformed to a finished product after going through a series of processing steps. Food packaging is one of the most important steps in food processing. This is because it protects the food during transportation, distribution, and storage but also serves to attract the buyer's attention. Then the product is consumed with the perception that it is safe and complies with certain quality standards and legislation. Quality control in food production is important to check and analyze that all the processes (i.e. raw materials, processing, packaging, etc.) used in producing the food comply with standards and legislation. Hence rapid methods (i.e. sensors, kit detection, etc.) are preferred, as they provide the faster data needed in the dynamic food industry.

Regarding food processing, nanotechnology can be deployed as encapsulation and carriers that help to protect aroma, flavor, color, and other ingredients in food and as anticaking agents, which help to improve consistency and prevent lump formation. This will produce better texture and appearance. Additives and nutraceuticals help to improve and enhance nutritional value in food, and gelatine agents help to improve food texture.[10] Among nanotechnology applications, major contributions are increasingly deployed as additives and ingredients. As additives, nanomaterials can function as preservatives (e.g. antimicrobials, antioxidants, and antibrowning agents), nutritional additives (e.g. vitamins and minerals), flavoring agents (e.g. sweeteners, natural and synthetic flavors, and flavor enhancers), coloring agents (e.g. natural and synthetic colorings), texturizing agents (e.g. emulsifiers and stabilizers), and other miscellaneous additives (e.g. chelating agents, enzymes, and antifoaming agents).

The utilization of nanoscale additives in food processing can improve product consistency; improve the potency and bioavailability of nutrients in food; maintain palatability and wholesomeness; enhance color and desired flavor; and improve food stability during processing and storage, which extends shelf life and prevents bacteria growth, oxidation, and other chemical changes.[11] Conventionally, food additives have been used to improve and enhance sensory properties of food (color, flavor, texture, taste). This is done to increase the likelihood of a consumer being attracted to purchase and consume the food.

10 Singh, *supra* note 8 at 3.

11 Ruud J.B. Peters et al., "Nanomaterials for Products and Application in Agriculture, Feed and Food" (2016) 54 Trends in Food Science & Technology. 155–61; Peter Murano, *Understanding Food Science and Technology* (New York, Thomson 2003), 178–99.

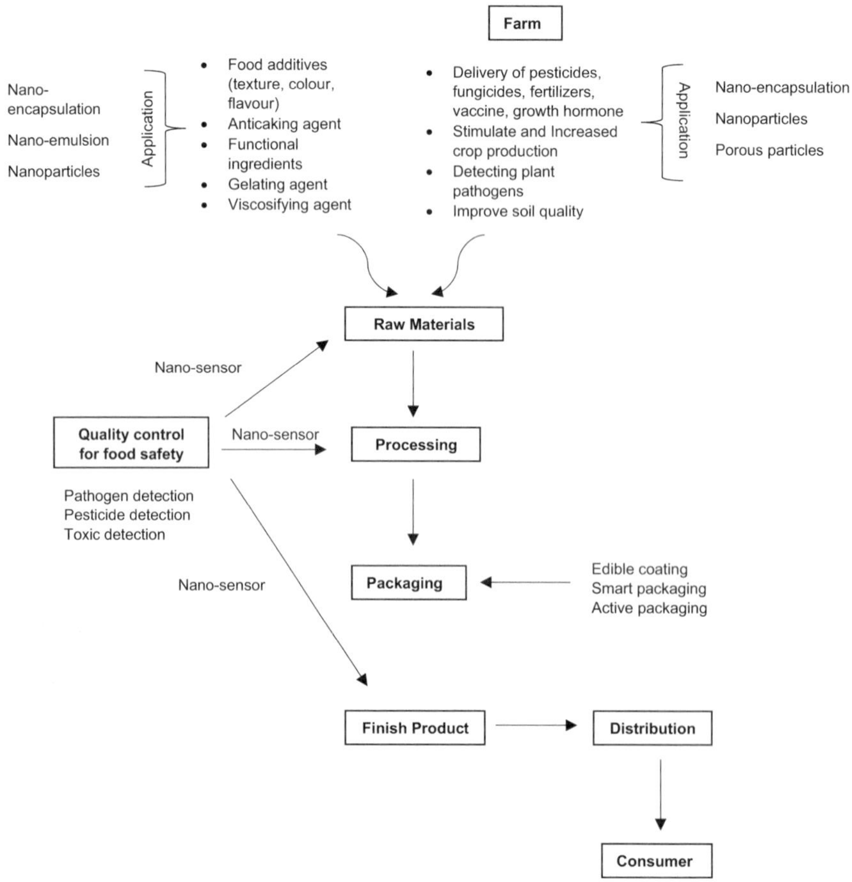

Figure 11.1 Food nanotechnology from farm to table[12]

Flavor is one of the important sensory characteristics of a food and involves a combination of two human senses: the gustatory and olfactory (i.e. orthonasal—sniffing of an aroma; retronasal—air pushed out from the back of the nose when we swallow).[13] It is retro nasal aromas that are combined with gustatory cues to give rise to flavors. Flavor will increase the enjoyment of a food, but the challenge is that flavors are volatile compounds that can be easily destroyed during processing, storage, and transportation when the food is exposed to heat or a harsh environment. Hence, encapsulation of flavors offers a solution to

12 The figure is adapted from Nile, *supra* note 6; Xiojia He & Huey-Min Hwang, "Nanotechnology in Food Science: Functionality, Applicability, and Safety Assessment" (2016) 24 Journal of Food and Drug Analysis. 671–81.

13 Paul Rozin, "Taste-Smell Confusions and the Duality of the Olfactory Sense" (1982) 31(4) Perception & Psychophysics. 399–400.

protect against unfavorable environments. Carriers such as carbohydrates (e.g. starch, maltodextrins, and dextrose), gums (e.g. gum arabic, alginates, and carrageenan), proteins (e.g. whey proteins and gelatine), and chitosan are popular carriers used to encapsulate flavors.[14] Solubility of the flavor and viscosity of the carrier must be considered when designing an encapsulation system to make sure carriers and flavors do not interact with each other.[15]

The usage of nanoencapsulation for flavors can be designed to control the release at the desired time and rate, which gives more flexibility and stability, especially during storage.[16] It gives sustained release by encapsulating a compound in appropriate nanocarriers, which will maintain physical stability under the expected performing conditions and durations.[17] Therefore, nanoencapsulation will provide better loading capacity and encapsulation efficiency, enhanced stability, and better control on the flavor release profile.[18] One of the factors that influences food choice and acceptance is the color of the food. For example, red apples tend to have better acceptance because they are perceived to be juicy, crunchy, and sweet. Depending on variety, unripe mangoes are green in color, hence they are perceived to be sour, and their texture is hard and less accepted. Color is one of the most significant factors that directly affects consumers' food choice and eating desires.[19] Coloring is used in food processing to restore natural color that was lost during processing and storage, enhance existing color, and strengthen weak color.[20]

Titanium dioxide (TiO_2) is used as coloring agent that can provide optical effects, such as the lightness and brightness of a food, that is, enhancing the white color of certain foods such as doughnuts, candies, desserts, and beverages.[21] It is also used as a flavor enhancer in a variety of foods (i.e. dried

14 Berta Nogueiro Estevinho and Fernando Rocha, "A Key for the Future of the Flavors in Food Industry: Nanoencapsulation and Microencapsulation" in A. E. Oprea & A. M. Grumezescu (eds.), *Nanotechnology Applications in Food: Flavor, Stability, Nutrition and Safety* (Oxford, Elsevier, 2017), 1–16.

15 Adem Gharsallaoui et al., "Applications of Spray-Drying in Microencapsulation of Food Ingredients: An Overview" (2007) 40(9) Food Research International. 1107–1121.

16 Berta Nogueiro Estevinho et al., "Microencapsulation with Chitosan by Spray Drying for Industry Applications—A Review" (2013) 31 Trends Food Science and Technology. 140.

17 *See* H Yu, *supra* note 8.

18 Md Saifullah et al, "Micro and Nano Encapsulation, Retention and Controlled Release of Flavor and Aroma Compounds: A Critical Review" (2016) 86 Trends in Food Science & Technology. 232–233.

19 Natalia Martins et al., "Food Colorants: Challenges, Opportunities and Current Desires of Agro-Industries to Ensure Consumer Expectations and Regulatory Practices" (2016) 52 Trends in Food Science & Technology. 1–2.

20 A. Aberoumand, "A Review Article on Edible Pigments Properties and Sources as Natural Biocolorants in Foodstuff and Food Industry" (2011) 6(1) World Journal of Dairy & Food Sciences. 71–73.

21 Alex Weir et al., "Titanium Dioxide Nanoparticles in Food and Personal Care Products" (2012) 46(4) Environmental Science & Technology. 2243–44.

vegetables, nuts, seeds, soups, and mustard) and as an antimicrobial agent.[22] The TiO_2 used in the food industry has a particle size of 100–300 nanometers to increase its light-scattering properties.[23] Iron oxide nanoparticles are widely used as industrial food pigments to color sweets, olives, or cheese rind.[24] They can also be used as source of bioavailable iron when food is being fortified with them. There are several forms of iron oxide that offer different colors; for example, magnetite (Fe_3O_4) is black, FeOOH is yellow, and hematite (Fe_2O_3) can be red or orange brown, depending on the crystalline structure.[25] Iron oxides are generally considered safe food pigments with low acute toxicity.[26] An anti-caking agent is a food additive that has the function of preventing lump formation and improving consistency. Nanoscale material such as silicon dioxide (SiO_2) is used for thickening of pastes (as an anticaking agent) to improve flow properties in powdered products and as a carrier for flavors or active compounds in food.[27]

In the primary production of food, application of nanotechnology in agriculture has the following benefits, including increasing productivity by utilizing nanopesticides and nanofertilizers, improving the quality of the soil by utilizing nanozeolites and hydrogels, stimulating plant growth by utilizing nanomaterials (SiO_2, TiO_2, and carbon nanotubes), and smart monitoring by utilizing nanosensors and wireless communication devices.[28] Nanotechnology has also contributed to formulating nanoscale carriers that enable the delivery of agriculture chemicals, that is, fertilizers, pesticides, and fungicides, that show beneficial effects over conventional ones.[29] Encapsulation of chitosan has been used as the delivery of pesticides, micronutrients, and fertilizers, which reduced the

22 *See* Peters, *supra* note 11; Touseff Amna et al., "Inactivation of Foodborne Pathogens by NiO/TiO2 Composite Nanofibers: A Novel Biomaterial System" (2013) 6(4) Food and Bioprocess Technology. 988–96.

23 Boris Jovanović, "Critical Review of Public Health Regulations of Titanium Dioxide, a Human Food Additive" (2015) 11(1) Integrated, Environmental Assessment and Management. 17.

24 European Food Safety Authority (EFSA), "Scientific Opinion on the Re-Evaluation of Iron Oxides and Hydroxides (E172) as Food Additives" (2015) 13(12) EFSA Journal. 4317.

25 Rochelle M. Cornell & Udo Schwertmann, *The Iron Oxides: Structure, Properties, Reactions, Occurrences and Uses, Second Edition* (Bern, Wiley-VCH 2006), 9.

26 Linn Voss et al., "The Presence of Iron Oxide Nanoparticles in the Food Pigment E172" (2020) 327 Food Chemistry. 1.

27 Satish Kumar Ameta et al., "Use of Nanomaterials in Food Science" in Mansor Ghorbanpour et al. (eds.), *Biogenic Nanoparticles and their Use in Agro-ecosystems* (Singapore, Springer, 2020), 457–88; Min-Ran Go et al., "Interactions Between Food Additive Silica Nanoparticles and Food Matrices" (2017) 8 Frontiers in Microbiology. 1013.

28 Leonardo F. Fraceto et al., "Nanotechnology in Agriculture: Which Innovation Potential Does It Have?" (2016) 4(20) Frontiers in Environmental Science. 2–3.

29 Narges Milani et al., "Fate of Zinc Oxide Nanoparticles Coated onto Macronutrient Fertilizers in an Alkaline Calcareous Soil" (2015) 2 *May Plos One*. 7–12; Hongda Chen & Rickey Yada, "Nanotechnologies in Agriculture: New Tools for Sustainable Development" (2011) 22 Trends Food Science Technology. 586–90.

required dosage for efficacy and ensured controlled delivery.[30] This reduction will help to address environmental issues (i.e. heavy metal pollution) raised by these agricultural chemicals. Controlled delivery mechanisms will allow the active ingredients to be slowly taken up to reduce the amount used and minimize the input and waste.[31] Upon harvesting, these agriculture products will be further processed, as they are used as raw materials in the making of value-added products.

B. Safety of Nanomaterials in Food

The use of nanomaterials in food raises concerns of whether conventional risk assessment will continue to apply to nanofood.[32] Unique characterization of substances used in food as compared to other food formulated at the micro-scale level, such as the determination of maximum permissible limit of daily intake for food based on weight in additives, contaminants, natural intoxicants, and dietary supplements are among the major problems facing the regulatory authorities.

With substantially different physiochemical and biological properties compared to their conventional form, the usage of nanomaterials can possibly create unpredictable hazards.[33] Little is known about the bioavailability, biodistribution, and routes of nanomaterials and the ultimate toxicity upon exposure to them.[34] Humans are likely to be exposed to nanomaterial toxicity via skin, gastrointestinal tract, lung, nasal cavity, and eyes, which are likely to redistribute or migrate it to other organs.[35] There are several potential mechanisms as a result of nanoparticle toxicity.[36] It is expected that there will be interference with normal gastrointestinal tract (GIT) function in which the presence of nanoparticles

30 HMN Abdel-Aziz et al, "Nano Chitosan-NPK Fertilizer Enhances the Growth and Productivity of Wheat Plants Grown in Sandy Soil. (2016) 14(1) Span. J. Agric. Res. 1–8; Prem Lal Kashyap, Xu Xiang & Patricia Heiden, "Chitosan Nanoparticle Based Delivery Systems for Sustainable Agriculture" (2015) 77 Int. J. Biol. Macromol 37–43, 46–48.

31 *See* Chen, *supra* note 29.

32 *See*, for instance, Chia-Fau Chau et al, "The Development of Regulations for Food Nanotechnology" (2007) 18 Trends in Food Science & Technology. 269–80; UK House of Lords, *Nanotechnologies in Food*, 1st Report of Session (London, The Stationery Office by Order of the House 2009–2010); Karinne Ludlow, "The Readiness of Australia Food Regulation for the Use of Nanotechnology in Food and Food Packaging," (2007) 26(2) The University of Tasmania Law Review. 177–202.

33 *See* Yu, *supra* note 8.

34 *See* Ameta, *supra* note 27; He and Hwang, *supra* note 12.

35 Valerian E. Kagan et al., "Fantastic Voyage and Opportunities of Engineered Nanomaterials: What Are the Potential Risks of Occupational Exposures?" (2010) 52 Journal Occupational Environmental Medicine. 943–46; Karen Tiede et al., "Detection and Characterization of Engineered Nanoparticles in Food and the Environment" (2008) 25(7) Food Additives and Contaminants. 795–821.

36 David Julian McClements & Hang Xiao, "Is Nano Safe in Foods? Establishing the Factors Impacting the Gastrointestinal Fate and Toxicity of Organic and Inorganic Food-Grade Nanoparticles"(2017) NPJ Sci Food. 1–10.

in gastrointestinal fluids could interfere with normal GIT functions. Concerns regarding high levels of nanoparticles (inorganic or some indigestible organics) could reduce the rate of digestion, whereas some types of inorganic nanoparticles may physically disrupt structures within the GIT (i.e. microvilli), which alters normal nutrient absorption and the protective function of the epithelium cells.[37] The presence of nanoparticles can stimulate an immune response, which could have adverse effects on human health. Accumulation within specific tissues, particularly the possibility of absorption of nanoparticles into the cells which are metabolized and transferred out of or accumulate within the cells may also occur. Accumulation of nanoparticles within specific tissues may lead to long-term problems if they exhibit toxic effects above a certain accumulation threshold.[38] This mechanism is most important for inorganic nanoparticles that are not normally digested or metabolized in the gastrointestinal tract.

Another possible effect is cytotoxicity and cellular malfunction, where inorganic nanoparticles generate reactive oxygen species (ROS) (i.e. singlet oxygen, superoxide, hydrogen peroxide, and hydroxyl radicals) and contribute to their toxicity.[39] ROS can cause damage to cell membranes, organelles, and nucleus when interacts with lipids, proteins, or nucleic acids.[40] As a result, many biochemical functions required to maintain cell viability (i.e. adenosine triphosphate production, DNA replication, and gene expression) are adversely affected.[41] This mechanism is important for inorganic nanoparticles that are absorbed by the intestinal cells, since most organic nanoparticles are digested before being absorbed.

Nanoparticle toxicity may also lead to altered location of bioactive release. The encapsulation of bioactive agents such as dietary supplements or nutraceuticals in nanoparticles may alter the location of their release and absorption within the gastrointestinal tract. This will upset the normal function of the digestive system, which could lead to gastrointestinal problems, whereas for enhancement of oral bioavailability, the biological effect of the bioactive agent will depend on exposure levels in the blood and specific tissue. If it is too low, the bioactive agent has little effect, but if it is too high, then it might be toxic. It is system dependent where it depends on the toxicity profile of the bioactive agent. For example, Vitamin E is essential for maintaining human health

37 Esther E Frohlich & Eleonore Frohlich, "Cytotoxicity of Nanoparticles Contained in Food on Intestinal Cells and the Gut Microbiota" (2016) 17 International Journal of Molecular Sciences. 1–22.

38 Erik Orfi & Janos Szebeni, "The Immune System of the Gut and Potential Adverse Effects of Oral Nanocarriers on Its Function" (2016) 106 Advanced Drug Delivery Review 402–9.

39 Haohao Wu et al., "Reactive Oxygen Species Related Activities of Nano-Iron Metal and Nano-Iron Oxides" (2014) 22 Journal Food Drug Analysis 86–94.

40 Ibid; Virender K. Sharma et al, "Organic-Coated Silver Nanoparticles in Biological and Environmental Conditions: Fate, Stability and Toxicity" (2014) 204 Journal of Advance Colloid and Interface Science 15–34.

41 Ibid.

at a specific dosage, but consumption at a high dosage will lead to chronic diseases.[42] This may also give rise to the enhancement of pesticide bioavailability: this mechanism is likely to be for foods containing lipid nanoparticles (nanoemulsions) that are consumed with foods containing high levels of hydrophobic pesticides or hormones. Finally, it would also cause interference with gut microbiota: As a result of the interaction of nanoparticles with colonic bacteria, it will alter the microflora and its surroundings. Hence, any change in the bacteria populating the human colon will have an effect on human health. It is likely that nanomaterials may enter our body during food production that may lead to DNA damage, cell membrane disruption, and cell death.[43]

III. Regulating Nanomaterials in Food as Product Category

The legal baseline of food safety practice is to provide safeguards to consumers from adverse health-related hazards. The classification of food is made according to product category and its intended use rather than technological applications. Pursuant to this classification, nanofood will not be left in a regulatory void. The current regulatory frameworks are the most suitable candidates to look for when trying to manage the potential adverse risk of food products or ingredients containing nanomaterials. While this proposition is legitimately held by many food safety authorities, there are different requirements applicable to certain product categories. In the US, the Food and Drug Administration (FDA), like majority food safety authorities, utilizes current food law regarding the current deployment of such substances in food ingredients and the absence of evidence on adverse risks to human health, whereas the EU introduces specific provisions regarding the notification obligation for manufacturers for the use or presence of nanomaterials in food products and information requirements for risk assessment. This section will elucidate the US and EU food laws' approaches as two leading jurisdictions in regulating nanoscale products and ingredients.

A. The United States

The US-FDA's authority of regulating food additives, food contact materials, and feed additives falls within the ambit of the Federal Food, Drug and Cosmetic Act (FFDCA). The broader regulatory guidance is encapsulated under the General Policy Principles of US Regulation under the Executive Order 13563—Improving Regulations and Regulatory Review. The policy requires all types of health and environmental risk regulation, including FFDCA, to

42 Edgar R. Miller et al., "Meta-Analysis: High-Dosage Vitamin E Supplementation May Increase All-Cause Mortality" (2005) 142 Annals of Internal Medicine. 37–46.

43 Nile, *supra* note 6.

be predictable, based on the best available science, and cost effective to the industry.[44] It assigns the FDA a wide margin of discretion in ensuring safety measures under the food safety law, and its threshold considers the information on the additive in question together with the chemical and pharmacological state of the substance in the diet.[45]

The US-FDA has not adopted a formal position on the definition of "nanotechnology." In its view, the general definition of nanomaterials of 1–100 nanometers is sufficiently robust to draw a distinction between nanofood and other products. Such a position is built upon a long history with cells and molecules such that products containing particulate novel materials in the same range can be treated as equivalent to nanofood or nanoscale substances.[46] Hence, the proposition that there should not be any discrimination as far as nanofood being "intrinsically benign or harmful" prevails.[47] This results in the US-FDA's stand of maintaining the regulatory *status quo* that traditional legal standards and safety measures apply to nanofood based on the product class and the purpose of its intended use. The equivalence study should be marked by reference to the risk profile of nanomaterials and whether it has changed the nutritional value of the products. As such, a new safety assessment should be carried out when the food incorporating nanomaterials poses an unreasonable risk to human health.[48]

It is a general obligation upon manufacturers to carry out pre-market review for new food additives. Food substances categorized under "generally recognized as safe" (GRAS) notification, dietary supplements, and prior sanctioned substances are expressly excluded from prior regulatory approval. In relation to nanoscale additives, the focus of US-FDA is to regulate based on product classes and corresponding legal standards. The safety of such additives must be established to a reasonable degree of clarity. Section 409(a) of the FFDCA prohibits the marketing of adulterated food in interstate commerce.[49] Any kind of food additive is deemed adulterated unless the US-FDA declares its intended use would be safe for human consumption. If an existing food additive exists in nanoscale form and is used for its intended purpose, its regulatory status might

44 White House, "General Principles of Regulation", Jan. 18, 2011, *available at* https://obamawhitehouse.archives.gov/the-press-office/2011/01/18/executive-order-13563-improving-regulation-and-regulatory-review.

45 FFDCA § 409(c)(5), 21 U.S.C. § 348(c)(5).

46 Chau, *supra* note 32.

47 US-FDA, "Draft Guidance for Industry: Considering Whether a FDA-Regulated Product Involves the Application of the Nanotechnology", *available at* www.fda.gov/regulatory-information/search-fda-guidance-documents/considering-whether-fda-regulated-product-involves-application-nanotechnology.

48 Gary Marchant, "Nanotechnology Regulation: The United States Approach" in *New Global Frontiers in Regulation: The Age of Nanotechnologies* (Cheltenham, Edward Elgar 2007), 189–211; Raj Bawa "FDA and Nanotech: Baby Steps Lead to Regulatory Uncertainty" in *Bio-Nanotechnology: A Revolution in Food, Biomedical and Health Sciences* (New York, John Wiley & Sons 2013), 720–32.

49 FFDCA § 301(a), 21 U.S.C. § 331(a).

change due to the presence and functionality use of the substance in food; hence, it is not established to be safe in case safety issues arise.[50] The safety level of food additives must also take into consideration information on the additive in question, coupled with the chemical and pharmacological state of the substance in the diet.

The voluntary notification of GRAS is based on the substance at its natural scale and conventional bulk form. There is also no discrimination on the type of substance with reference to its particle size, and no clear permissible safety threshold limit of particle size is available for scientific and regulatory purposes due to the lack of consensus over the definition of nanomaterials. In this situation, it would be difficult for the US-FDA to treat a nanoscale substance as completely safe despite its being a prior sanctioned substance in macroscale form as GRAS. While food manufacturers can submit a statement that they have determined that the intended condition of use for a food ingredient is GRAS, the US-FDA has the authority to require a new pre-market review should there be any objection to the previous notification. On science questions, the US-FDA Nanotechnology Task Force outlined two methods of establishing safety for any US-FDA-regulated products: first by understanding the interactions of nanomaterials with biological systems and second the adequacy of testing approaches for assessing the safety and quality of products containing nanomaterials.[51]

GRAS is founded on the basis of determining "the safety of new additives against the benefits of promoting innovation in food science, without exposing to pre-market approval the majority of ingredients that had already been sanctioned for use or that were generally recognized as safe."[52] Therefore, nanoproducts need to be regulated or subject to the regulatory intervention of the US-FDA in situations where the risk may threaten human health.[53] In consequence, companies are not obliged to provide scientific information and undergo application for approval, considering there is substantial equivalence of data already available for the GRAS category of food substances. This, however, would not give the US-FDA any leeway to ensure safety is implemented. The guidance would be useful to provide additional standards and protocols with respect to case-by-case product review.[54]

50 US-FDA, "Consideration of FDA-Regulated Products That May Contain Nanoscale Materials", *available at* www.fda.gov/regulatory-information/search-fda-guidance-documents/considering-whether-fda-regulated-product-involves-application-nanotechnology (last accessed Nov. 19, 2021).

51 US-FDA, "Nanotechnology over a Decade of Progress and Innovation: A Report by the U.S. Food and Drug Administration", July 2020, *available at* www.fda.gov/media/140395/download.

52 Ibid.

53 Ibid.

54 Brianna M. Sandoval, "Perspectives on FDA's Regulation of Nanotechnology: Emerging Challenges and Potential Solution" (2009) 8(4) Comprehensive Review in Food Science and Food Safety. 387.

B. The European Union

The White Paper on Food Safety contains assurance for high-level protection of human and consumer interests in relation to food[55] and later becomes a guiding legal principle of EU food safety law and policy in Regulation (EC) 178/2002, which lays down General Principles and Requirements for Food Law.[56] The scientific scheme highlighted in both documents is "to use the best available science in developing food safety measures."[57] In order to support science-based risk management practice, the European Food Safety Authority (EFSA) was created as an EU-wide risk assessment body to provide scientific opinion for reference by its Member States and non-EU countries. While the EFSA's opinion does not have the status of law, any disagreement with or difference from its published opinion is allowable only on the grounds of public health and safety.[58]

The EU's approach to nanotechnology challenges the notion that it can be simply covered by the existing authorization procedure. Contrary to the US and other countries' approach, the EU views that no nanofood would make its way into the consumer market in the absence of sufficient evidence of safety to health and the environment. Several policy and legal documents shed light on using science as a prerequisite to approve the product's entry into consumer markets—that means no safety data, no market for nanofood.

Regulation of food and food ingredients incorporating nanomaterials in the EU depends on their intended use or purpose, either as novel food and novel food ingredients, food additives, food supplements, vitamins, minerals, or food contact materials. The use of food and feed additives in the EU is controlled by the European Parliament and Council legislation, which sets out lists of permitted additives, the foods in which they can be used, and maximum levels of use.[59] All permitted additives have been assessed for safety by the independent scientific committees that advise the European Commission, a role now performed by EFSA.[60] In addition, each additive must comply with specific purity criteria laid down in corresponding European Commission Directives. The criteria dictate the chemical structure and purity of each additive. However, minimum particle size is only specified in the case of microcrystalline cellulose (E460 (i)), while the specification for carrageenan (E407) limits the molecular weight distribution (which may indirectly limit particle size).

55 European Commission, *White Paper on Food Safety* 2000 (COM (1999)) 719 final 14–21.

56 Regulation (EC) 178/2002 of the European Parliament and of the Council of January 2002 laying down the general principles and requirements of food law, establishing the European Food Safety Authority and laying down procedures in matters of food safety, Article 5(1).

57 European Commission, *supra* note 55.

58 *Pfizer Animal Health v. Council of the European Union* [2002] ECR II-3305, 380–82.

59 Regulation (EC) 133/2008 of the European Parliament and of the Council of 16 December 2008 on Food Additives, Article 10. *See* also Ioana Ratescu, "Safe Use of Food Additives under EU Law" (2010) 4 European Journal of Risk Regulation. 402–4.

60 Ibid., Recital 11 and Article 12.

The latest novel food law, Regulation (EU) No. 2015/2283, has resolved many years of debates[61] among EU institutions on whether nanofood should be treated as novel food.[62] It provides the legal definition of "engineered nanomaterials," which maintains the basic range of 1–100 nanometers for nanomaterials with consideration of the surface, structures, agglomerates, or aggregates. The properties of nanoscale materials include those related to the large specific surface area of the materials or physicochemical properties that are distinct from those of the bulk or non-nano form of the same materials.[63] Since nanofood is a separate category of novel food, the proof of significant changes in the composition or structure of food affecting nutritional value, metabolism or level of undesirable substance,[64] or the prior history of safe use for at least 25 years does not apply.[65] The EFSA's scientific opinion and the Organisation for Economic Cooperation and Development (OECD) Council Recommendation are considered, in which general safety testing is appropriate for nanomaterials, but the test method must be adapted to the specific properties of nanomaterials.

The general rules governing food additives, enzymes, and flavoring require pre-market assessment and authorization before entry into the market. The applicable regulations are Regulation (EC) 1332/2008 on food enzymes;[66] Regulation (EC) 1334/2008 on flavorings and certain food ingredients with flavoring properties;[67] and Directive 2002/46/EC on food supplements, minerals, and vitamins.[68] Regulation (EC) 1333/2008 contains authorization procedures that scientific risk assessment must be carried out to ensure safe ingredients are contained in food. Any changes in the starting material used in the production method of an additive, including change of particle size, are not covered by existing authorization. Therefore, it must pass through a new safety assessment.[69] So any food additives approved for the market that have been used for many years, such as anti-caking agents, vegetable carbon, silver, and gold,

61 *See*, for instance, Naomi Salmon, "What's Cooking? From GM Food to Nanofood: Regulating Risk and Trade in Europe" (2009) 11(2) Environmental Law Review. 97–115.

62 Regulation (EU) 2015/2283 of the European Parliament and of the Council of 25 November 2015 on novel foods, amending Regulation (EU) No 1169/2011 of the European Parliament and of the Council and repealing Regulation (EC) No 258/97 of the European Parliament and of the Council and Commission Regulation (EC) No 1852/2001.

63 Regulation (EU) No. 2015/2283, Article 3(f).

64 Ibid., Recital 12.

65 Ibid., Recital 15.

66 European Parliament and Council of Europe, *supra* note 59.

67 Regulation (EC) No 1334/2008 of the European Parliament and of the Council of Dec. 16, 2008 on flavourings and certain food ingredients with flavouring properties for use in and on foods and amending Council Regulation (EEC) No 1601/91, Regulations (EC) No 2232/96 and (EC) No 110/2008 and Directive 2000/13/EC

68 Directive 2002/46/EC of the European Parliament and of the Council of June 10, 2002 on the approximation of the laws of the Member States relating to food supplements.

69 Valeria Amenta et al., "Regulatory Aspects of Nanotechnology in the Agri/Feed/Food Sector in EU and Non-EU Countries" (2015) 73 Regulatory Toxicology and Pharmacology. 467.

are subject to re-evaluation by the EFSA.[70] Some of the substances or materials used in the nanoparticle size range so far have not raised any health concerns for calcium carbonate as a food additive.[71] Other substances, such as nanosilver, SAS (E551), may possibly pose a health risk with the integration of nanoparticles. However, a detailed risk assessment should be carried out to identify the knowledge gaps and safety evaluation. Therefore, any food or food ingredients are not subject to prior approval unless it is required by the law, such as the purpose of its use in food as additives and flavorings—which happens to be the case for nanoscale substances in food ingredients.[72] The EFSA's opinion suggests that the current risk assessment method may not be appropriate to evaluate the risk posed by the unique properties of nanomaterials.[73] Hence, generation of scientific depository targeting at specific products and process must consider a wide range of factors, such as chemical composition, physicochemical properties, interaction with tissues, and potential exposure level to overcome the dearth of science facing the risk assessors.[74]

C. *Risk Assessment of Joint FAO/WHO Expert Committee on Food Additives*

Numerous risk assessment policies and procedures in relation to food products, such as additives or pesticides, are implemented by the Joint FAO/WHO Expert Committee on Food Additives (JECFA). The role of JECFA is independent of the Codex Alimentarius Commission structure. It develops principles for safety assessment of chemicals in food consistent with the mainstream thinking of risk assessment and in consideration of comprehensive studies on toxicology and other related disciplines.[75] In relation to the applicability of nanotechnology in food products, JEFCA emphasizes that "the current risk assessment approach used by the FAO and WHO is suitable for engineered nano-scale in food and agriculture, including the effects on animal health."[76] As an international risk assessor, the role of JECFA can benefit the ASEAN food

70 Eveline Verleysen, "Physicochemical Characterization of Nanoparticles in Food Additives in the Context of Risk Identification" (2021) EFSA Supporting Publication. EN-9992.

71 EFSA Panel on Food Additives and Nutrient Sources added to Food (ANS), "Scientific Opinion on Re-Evaluation of Calcium Carbonate (E 170) as a Food Additive" (2011) 9(7) EFSA Journal. 2318.

72 Amenta, *supra* note 69.

73 EFSA, "The Potential Risks Arising from Nanoscience and Nanotechnologies on Food and Feed Safety" (2009) 958 EFSA Journal. 1–39.

74 EFSA, "Guidance on the Risk Assessment of the Application of Nanoscience and Nanotechnologies in the Food and Feed Chain" (2011) 9(5) EFSA Journal. 2140.

75 FAO, "Joint FAO/WHO Expert Committee on Food Additives (JECFA)", *available at* www.fao.org/food-safety/scientific-advice/jecfa/en/.

76 FAO/WHO, "State of the Art on the Initiatives and Activities Relevant to Risk Assessment and Risk Management of Nanotechnologies in the Food and Agriculture Sectors" in *Food and Agriculture Organization of the United Nations and World Health Organization* (Rome, FAO/WHO 2013), 36.

safety authorities about the quality and adequacy of scientific data and safety assessment of food additives. JECFA has noted that neither the specification nor the amount of daily intake (ADI) for food additives has been evaluated to apply to specified intended use in food in nanoscale form.[77]

IV. Regulatory Responses to the Use of Nanoscale Substances in Food in ASEAN

Food safety systems in ASEAN are governed by the respective national legislations.[78] At the regional level, the Member States crafted an ASEAN Food Policy that became the common point of policy and regulatory structures for the ASEAN Food Regulatory Framework. The framework is intended to address issues across the food supply chain and undertake coordination mechanisms for implementing the ASEAN Food Safety Policy.[79] The ASEAN Food Regulatory Framework further establishes the Prepared Foodstuffs Products Working Group (PFPWG) under relevant teams under the ASEAN Ministers of Agriculture and Forestry Meeting and the ASEAN Health Ministers Meeting.

At the industry level, the manipulation of nanoscale materials into existing products and processes has begun in ASEAN over the past few decades. The policy document addressing nanotechnology development and safety, however, is relatively nascent in this region. Thailand[80] is the only Member State that has introduced a national nanosafety policy. The policy document highlights national policies and the lack of comprehensive laws covering the entire lifecycle of nanomaterials, which ranges from the production to importation and exportation of nanomaterials. Other countries, such as Malaysia, prepared the National Nanotechnology Strategy and Action Plan, which became the reference document as the draft National Nanotechnology Policy. The government plans to introduce the National Nanotechnology Industry Development Act to regulate activities relating to research, development, and commercialization of nanotechnology. The document also proposes a re-alignment of the existing national laws and obligations under various treaties[81] and adoption of best

77 Ibid.

78 The main national food legislations in the ASEAN Member States are the Food Act 1983 (Act 281) and Food Regulations (Malaysia); the Sales of Food Act (Chapter 283 (Singapore); Law 18 of 2002 on Food (Indonesia); the Food Safety Act of 2013 Republic Act (RA) No. 10611 (Philippines); Food Act B.E 2252 1979 (Thailand); Law No.55/2010/QH12 on Food Safety (Vietnam); the Food Safety Law of 1997 (Cambodia) and the Public Health (Food) Act (Chapter 182) (Brunei).

79 *See* for instance Ching-Fu Lin, "The Emergence of ASEAN Regional Food Safety Governance: Structure, Substance, and Context" (2019) 74 Food and Drug Law Journal. 85–96.

80 The Nanosafety and Ethics Strategic Plan, *available at* www.nanotec.or.th/en/wp-content/uploads/2018/09/Nanosafety-Soft-file.pdf (last accessed May 20, 2021).

81 National Nanotechnology Directorate, *Nanotechnology—The Malaysian Landscape, National Nanotechnology Strategic Direction and Roadmap,* February 2014 (restricted access—on file with author).

risk management practices from other countries.[82] At the moment, there is no dedicated policy on the safety of nanotechnology in food being formulated at the national and regional level.

A. The Relevance of Current Food Law to Nanotechnology

In the wake of emerging nanotechnology innovation in the food sector, it is timely for the food safety authorities in ASEAN to review the relevance of existing food regulatory frameworks to manage potentially unique risks posed by nanotechnology applications, products, and processes. The laws were also passed without the need of addressing any particular technology at the time of drafting. The absence of dedicated provisions nonetheless does not necessarily leave nanotechnology in a regulatory void. The product class approach is sufficiently robust to govern food and its specified condition of use in food at nanoscale level. They are designed in such a way to be inclusive to any kind of novel technologies, including nanotechnologies. The US, Ireland, Hong Kong, Australia, and New Zealand are among prominent jurisdictions that rely on the general food law to regulate nanotechnology products and safety.[83]

No Member States in ASEAN have introduced additional provisions just to specifically cater to the use and applications of food nanotechnology. In the FAO/WHO Joint Expert Meeting on Nanotehnologies in Food report, Malaysia submitted that:

> At present there are no specific regulations applicable to the risk assessment of nanotechnology. All food imported or produced domestically including those containing nanoscale particles, must comply with the Food Act 1983 and related regulations, and must be safe for human consumption. In addition, risk assessment is conducted to address potential health risks and is not limited to nanotechnology.[84]

The safety of nanoproducts is routinely seen using the general food safety provision under the food law. Any importation or production of food and food ingredients, including those containing nanoscale substances, must comply

82 National Nanotechnology Directorate & NanoMalaysia Ltd., "Towards a Malaysian Regulatory Framework", *Asia Nano Forum Nanotech 2013*, Japan, Jan. 31, 2013.

83 Amenta, *supra* note 69 at 469–71; Ludlow, *supra* note 32 at 200–1; Nick Flecther & Andrew Bartholomaeus, "Regulation of Nanotechnologies in Food in Australia and New Zealand" (2011) 1(2) International Food Risk Analysis Journal. 37; Food Safety Authority of Ireland, *The Relevance for Food Safety of Applications of Nanotechnology in the Food and Feed Industries* (Dublin, Food Safety Authority of Ireland), 47–53.

84 FAO/WHO. "State of the Art on the Initiatives and Activities Relevant to Risk Assessment and Risk Management of Nanotechnologies in the Food and Agriculture Sectors," *Food and Agriculture Organization of the United Nations and World Health Organization* (Rome: FAO/WHO: 2013), 14.

with the general food law.[85] This has been the common norm of regulatory practice in many jurisdictions as well.[86] The lack of explicitness in the definition of nanotechnology, the information and notification requirements challenges the food safety authority in coming up with the rules of labeling and marketing authorization upon manufacturers incorporating nanomaterials in food products.

B. *Nanomaterials as "Inclusive" Criteria of Existing Product Categories*

Within ASEAN, "food" is defined broadly to include any form and substance added to it according to the product category and its specified condition of use. The range of particle size is not the sole factor to determine the risk profile of food or food ingredients.[87] The permissibility level of food additives under the Food Regulations 1985 (Malaysia) is determined by reference to the safety threshold based on the list of authorized ingredients, the proportion of additives or total proportion which does not exceed the maximum residue limits, and where the food containing the additives is not in a greater quantity than those made under proper technological conditions and in line with sound manufacturing practices.

In Singapore, a safe additives must conform to the limits of the types of additives prescribed under the Food Regulations.[88] As for preservatives, the approved limits must not exceed 4% of the substance itself, 400 milligrams of benzoic acid, and an acidity regulator as permitted conditioner. As for flavoring substances, certification issued by the national food authorities from the country of origin and manufacture, and the approval of the director general of Ministry of Health is required.[89] In the US, Australia, and New Zealand, the permissible limits are determined by reference to the positive and negative lists of additives. The list bucket system does not apply in the ASEAN food safety system. In this regard, the national food safety authorities will rely on the risk assessment results published by reputable authorities, such as EFSA, US-FDA, Food Standards Australia New Zealand (FSANZ), or JECFA/CAC.[90]

85 The applicable food laws in the countries are the Food Act 1983 and Food Regulations 1985 (Malaysia), and Law Number 18 of 2012 concerning Food (Indonesia).

86 *See* the country reports in FAO/WHO, *State of the Art on the Initiatives and Activities Relevant to Risk Assessment and Risk Management of Nanotechnologies in the Food and Agriculture Sectors*, (Rome: FAO/WHO, 2013), 8–20.

87 Muhammad Nizam Awang, 'Regulating Safety of Nanotechnology in Food: The Legal Case for Malaysia' in *Responsibility and Emerging Technologies: Experiences, Education and Beyond*, ed. Diana M. Bowman et al (Berlin: IOS Press), 95.

88 Sale of Food Act (Chapter 283) (Singapore), section 56(1) and Food Regulations 1985 (Malaysia), Regulation 15.

89 Food Regulations 1985 (Malaysia), Regulations 20(1) & (2).

90 Awang, *supra* note 87 at 97–98.

C. Novel Food

Some Member States, such as Thailand and Singapore, consider the regulation of food incorporating nanomaterials under the scope of novel food. The classification of novel food is made based on the "history of safe use" approach, where

> the substance used as food or food ingredients has not been currently used in a production process that gives rise to significant changes in the composition or structure of such food which affect their nutritional value, metabolism or level of undesirable substances.[91]

In Thailand, there must neither be any history of consumption over the last 15 years nor current usage in a production process, whereas in Singapore, there must be a minimum period of at least 20 years without any report of adverse health effects.[92]

The guidelines on safety assessment issued by the Singapore Food Agency (SFA) indicate the information required for the application: the length of consumption or use of the ingredients, that is, how many years the ingredients have been consumed as food or used in food; the extent of particular ingredients being used or consumed by the respective population; the quantity of use; and the purpose of use or any available evidence suggesting side effects to human health during the period of use as food.[93] With regard to the substance, the SFA will look into the information on the use of the substance in the manufacturing process; the intended use and proposed use levels of the substance in food; *in-vitro* and *in-vivo* toxicity studies, such as acute, short-term, and long-term toxicity studies, carcinogenicity studies, reproductive toxicity studies, developmental toxicity studies, and genotoxicity studies; or metabolism or toxicokinetic studies, where relevant, including absorption, distribution, metabolism, and excretion (ADME) studies.[94] Where no local safety assessment data is available, the SFA may consult reports published by other credible food safety authorities, such as Australia, Canada, New Zealand, Japan, the EU, and the US on the definition, scope, and legal processes verifying novel food and food ingredients; published or unpublished scientific studies; or any studies that

91 Ministry of Public Health Thailand, "The Notification of Ministry of Public Health (NO. 376) B.E. 2559 (2016) Clause 1, http://food.fda.moph.go.th/law/data/announ_moph/V.English/No.376_Re_Novel_food.pdf (last visited 10 October 2021).

92 Singapore Food Agency (SFA), "Requirements for the Safety Assessment of Novel Foods", 23 November 2020, www.sfa.gov.sg/docs/default-source/food-import-and-export/Requirements-on-safety-assessment-of-novel-foods_23-Nov-2020.pdf (last visited 29 October 2021).

93 *Ibid.*

94 Food Standards Australia and New Zealand (FSAZ), "Potential Health Risks Associated with Nanotechnologies in Existing Food Additives," May 2016, www.foodstandards.gov.au/publications/Documents/Safety%20of%20nanotechnology%20in%20food.pdf (last visited 19 November 2021).

have been carried out in accordance with the reference documents published by national and international risk assessment agencies, such as US-FDA, EFSA, and JECFA.

The legal position of nanofood and food ingredients as novel foods in ASEAN is not fully explored yet. While it fits within the definition of novel food as food prepared using unconventional processes, it remains to be seen how the food safety authorities will evaluate the specific properties of nanomaterials and whether the history of safe consumption would still apply. In the first draft of a public consultation document, the SFA illustrated a category of novel to include "food consisting of intentionally engineered nanomaterial."[95] It was removed in the final version, presumably because the industry and authorities prefer the guidelines to be general and not restricted to nanotechnologies. This could possibly suggest the market authorization procedure and safety assessment of nanofood could dispense with the history of consumption.

V. Conclusion

The primary goal of food safety regulation is to ensure a high level of health protection to the consumer against food-related hazards. The rise of food products and ingredients incorporating nanomaterials in the food market has pushed national food authorities around the world and in the ASEAN region to assess how far the existing legal and safety standards are still relevant to manage potential risk associated with them. Except for the EU, the current regulatory frameworks make no reference to particle size to determine the safety threshold of a food category. The frameworks are sufficiently robust, but the use of specific properties of nanomaterials used in food as additives, flavoring, enzymes, coloring, or contaminants may require a re-evaluation of food safety. Hence, a comprehensive review of the safety assessment and pre-marketing authorization procedures, particularly on food additives, among the Member States should be emphasized at the regional level. Some substances, such TiO_2, have been widely used as nanoscale additives despite not being mentioned as permitted additives in food regulations. As a newly developed food additive, the substance needs to pass through the evaluation of a safety assessment and pre-market review. The ASEAN Member States also should verify the safety data with other reputable risk assessment bodies. The existing intergovernmental platform can be leveraged to promote the exchange of best practices, including the publication of stable and low-risk nanomaterials in food. They

95 Singapore Food Agency (SFA) (formerly known as Agri-Food and Veterinary Authority [AVA]), *First Public Consultation on Proposed Regulatory Framework For Novel Food And Novel Food Ingredients In Singapore*, From: www.sfa.gov.sg/docs/default-source/legislation/sale-of-food-act/first-public-consultation-on-proposed-regulatory-framework-for-novel-foo.pdf (last visited 20 March 2021).

can also extrapolate useful lessons from the regulatory practices of developed countries on how they manage the regulatory competencies and expertise in dealing with nanomaterial use in food. As such, any safety measure must be grounded in sound and available science and be carried out with ultimate transparency to improve the public trust placed in them in protecting human health.

Part IV

Health/Functional Food Regulation from a Comparative Perspective

12 Contested Discourses of the Use of Health Foods in Japan

Tomiko Yamaguchi

I. Introduction

Over the course of the last few decades, the food and agricultural sector in Japan has faced challenges in the form of a series of food safety issues, exemplified by the social controversies surrounding bovine spongiform encephalopathy.[1] Similar intense social conflicts, driven by food safety concerns, erupted over the plan to introduce genetically modified food in the late 1990s.[2] More recently, food safety concerns have arisen over radiation contamination of food in the wake of the explosion of the Fukushima nuclear power plants.[3] Through these experiences, food safety concerns have become central issues in Japanese society.

Another phenomenon worth noting is at present Japan is undergoing is the rapid transformation of the food and agricultural sector through the use of science and technology for food production and processing. As exemplified by gene edited foods and cultured meat, science and technology have given rise to novel ways of making and altering foods.[4] These are coupled with government policies that favor deregulation, policies reflected in trade agreements such as

1 K. Tanaka, "Seven Samurai to Protect "Our" Food: the Reform of the Food Safety Regulatory System in Japan After the BSE Crisis of 2001" (2008) 25 *Agriculture and Human Values* 567, 567–580.

2 Y. Otsuka, *Naze Idenshikumikae Sakumotu wa Kaihatsu Saretanoka: Biotechnology no Shakaigaku [Why have GMOs been Developed? Sociology of Biotechnology]* (Akashi Shoten, 1999); T. Yamaguchi and F. Suda, "Changing Social Order and the Quest for Justification: GMO Controversies in Japan" (2009) 35:3 *Science, Technology, & Human Values*, 382, 382–407.

3 Y. Igarashi, *Minnade Kimeta "Anshin" no Katachi [Community-Led Food Safety Standards]* (Tokyo, Akishobou 2012); AH Kimura, *Radiation Brain Moms and Citizen Scientists: The Gender Politics of Food Contamination after Fukushima* (Durham, Duke University Press 2016); C. Reiher, "Food safety and consumer trust in post-Fukushima Japan" (2017) 29:1 *Japan Forum* 53, 53–76; N. Sternsdorff-Cisterna, "Food after Fukushima: Risk and Scientific Citizenship in Japan" (2015) 117:3 *American Anthropologist* 455, 455–467; A. H. Kimura, *Radiation Brain Moms and Citizen Scientists: The Gender Politics of Food Contamination after Fukushima.* (Duke University Press, 2016); T. Yamaguchi, and J. Joo-Young, "Coping with Food Safety Risks Information Sources and Responses by Residents in Japan in the Aftermath of the Fukushima Nuclear Accident." In T. Mayer and M. D. Anderson (eds), *Food Insecurity: A Matter of Justice, Sovereignty, and Survival* (Taylor & Francis, 2020), 197–213.

4 A Shukla-Jones et al., "Gene Editing in an International Context: Scientific, Economic and Social Issues Across Sectors" (2018) OECD Science, Technology and Industry Working Papers 2018/04;

DOI: 10.4324/9781003271918-16

the Comprehensive and Progressive Agreement for the Trans-Pacific Partnership, which went into force in 2018, and the EU-Japan Economic Partnership Agreement in 2019. These changes have built the expectations of people in industry who hope to expand their market while creating additional tensions for those who are concerned about the safety of novel foods.

One arena in which societal tensions surface is the use of health foods. Health foods are met with high expectations from people in industry, both domestic and abroad, who are trying to enter into the Japanese market or expand their market share, yet at the same time, such foods also raise safety concerns. Japan's health food market is currently said to be the world's third largest and is expected to grow further,[5] but health consequences of the misuse and overuse of health foods have been observed.[6] These observations suggest that in trying to understand the issues related to the food and agricultural sector in contemporary society, it is important to understand the concerns that arise over the safety and quality of food in the wake of expectations of future market growth.

Against this backdrop, this chapter sheds light on discourses surrounding the use of health foods, in particular where societal concerns over safety and expectations about the use of science and technology in making novel foods intersect with expectations of market expansion. Given that there are multiple interests and issues at stake, it will be useful to map out conflicting social phenomena and competing interpretations on the use of health improvement food. The chapter introduces two relevant cases in Japan: one an incident connected to controversies that surround "foods for specified health uses (FoSHU)-labeled" food products and the second a set of food labeling policies that was introduced in 2015 called "Foods with Functional Claims." In this chapter, I draw on an analysis of regulatory texts such as minutes of expert committees, governmental reports, and reports and letters published by consumer groups as well as data obtained from participant observation of seminars and forums that relate to health foods. Section II introduces the analytical lenses that are used to understand the two cases. Section III provides background to this study by introducing how health foods are regulated in Japan. Then cases are described and analyzed.

II. Analytical Lens to Map Out Contours of Controversies

In any situation where multiple interests compete, varying conceptions of moral values surface by which actors attempt to convey their opinions and ideas

RD Warner, "Review: Analysis of the Process and Drivers for Cellular Meat Production" (2019) 13:12 Animal 3041.

5 USDA, "Japan Health Foods Market Overview" (USDA FAS) <https://www.fas.usda.gov/regions/japan> last accessed 20 April 2021.

6 T Fukushima, "Shiroutoniyoru Kenkoshokuhin no Riyo [The Use of Healthy Food by Lay People]" (2014) 24:2, *The Japanese Journal of Health and Medical Sociology* Hoken 48; K Umegaki, "Positive and Negative Aspects of Food with Health Claims in Japan" (2015) 61, *Journal of Nutritional Science and Vitaminology* S133.

while also appealing to a sense of the common good that transcends particular interests. When controversies erupt with regard to safety concerns over food, discourses are frequently driven by these. *Cité*, a concept that lays out the varying values that individuals may hold with respect to the social order, will help us understand varying meanings about the issue in contention.[7] What this concept suggests is that issues surrounding the novel foods are not static but are rather an emergent arising from the negotiation of meanings about the novel foods. There are six *cités* (or orders of moral value) which are suggested by Boltanski and Thévenot, of which four are relevant for the present discussion. *Civic* worth is based on the idea of what is best for a collective, such as an organization, city, or nation. Actors lay claim to worthiness by presenting themselves as representatives of the interests of the collective. Stakeholders negotiating within this order attempt to justify their positions or actions using the collective conscience as the basis for their claims. Scientific methods and technological objects have their place in the order of *Industrial* worth. Claims are framed in terms of technical efficiency, scalability, and proper functionality. Within this order of worth, the evidence presented to support claims of legitimacy is technical and objectively measurable. A system is organized in such a way that things are technically predictable. *Market* worth is distinct from Industrial justification. Whereas Industrial justification appeals to notions such as effectiveness, Market justification is based on the desires of individuals to own the same objects as others or to acquire rare things, driving a sense of competition. Within this order of worth, price is a signal of value. For instance, firms appeal to the Market order of worth when they reference their product's position in the marketplace (such as "The number-one seller") or speak in terms of "beating the competition." *Domestic* worth draws on notions pertaining to the family and to ideas of tradition, loyalty, and trustworthiness. Within the Domestic order of worth, hierarchies (such as the distinction between those who have greater expertise and those who have less) come with a duty of care: superiors are expected to provide care to subordinates. For example, firms draw on the values of the Domestic order when they refer to such concepts as loyalty, trust, and a commitment to their customers' well-being. As we will see, all four of these orders of worth come into play in discourse concerning health foods.

III. Health Food Regulations in Japan

Health food regulation is primarily built on the Industrial order of worth; the dominant idea is that health food regulation functions properly as long as the system is built logically and rationally—for instance, using scientific data. The assumption is that consumers will use the available information, such as facts provided on product labels, to make reasoned decisions about which products will be best for their health.

7 L. Boltanski and L. Thévenot, *On Justification: Economies of Worth* (Princeton University Press, 2006).

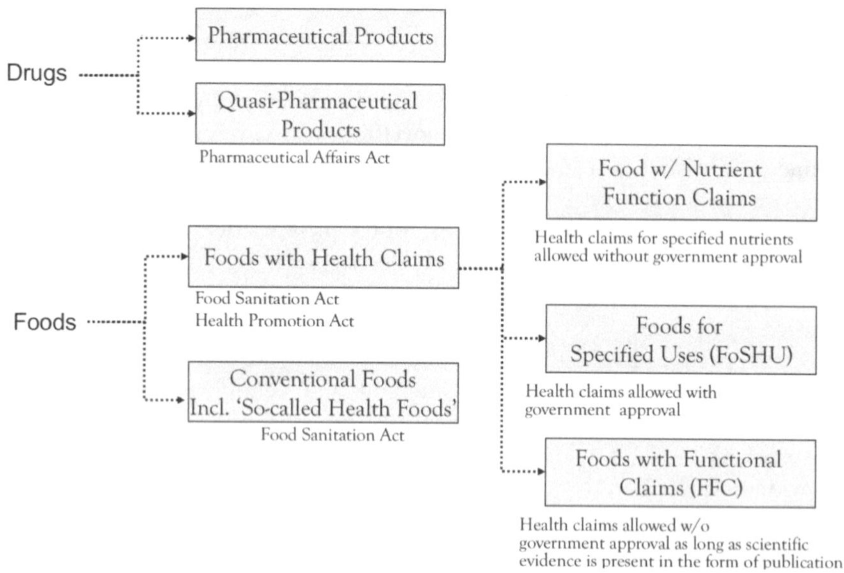

Figure 12.1 Classification of foods and drugs in Japan

Source: Translated by the author from the information available at www.caa.go.jp/policies/policy/food_labeling/foods_with_function_claims/pdf/150810_2.pdf

Health food regulation in Japan is organized in terms of the regulatory categories "Foods with Health Claims" (FHC), "So-Called 'Health Foods'," and "General Foods" (see Figure 12.1). FHC are defined as foods that alter physiological functions and have characteristics partway between those of a drug and those of a conventional food.[8] FHC are divided further into three subcategories defined by differences in purpose and function: "Foods with Nutrient Function Claims" (FNFC), "FoSHU" and "Foods with Functional Claims" (FFC). FNFC refers to foods that are labeled with the functions of nutritional ingredients (vitamins and minerals). FNFC do not require the government's permission for health claims for specified nutrients. FoSHU carry a health claim that indicates a physiological effect on the human body, and manufacturers are required to submit data from clinical trials of the product if FoSHU certification is sought. Foods categorized as FFC, a category newly introduced in 2015, also carry functional claims on the labels, but the FFC category does not require governmental approval or oversight; instead, manufacturers are responsible for determining the safety and functionality of their products by

8 H Ohama et al., "Health Food and Foods with Health Claims in Japan," in D Bagchi (ed), *Nutraceutical and Functional Food Regulations in the United States and Around the World* (Amsterdam, Elsevier 2008).

substantiating them in published literature.[9] Then there is the category of Non-FoSHU products (which are called "So-Called 'Health Foods") that may have the appearance of food, drinks, or tablets; these do not require permission from the Consumer Affairs Agency (CAA), the governmental organization charged with oversight of food standards and health claims. Labeling regulations prohibit manufacturers from making specific health or nutrient claims for products in this category.

Put differently, the regulatory framework recognizes four different types of foods, governed by different types of laws: FNFC do not require application, registration, or prior notification to the government as long as companies meet the standards set by Japan's Consumer Affairs Agency; FoSHU involve safety evaluation and approval by the government; with regard to FFC, companies must notify and provide the CAA with scientific information on the safety and functionality of their products, but marketing is not subject to government permission. Meanwhile, foods that are categorized as "So-Called Health Foods" require no special oversight but cannot be accompanied by specific claims about health effects.

Given this patchwork of multiple regulatory categories under which health-promoting foods are designated, it may not be surprising that consumers are sometimes misdirected or misinterpret information about health claims. The types of health foods sold in the marketplace range from general foods to functional foods and from food-like dietary supplements to medicine-like supplements, and government authorities require widely varying amounts of scientific evidence and oversight to ensure the safety and efficacy of each of these foods. Indeed, the rise of health foods blurs the boundaries between food and drugs in the eyes of consumers. The result is that health foods are met with high expectations of drug-like health effects by some, but because they are understood by others to be foods, the possibility of health risks arising from misuse, overconsumption, or drug interactions is not widely recognized. Thus, the possibility that such foods might, similarly to drugs, have unforeseen side effects is not taken into consideration by consumers.[10] These circumstances present a challenge to the governing authorities because consumers' blanket understanding that "health food" that is sold in the market is safe and effective sets the stage for social confusion and in some cases leads to health problems.

Indeed, cases have been reported in which ingestion of certain types of health foods have led to health problems, generating side effects or allergic reactions, sometimes even resulting in death. For example, the National Consumer Affairs Center (NCAC) of Japan, an independent administrative agency

9 A. Saito, *"Daisan no Seido 'Kinousei Hyouji Shokuhin' no Gaiyo to Kadai" [The Third Institution: Overview and Challenges of "Foods with Functional Claims"]'* in *Rippo* to Chosa 368 (Bureau of House of Councilors, 2015), 86–100.

10 Cabinet Office, *Shōhisha no [Kenkou Shokuhin] no Riyou ni kansuru Jittaichōsa [Report on the Consumers' Use of Health Foods]* (The Consumer Commission, 2019), <https://www.cao.go.jp/consumer/doc/20120605_chōsa houkoku.pdf >.

for consumer advocacy, reports a substantial number of incidents that required medical attention.[11] Further, the Japan Medical Association (JMA) acknowledges that the misuse and overuse of health foods constitutes a serious public health threat for Japanese society and has been carrying out projects to establish a system for medical doctors who are members of the JMA to share information regarding health problems related to health foods. It has also been trying to establish a systematic method for clinics to disseminate information to patients about the proper use of health foods.[12] Although the number of cases may appear small in proportion to the Japanese population overall, the problem is serious and includes reported fatalities.

The present medical infrastructure is not set up to provide an effective response to these problems because thus far health problems arising from health foods—such as interactions between drugs and health foods—have not been addressed carefully by either patients or medical doctors. Patients rarely mention the use of health foods to medical doctors at the clinic, and medical doctors rarely ask patients about the use of health foods when prescribing drugs. Insufficient clinical data have been collected on drug interactions with health foods,[13] simply because the concept of such interactions was not recognized until very recently. Combined with the complex regulatory framework, the lack of clinical data underscores the point that consumers are not as protected as they think they are. Health claim labeling policies were meant to empower consumers make informed choices about what to eat, based on the assumption that consumers would read and be able to understand what is written on the labels and would then be able to figure out how to relate daily intake of those foods to their everyday eating practices. In summary, regulations applying to functional foods rest on the assumptions of the *Industrial order of worth*, whereby informed consumers will use information provided by regulatory agencies to promote and protect their health. Other societal considerations, such as practical and economic needs or social relational and symbolic influences of the use of health foods are not a part of the logic that shapes the existing regulatory framework.[14]

IV. Controversies Over FoSHU Products

The market demand for health-promoting foods such as functional foods is high in Japan, and food manufacturers continue to innovate, bringing new products to market. Among companies selling health-promoting foods, Fima,[15] a chemical and cosmetics company, has kept its presence in the market by

11 National Consumers Affairs Center, *Annual Report on Consumer Affairs*. (Tokyo: NCAC, 2014).

12 Japan Medical Association, *Iwayuru Kenko Shokuhin ni tsuite – Nihon-ishikai no Tachiba kara [Assessing health foods from medical stand points]*. (Handout distributed at the Second Expert Meeting on Labeling of Health Foods, 2009).

13 Ibid.

14 L. Holm, "Food Health Policies and Ethics: Lay Perspectives on Functional Foods", (2003) 16:6 *Journal of Agricultural and Environmental Ethics*, 531, 531–544.

15 Pseudonym.

selling cooking oil, salad dressing, and mayonnaise that are certified as Foods for Specified Health Uses since 1999.[16] FoSHU is a category of food which has "functional ingredients" that provide the special health benefits claimed on the label.[17] Its specially branded line of FoSHU products sold well. They were seen as helpful in preventing the rise of neutral fats in the blood and in lowering cholesterol levels. Its cooking oil was a huge commercial success. Major news companies and TV programs carried stories about the products when they were first introduced to the market in 1999, and the products sold out quickly once they were on store shelves.[18] Its label carried the seal of FoSHU approval and also a recommendation by expert groups such as the Japan Society of Ningen Dock, all of which endorsed the safety of its use and the validity of its health claims.

An uproar about the product erupted ten years after the product launch due to food safety concerns reported in the news. The issue was the presence of high levels of glycidol esters in this cooking oil, substances which "may" transform into glycidol during the deodorization processes. Glycidol (unlike glycidol esters) is classified as "probably carcinogenic to humans" by the International Agency for Research on Cancer (IARC), a part of the World Health Organization specializing in cancer prevention and control.[19] As in the case of other food safety problems, regulators in Japan began to look into the problem in an effort to determine any safety risks. For instance, the Food Safety Commission recommended that "Investigation of health effects [should] be done immediately," a statement which was reported in the newspaper,[20] triggering consumer interest groups to act upon this incident. However, to date, the scientific knowledge available does not provide a definitive answer to the problem, as evidenced in IARC's use of the term "may." In particular, the question of the extent to which glycidol esters will transform into glycidol, and the extent to which glycidol will morph into a suspected carcinogen after it is in the human body, are uncertain.[21] Finally, one additional important reason that this incident was seen as highly problematic was that this particular vegetable cooking oil carried the government-approved FoSHU label, which suggests that the safety and efficacy of the product were scientifically demonstrated by the manufacturer and subsequently confirmed by the government.[22]

16 MJ Nikkei, *Shokuyo Abura [Cooking oil]* (2005).

17 R.Bailey, "Functional Foods in Japan: FOSHU and "Foods with Nutrient Function Claims," in Clare M. Hasler (ed.), *Regulation of Functional Foods and Nutraceuticals: A Global Perspective* (IFT Press, 2005) 247, 247–262.

18 S. Nikkei, *Shokuyo Abura Takakutemo Tokuho [Cooking oil, expensive but Tokuho]* (2008).

19 IARC's summaries and evaluations of glycidol are found, *available at* www.inchem.org/documents/iarc/vol77/77-14 (last accessed Jan. 3, 2021).

20 Mainichi Shinbun, *Econa Shohin Hanbai Teishi [Sales of Econa Stops]* (2009).

21 Y. Katsuragi, "Recent Glycidyl Gatty Acid Esters in Food Safety" (2016) 25(1) *Journal of Lipid Nutrition* 15, 15–24.

22 H. Yoshida, "Daihittoshohin de Roteishita Tokuho no Kekkan" [Issues of FoSHU: Problems Emerged from the Discontinued Sales of Econa] (2009) 44:21 *Keizaikai* 58, 58–60.

Sparked by concerns about the unintended amount of glycidol esters present that "may" transform into a carcinogenic substance once ingested, discussions took place in various arenas, including government-commissioned expert committees involving multiple stakeholders such as representatives of industry, consumer groups, and mass media, as well as lobbying efforts by consumer groups. Concerns were expressed about the safety of this specific product and at the same time about the current FoSHU approval system, such as how the government will deal with the situation if a new risk factor is later found with a FoSHU-approved product. Appealing to collective conscience, consumer interest groups demanded that scientists develop methods to determine risks, that regulators translate the scientific data into more precautionary policy prescriptions, and that companies disclose any relevant scientific data about the hazardous substances and the measures taken to deal with the risks.[23]

In response to the situation, Fima moved quickly to suspend its use of the FoSHU label and recall products that were on the market before the Consumer Affairs Agency, an agency newly established in 2009 with jurisdiction over a range of consumer problems, including oversight of food safety–related matters, could make a decision to revoke FoSHU status. Meanwhile, voices calling into question the credibility of the FoSHU approval system and the effectiveness of regulatory oversight were heard in popular magazines and on various web sites. For instance, a lengthy article covering this incident and criticizing the regulatory procedures appeared in places such as a popular weekly women's magazine.[24] Meanwhile, consumer hotlines were established at the company. In the end, on September 16, 2009, Fima suspended shipments within Japan of its 59 Directed Acyclic Graph (DAG)-based products, citing the presence of glycidol esters in high density.

> We are taking immediate action by temporarily halting the sale and shipment of these products until the amount of *fatty acid glycidol esters* in [brand name of the cooking oil] and related products can be lowered to levels similar to common cooking oils. . . . While we believe our products have been and are safe, we are nevertheless taking this extra precaution as a way to assure our customers that they can continue to enjoy our products with confidence.
>
> (News Release by the Company, September 16, 2009)[25]

Although the CAA said on October 8, 2009, that it would move to revoke FoSHU status for Fima's DAG-based product line, the company had already

23 Shufuren (Japan Housewives Association), "Opinion Statement for Revoking FoSHU Status of Econa Cooking Oil" (*Shufuren*, 11 September 2009) <https://shufuren.net/requests/requests112/> last accessed 20 April 2021.

24 Jyosei Seven, *Shokuno Anzen Gray Zone [Gray Zone of Food Safety]* (Tokyo, Shogakukan （日文：小学館), Oct. 8 2009).

25 *Available at* www.kao.com/jp/corp_news/2009/20090916_002.html (last accessed June 13, 2018).

voluntarily relinquished the FoSHU label before the agency could take action. This move allowed the company to make a public display of commitment to values shared with the consumers: the company implies that it is staying fully informed about the science relevant to DAG-based cooking oil, that it is committed to developing and selling what is safe and effective, and that it is committed to giving consumers healthier choices in food. Moreover, it implies that it is committed to not only providing information to consumers but also listening to the needs and demands of consumers, thus fulfilling its role as a caretaker of consumers.

Seeing this as a serious problem, an array of consumer interest groups such as the Nippon Association of Consumer Specialists, Consumers Union of Japan, National Consumers' Group Communications Association, Housewives' Federation, Japanese Consumers' Cooperative Union, and others have become actively involved in issues related to the glycidol esters incident. Some are represented on the commissions at the regulatory agencies such as the Consumer Commission, while others have worked on this issue outside the public policy arena, forming external pressure groups to influence regulatory agencies and industry. Although there are diverse perspectives on food and its safety among these interest groups, consumer interest groups across the board see problems with the current health food system—inadequate labeling, misleading advertisements, lack of information about its safety and efficacy—all of which have led to difficulties in understanding the safety and efficacy of health foods; all felt that something needed to be done. Among consumer interest groups, the Food Safety Citizens' Watch, Consumer Union of Japan, and Housewives' Federation took a clear position on DAG-based cooking oil much earlier than the time at which the problem became widely known. They requested regulatory agencies to withdraw approval of FoSHU from their product lines, to ban the sale of products, to disclose scientific data and explain problems in a way that non-expert consumers can understand, to manage problems by taking a "worst-case scenario" stance, and to carry out health impact studies on consumers who have used the products long term. Throughout the time until the company removed the products from the shelf, these groups monitored how the problem was dealt with—or not dealt with—by regulatory agencies and described what they believed needed to be done, using their web sites and petitions to regulatory agencies based on their model of the role and responsibilities of the regulatory agencies. The logic underlying these actions is in tension with the prevailing reality that the choice to introduce a novel food is rooted in reasoning within the Industrial and Market orders of worth, in which government and industries expect that individual consumers will be responsible for their choices, and reasoning within the Civic and Domestic orders of worth, in which consumer groups attempt to represent the interests of individual consumers while also asking for the company's commitment to consumers' well-being. At an emergency public forum organized by a consumer interest group immediately after the incidence, voices were heard from the floor saying "We thought that the Consumer Affairs Agency was established to work from the

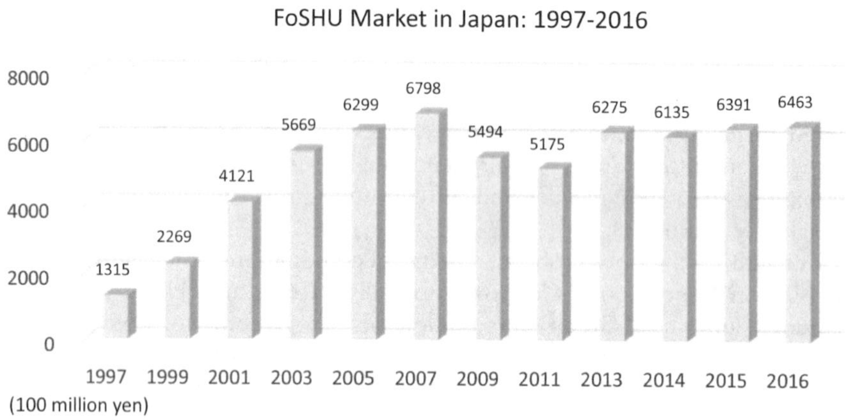

Figure 12.2 FoSHU market in Japan: 1997–2016

Adapted and translated from the web site of Japan Health Food & Nutrition Association, 2016, https://jhnfa.org/tokuho-market.html

perspective of consumers"—directly calling into question assumptions about the responsibility assigned to individual consumers in this situation.

Fima published a risk communication brochure one year after the incident. In that document, the director of Consumer Communication Center of the company reflects upon what had and had not been done and what could and should have been done. In those reflections, phrases and words such as "a consumer-oriented company," "trust," "consumers' right to know," and "stands by consumers" are heavily used, such that one could clearly see how the company is trying to appeal to consumers by using values in the realm of the Domestic order of worth: sending the message that they are being looked after. A closer look at the way this situation unfolded reveals some of the ways in which the discourse around FoSHU-certified foods is shaped by negotiations structured within different orders of worth. These differences arguably contribute to confusion and mismatches between consumers' expectations and the reality that surrounds the use of health-promoting foods.

V. New Food Labeling Policies Adopted in 2015

From the early years of introducing functional foods, values hinging on Market orders of worth have prevailed. While the link between food and health is not new in Japan, as exemplified by the idiom *Ishoku Dogen*; "a balanced diet leads to a healthy body"), the concept of functional foods did not gain widespread recognition until the early 1980s, when the world's first functional food, a sports drink called "Pocari Sweat," launched in Japan. Seeing the market potential, food companies have actively promoted functional foods since then.[26] As industry responded to a high demand for such foods as calcium-fortified foods, dietary fiber drinks, and fermented soy protein drinks, and so on, by 2004, the size of the Japanese market for FoSHU is said to have reached more than 1 trillion yen (10 billion US dollars)[27] and then again doubled in the following 10 years.[28] Occupying a middle ground between food and drugs, functional foods are seen by industry as offering endless marketing opportunities to health-conscious consumers in Japan and are a fast-growing, multi-billion-dollar industry. Indeed, functional foods maintained a significant presence in the Japanese market over the ten-year period beginning in 1997.

Though functional foods have gained a prominent position in the market, one needs to recall that the term "functional foods" is primarily a marketing term referring to varying types of foods, such as traditional foods with newly defined significance or newly formulated foods whose ingredients or formulation may be novel. The term "functional food" is commonly used in our daily life, and there is a scientific journal dedicated to the subject, but there remains a lack of consensus on a definition of the term.

Interestingly, for Japanese consumers, the *Market order of worth* plays a role in determining the desirability of foods. When health-promoting foods are available in the market, price is read by consumers as a signal of quality; thus a signal within the Market order of worth may be used by both manufacturers and consumers to evaluate quality of functional foods. For instance, a consumer participant at a government-organized public forum on health foods points out:[29]

> It is true that we tend to be attracted to expensive health improvement foods because it seems that expensive ones have more effect than others. [If they are expensive], naturally we expect those will have more effects.
>
> (comments by a participant in the public forum)

The 2015 Reform was an extension of this thinking. Drawing on assumptions within the Market order of worth, people in policy circles and businesses shared the sense that the food regulations that existed before 2015 were hindering businesses from being competitive in the market. Among the three categories of foods with health claims, namely FNFC, FoSHU, and

26 T Takeda and Y Fujita, *Hitto o Sodateru! Shokuhin no Kinousei Marketing [Creating a Hit! Marking of Nutritional Components]* (Tokyo, Nikkei BP 2017).

27 CMC Books, *Kinousei Shokuhinsozai no Shijyodoko [Market Trends of New Food Materials]*. (CMC, 2005).

28 Association of Health Economics Research Social Insurance and Welfare, *Shokuhinkino to Kenko nikansuru Anketo Hokokusho [A Report on the Survey on Food Function and Health)]* (Shokuhinkino to Kenko-vision Kenkyukai, 2009).

29 The Ministry of Health, Labor and Welfare organized a risk communication program in 2006. Minutes, *available at* http://kouseikyoku.mhlw.go.jp/hokkaido/gyomu/bu_ka/shokuhin/risuku_090309.html (last accessed June 10, 2018).

FFC, FoSHU occupied the largest market share, but people in business saw some signs that the market was no longer growing by 2009, particularly when trends were compared with the upward trend witnessed from late the 1990s to early 2000s[30] (see Figure 12.2). Parallel to this was the announcement by Prime Minister Shinzo Abe that the government would reform health claims of foods for the purpose of enabling consumers to make informed decisions about foods that would help them to lead a healthy life.[31] In line with the usual pattern of food policy decision-making processes, once such statement was made by the prime minister, there were cascading activities by councils and committees mandated to work on details about the content and workings of the rules. For instance, following up on what was stated by the prime minister, the Regulation Reform Council (RRC) suggested that the then-current regulatory framework of FNFC and FoSHU was limiting the capabilities of Japanese companies that might otherwise be able to expand on their product lines and increase market share and was preventing some, especially small and medium-sized companies, from entering into the health food market. Using the US Dietary Supplement Health and Education Act as a model, the RRC indicated that Japan would consider yet another category of foods with health claims, by which companies are required only to notify the government about their launch of new lines of products as long as their safety and efficacy have been proven in existing scientific literature. The council again reiterated that these efforts are made in light of people's desire to lead long and healthy lives. Thereafter, an expert committee mandated to give advice to the government was convened, consisting of scientists such as nutrition scientists, molecular nutritionists, a clinical doctor, a magazine editor, people representing industry associations, and a representative of consumer groups, along with others. This committee was tasked with working out the details of how to put the category of Food with Functional Claims in place, not with making the basic decision as to whether to introduce a new category of foods with health claims.[32]

A series of meetings was held by the committee, and in April 2015, the CAA announced to the public that the Japanese government would introduce the third category of health claim labeling for food. This category of voluntary labeling, FFC, allows companies to display a product's specific health benefits on retail food packaging. Unlike the situation with FoSHU certification, no government approval is required for the labels of foods designated FFC. While the FoSHU label states that the product has been approved by the CAA, the label for FFC says the product's function claims have not been individually reviewed by the agency.

30 M. Emoto, *Hoken Kinoushokuhin no Shijyokaihatsu to Kadai [Market Development of Functional Foods and Its Challenge]* (JAS Net, 2016).

31 The text of the speech "The Third Growth Strategy" by Prime Minster Abe, *available at* www.kantei.go.jp/jp/96_abe/statement/2013/0605speech.html (last accessed July 5, 2020).

32 Material distributed at the advisory committee, *available at* www.caa.go.jp/policies/policy/food_labeling/other/review_meeting_003/ (last accessed July 5, 2020).

Businesses have shown strong interest in the new system. From the perspective of people in business, the reform that took place in 2015 is seen as a deregulation of functional foods, because the government's requirements are much less rigorous than those for obtaining FoSHU certification; the result is more rapid introduction of products with smaller product-development costs. In fact, the development of a FoSHU product typically takes three to five years, whereas FNFC require two years at maximum. For a food product to quality for a FoSHU level to prove its safety and efficacy, clinical tests are required to obtain data. The questionnaire carried out by the Institute for Health Economics and Policy (2009) demonstrated that the majority of the 1,556 Japanese companies that responded to their questionnaire reported that they spent 20 million yen (approximately 200,000 US dollars) for the development of a FoSHU product, while as much as 36% of the companies responded that they had spent more than 40 million yen (approximately 400,000 US dollars) for such development, while another 12% of respondents indicated that they had spent more than 100 million yen (approximately 1 million US dollars). Responses to the questionnaire suggested that the costs incurred for research and development of a new line of FoSHU product are exorbitant to the point that the regulatory framework has been hindering the entry of small and medium-sized companies into the market, even though the market seems to be lucrative. In other words, the FoSHU system has had a serious scale bias from an industry point of view.

Seen as a newly emergent business opportunity, the changes made in 2015 were also welcomed by people outside Japan. For example, a US government report candidly stated:

> . . . this new FFC registration process is more affordable and faster than the registration process for Food for Specialized Health Uses (FoSHU). CAA also revised its regulations for Food with Nutrient Functional Claims (FNFC) to increase product eligibility, to expand the list of eligible nutrients, and to include fresh foods. These changes by the CAA should create new opportunities for U.S. exporters to the world's third largest health food market.[33]

Ideas hinging on Market justification have triggered various visible phenomena. Among many noticeable changes was a dramatic increase in the number of notifications regarding FFC, while the number of applications to be certified for FoSHU has been declining. The change in food labeling policies has transformed the Japanese market structure rapidly.[34]

33 United States Department of Agriculture, Foreign Agricultural Service, 'Japan's New Health Claims Labeling System Creates Opportunities' (2015), <https://www.fas.usda.gov/data/japan-japan-s-new-health-claims-labeling-system-creates-opportunities>.

34 Japan Health Food and Nutrition Association, "Tokuho Shijyo 6,391-oku Yen, Kako Nibanme no Kibo ni Shinchou [FoSHU Market Reached 631.1 Billion Yen, Becoming The Second Biggest Market]" (*JHFNA*, 1 April 2019) <https://www.jhnfa.org/tokuho2018.pdf>.

The 2015 Reform highlights issues of the food policy decision-making process in Japan that pertain to competing public policy agendas such as responding to the public's concerns while promoting the growth of industry. The way in which the government justified the 2015 Reform was to state that introducing the new category of health claims to food would support the dual goals of growth in the Japanese economy and making a contribution to public health. Food labels that carry functional claims are framed as an appropriate mechanism for consumers to make informed choices and for businesses to be given an opportunity to enter the market or expand their market share. However, not everyone necessarily agreed with the statements that the government made. Critics with expertise in food safety as well as representatives of consumers groups have raised concerns about the varying ways in which the information on labels can be interpreted (similar to the case of other types of health foods) as well as the varying ways in which businesses within the food industry define an adequate level of evidence to claim foods as safe. Within the community of food safety experts, the standard for determining the safety of substances in food is using "the empirical evidence from prior history of safe use." In the absence of a prior history of safe use, potential new functional ingredients must be evaluated for safety before introduction into the market. If that is the case, the safety evaluation of new functional ingredients should adhere to the same safety testing principles used for other substances and should replicate the intended use levels.[35] The Committee which worked on the details of 2015 Reform chose not to specify years required for history of safe use and suggested that the required years would vary "case by case." This stance has led companies to define safety in varying ways, resulting in a situation in which some companies interpret a scientific protocol in a precautionary manner, while others proceed to sell products that might not necessarily have sufficient evidence. In principle, the safety evaluation of new functional ingredients should adhere to the same safety testing principles used for other substances and should replicate the intended use levels, but that has not always been the case, as indicated in the government report.[36]

VI. Consumer Perspectives

While technology-induced change in food is not new, the rise of functional foods adds a new dimension that could initiate changes in the practices of consumers. The influx of new ideas reflecting conventions of the Industrial order of worth requires consumers to reconfigure their understanding of

35 S. U. Fabiansson, "Safety Consideration in Developing Functional Foods in Yasmine Motarjemi", Gerald Moy and E.C.D. Todd, Yasmine (eds.), *Encyclopedia of Food Safety* (CA: Academic Press, 2014) 422, 422–426.

36 Report, *available at* www.caa.go.jp/policies/policy/food_labeling/other/review_meeting_008/ (last accessed Jan. 24, 2021).

health-promoting foods and their uses. The proliferation of health-promoting foods continues and presents a new challenge to consumers: determining how one can evaluate the quality of these novel foods in terms of their safety and figure out the efficacy of their purported nutritional benefits for oneself.[37] Some food packages claim that their contents promote good health, while others make more dubious claims, such as acting as defense against diseases. For consumers, making the "right" choice for their needs is becoming increasingly difficult, given the complexity arising from the existence of various types of health-promoting foods with widely varying amounts of scientific evidence provided for the safety and efficacy of each one.

Regardless of health incidents that arise from the misuse and overuse of healthy foods, the presence of health-promoting foods in the Japanese market is strong.[38] It is interesting to note that, in contrast to the situation with genetically modified foods, which have a very limited market presence, and which have faced intense opposition in Japanese society, conflicts over functional foods have been less intense; in general, their use is socially accepted, and fewer concerns are expressed. One reason is that consumers perceive functional foods as foods, first and foremost, and thus treat them as foods (unless and until there is a specific health scare involving some food, such as the BSE outbreak). In this sense, health-promoting foods are likely to be evaluated by consumers within the Domestic order of worth. Food is seen as something that is traditional, thus reliable, associated with family and with nourishment[39]—all themes within the Domestic order of worth. But at the same time, consumers rely on Industrial-order claims of efficacy and thus have high expectations that functional foods will be safe and have drug-like health effects. Because these products are seen as food and interpreted within the Domestic order of worth, health risks arising from misuse or overconsumption are not widely recognized. Instead, Japanese consumers appear to be guided by the expectation that industry and the government will perform the functions of ensuring absolute safety. The longstanding cultural expectation of *anzen-anshin* (Japanese idiom, roughly translatable as "safety and peace of mind" but implying "absolute absence of risk") reinforces the expectation that foods distributed in the market have been thoroughly investigated by the government and that products will not be allowed on the market if there is any doubt as to safety.[40] This expectation reflects the values

37 T Chiba et al., "Inappropriate Application of Food for Specified Health Uses" (2014) 67(4) Nippon Eiyo Shokuryo Gakkaishi 177; Consumer Affairs Agency, *Kinōsei Hyōji Shokuhinsedo nitaisuru Shōhishaikoutouni kansuru Chōsajigyohoukokusho [Report of the Consumer Survey of Foods with Functional Claim]* (CAA, 2017).

38 Japan Health Food and Nutrition Food Association., *Kenko Shokuhin ni kansuru Chosa [A Report on Survey on Health Foods]* (JHFNA. 2003).

39 A. Allison, "Japanese Mothers and Obentōs: The Lunch-Box as Ideological State Apparatus", (1991) 64:4 *Anthropological Quarterly* 195, 195–208.

40 T. Yamaguchi, "Social Imaginary and Dilemmas of Policy Practice: The Food Safety Arena in Japan" (2014) 45 *Food Policy* 167, 167–173.

of the Domestic order of worth, in which hierarchical relationships determine a duty of care on the part of the powerful (in this case, both government and industry) towards the less powerful.

Some consumer advocacy groups are aware of the ways in which consumers are misled by interests within the Market and Industrial orders of worth. For instance, at a public forum,[41] a consumer participant said:

> What confuses many of us consumers is that the fliers from the drug stores frequently advertise information on drugs and health foods in the same section. For example, it says "for helping to build a health body" or "for a party season", then puts drugs and health foods in the same section. Even at the drug stores, drugs and health foods are sold on the same shelf. We cannot help but think that health foods are similar to over-the-counter drugs.

Another attendee said:

> The name "health food" is misleading because it raises our expectation of having a positive health effect. Ads at the stores are not helpful either because they only emphasize the effects, not the risks.

There are plenty of misleading or extravagant advertisements that emphasize the health effects of health foods, raising high expectations by consumers that these foods will enable them to be proactive in making healthy choices and protecting their health, but consumers do not realize the irony that all the innovations taking place may actually be taking away some of the control of their life by introducing new, unexpected risk factors. In other words, because of the ways in which health foods are presented to them in the marketplace, consumers are misled and misinterpret what it means to buy and use the health foods available at the stores.

VII. Conclusion

This chapter attempted to map out contours of interpretations that surround health improvement foods in Japan, especially foods known as functional foods, which have been expected to offer consumers greater control over their health and nutritional choices and allow them to make informed choices. I argued that confusion on the part of consumers over the safety and efficacy of health-promoting foods cannot be resolved easily by the evidence-based solutions presented by the government, such as to manage risks and introduce food labels,

41 Ministry of Health, Labor and Welfare organized a risk communication program in 2006. Minutes, *available at* http://kouseikyoku.mhlw.go.jp/hokkaido/gyomu/bu_ka/shokuhin/risuku_090309.html (last accessed June 10, 2018).

that interpret the issues related to health-promoting foods within the Industrial order of worth. At the same time, what makes the situation more complex is the fact that people in industry value health-promoting foods in terms of market worthiness or competitiveness in the market, but their messages to the public tend to be framed using the values that lie in the Domestic order of worth. In other words, what complicates the use of health-promoting foods such as functional foods is that in lieu of actual, practical contributions to solving the problem, industry and government attempt to express how committed they are to supporting the core values of consumers, thus creating an illusion for consumers that somebody else is ensuring food safety for them.

Furthermore, shifting the emphasis of evaluation of the quality of food to the Industrial order of worth puts consumers in a vulnerable position when choosing foods. Health-promoting foods are regulated, and food labels are there, but how much data is available and to what extent the information on labels represents a real exchange of information are both highly questionable. After all, consumers, industry, and government have fundamentally different agendas for functional foods, with industry trying to sell its products, government trying to provide a certain amount of oversight while enabling the growth of an industry that is expected to help solve certain problems facing Japan, and consumers attempting to select foods that will meet their needs. The varied meanings which each group gives to the situation deriving from differing orders of worth manifest in the social processes that lead people to the consumption of health-promoting food, sometimes resulting in health problems. It should be noted that an opportunity was lost to actually translate the ideal of "informed consumers," which frequently appears in public policy statements, into reality. Consumers have the expectation that they will have all the necessary information to enable them to decide whether a food is safe or meets their needs, but in reality, multiple agendas are brought into the social arena that might not match one's expectation and values.

Given the importance of health-promoting foods for economy, the main food choice trends may shift increasingly to ones that reflect the Industrial order of worth, representing a convergence of perspectives on worth by industry and government. These trends will further blur the boundaries of food and drugs. Seeing health-promoting foods in this light helps us understand that in the end, conflicts over food safety are expressions of the kind of world that one wants to live in. Thus, respecting the existence of differing systems of values and orders of worth becomes all the more important in trying to envision an ideal food safety governance.

13 Effective Health Foods Versus Ineffective Drugs

Governing and Marketing Glucosamine Products in Taiwan

Yeh-Han Wang

I. Introduction: Defining "Health Food" in Taiwan

Food and drugs have long been established categories, but they are not necessarily dichotomous. The development and marketing of health food redefines the boundary of food and drugs, leading to difficulty in regulation. The potential controversy is not easily understood in people's daily lives, especially from the viewpoint of people in East Asia. Throughout the history of East Asian traditional medicine, "medicine–food homology," wherein people believe that certain foods are considerably healthier than others and can even substitute for drugs in treating or managing diseases, has been a widely accepted concept. This continues to the present day, with numerous food products on the market claiming to have medical benefits despite a lack of scientific justification. In Taiwan, the most common health foods are supplements (in tablet or capsule form) developed from herbs used in traditional Chinese medicine. The marketing of such supplements emphasizes their health effects, and their presentation blurs the distinction between food and drug. This ambiguity can be problematic. Furthermore, industry consensus on the boundaries between food and drugs is difficult to reach, leading to food safety concerns and complicating relevant regulation by the government.

Since the passing of the 1999 Health Food Control Act,[1] wherein it is defined as "food with healthcare effects," "Health Food" has been a formal legal term in Taiwan. Herein, I distinguish this term from health food in the everyday sense by capitalizing it. According to Article 2 of the Act, "health care effects" are only those that "have been scientifically proven to be capable of improving people's health and decreasing the harms and risks of diseases." Therefore, not every food with health claims is a Health Food by law. The law distinguishes Health Foods from drugs by noting that these health effects cannot involve "medical treatments aimed at treating or remedying human

1 The Act has been amended 5 times to date, and the latest amendment was in 2018. Laws & Regulations Database of the Republic of China, *available at* https://law.moj.gov.tw/ENG/LawClass/LawHistory.aspx?pcode=L0040012 (last accessed Jun. 23, 2020).

DOI: 10.4324/9781003271918-17

diseases." Furthermore, Health Foods "shall be announced [as such] by the central competent authority."[2]

After its amendment in 2006, the Health Food review and approval process has had two tracks. Track 1 reviews cases individually based on scientific evidence of the food's safety and healthcare effects, whereas Track 2 sets specific standards for individual ingredients or components. Currently, Track 1 approval for foods can be applied for under 13 categories of healthcare claims; a Health Food permit cannot be applied for any food with health claims outside the 13 categories. Many popular products are thus excluded from Health Food status application, such as those with claims of weight control or weight loss benefits, cosmetic functions, or relief of postmenopausal symptoms.[3] Among the thousands of health foods on the Taiwanese market, only 366 and 67 have obtained Health Food permits through Track 1 and Track 2, respectively.[4] To date, only two Track 2 ingredients have been announced by the Taiwan Food and Drug Administration (TFDA); the foods for which applications can be submitted through Track 2 are limited.[5] Therefore, the law only regulates a minority of so-called health foods. Health Foods should not be regarded as products on the food–drug spectrum but rather as a new socially and legally constructed category that overlaps with both food and drugs but is accompanied by distinct regulations. Numerous researchers in Taiwan have made similar arguments to mine. Cheng and Chen used the term "health techno-food" to describe various modern health foods and stress the effects on the food industry of emerging genetic technology and the adoption of modern medical knowledge. Cheng viewed the invention of Health Foods as a technosocial complex of policy, which created a new network encompassing the biotechnology, biomedical, and healthcare management industries.[6]

Most case studies centered on the technoscientific social network surrounding Health Foods have limited their discussions to herbal products, including those developed using traditional Chinese medicine ingredients. In one

2 Laws & Regulations Database of the Republic of China, *available at* https://law.moj.gov.tw/ENG/LawClass/LawHistory.aspx?pcode=L0040012 (last accessed Jun. 23, 2020).

3 The 13 categories of healthcare claims in Track 1 are: (1) improving gastrointestinal functions, (2) alleviating osteoporosis, (3) maintaining dental health, (4) modulating immune system, (5) protecting liver, (6) anti-fatigue, (7) delaying aging, (8) increasing intake of iron, (9) aiding blood pressure control, (10) avoiding body fat accumulation, (11) aiding the modulation of allergy status, (12) regulating blood sugar, and (13) lipid level. Only two ingredients have been announced to be applicable for Track 2: red rice yeast and fish oil.

4 Fei-Wen Cheng & Yinting Chen, "Risk, Technology and Food Safety—A Sociology Analysis of Taiwan Health Food" in Fu-Shih Lin (ed), *Food Technology and Modern Civilization* (New Taipei, Daw Shiang Publishing Co. 2010), at 146.

5 Database search of Health Food approved by Ministry of Health and Welfare, *available at* https://consumer.fda.gov.tw/Food/InfoHealthFood.aspx?nodeID=162 (last accessed Jun. 23, 2020).

6 Fei-Wen Cheng, "The Sociology of Techno-Food: An STS analysis of Health Food in Taiwan" in Fu-Shih Lin (ed), *Food Technology and Modern Civilization* (New Taipei, Daw Shiang Publishing Co. 2010), at 49–120.

study, An observed that the emergence of the Health Food category in Taiwan bridged the gap between food and drug regulations. The classification of a herbal product can changed from one category to the other if it is approved as a Health Food. For example, herbal products developed from traditional Chinese medicine–related knowledge or ingredients would initially be classified as being part of a broad food category, for the regulation is loose for food production. Later, testing of such products under TFDA-approved experimental protocols can provide scientific evidence of their health effects. Thus, the opportunity for their entry into the global pharmaceutical market may arise.[7] However, herbal products do not always successfully transition from food to drug. Red yeast rice is an example of a Health Food that was demonstrated in trials to be effective but was not accepted by medical professionals and failed to be classified as a drug.[8]

Separate from the issues of products derived from traditional herbal medicines, the use of certain agents as drugs in Western medicine has sparked controversy surrounding Health Food regulation in Taiwan. Herein, I present a case study of glucosamine, an ingredient widely used in drugs and health foods worldwide to manage degenerating osteoarthritis. The TFDA has not yet established a standard protocol for the use of glucosamine in animal experiments to prove its health effects. Therefore, glucosamine products are not classified as Health Foods in Taiwan. According to the TFDA's scientific review, glucosamine products can be classified as foods or drugs depending on the ingredients. This chapter describes how between-country or between-region differences in regulatory frameworks redefine the trajectory of objects, how industries or distributors shape the scientific discourse in coping with obscured food–drug boundaries, and how the Health Food Control Act failed to regulate glucosamine in Taiwan. The coproduction of scientific knowledge from the classification and regulation of foods and drugs in and across countries and regions is highlighted.

II. The Social Life of a Hybrid

I employ two central concepts derived from science, technology, and society (STS), namely classification and the social life of objects, to focus on the classifications and trajectories of health foods and the social processes they undergo.

Classification is almost always a political practice that is embedded in our daily lives, and the process is so natural that most people are not consciously aware of it. The classification process can be regarded as "naturalization" that "strip[s] away the contingencies of an object's creation and its situated nature"

7 Chin-Chih An, *From Four Agent Soup to Functional Foods: Biographies of Chinese Herbs in Contemporary Taiwan (1990–2008)* (Master's thesis, National Taiwan University 2008).

8 Yinting Chen, *Biotechnology Industry, Food Technology, and Commodifization: A Case Study of Red Rice Yeast Health Food in Taiwan* (Master's thesis, Tunghai University 2010).

(p. 299).[9] Classification also encounters resistance arising from the coexistence of multiple created identities. The multiplicity of identities blurs category boundaries, generating a "borderland" where an object has difficulty being classified. Multiple concepts, such as "boundary objects"[10] and "monsters,"[11] have been proposed for describing the interaction and politics of identities and categories.

I use a more general term, "hybrid," to cover the concepts of both boundary objects and monsters. Hybrid refers to an object with memberships in multiple categories. A hybrid is inevitably cultivated in a borderland, and the classification of a hybrid is so problematic that a resistance to naturalization is often encountered.[12] Hybrids also have a "plastic" nature that allows them "to adapt to local needs and the constraints of the several parties employing them."[13] Therefore, a hybrid dynamically outlines the boundaries and differentiates the membership, creating experiences of anomalies in practice.

Health food is a hybrid that obscures the boundary between food and drug. This causes issues for regulatory frameworks that are primarily established on the basis of the differences between a food and a drug. Given that classification can produce knowledge and regulate the flow of an object in terms of the exchange of commodities, regulating a hybrid is not only a political practice but also a process of creating or shaping a technoscientific social network. By generating uncertainty regarding the two categorical boundaries, this interactive process opens a regulatory system to the possibility of health food innovation.[14] Values from new products induce circulations of objects as commodities in society, which implies the transformation of identities across categories. Appadurai proposed the concept of the social life of objects to demonstrate that the value of commodities is defined by the process of exchange. With embedded values, complex standards and criteria that are gradually established at the intersection of temporal, cultural, and social factors govern the exchangeability of objects. However, both these standards and the process of exchange are constantly evolving in cultural and social contexts. As objects are exchanged,

9 Geoffrey C. Bowker & Susan L. Star, *Sorting Things Out: Classification and Its Consequences* (Cambridge, The MIT Press 1999).

10 Susan L. Star & James Griesemer, "Ecology, 'Translations' and Boundary Objects: Amateurs and Professionals in Berkeley's Museum of Vertebrate Zoology, 1907–39" (1989) 19(3) Soc. Stud. Sci. 387–420.

11 Donna Haraway, "The Promises of Monsters: A Regenerative Politics for Inappropriate/d Others" in Paula Treichler et al. (eds), *Cultural Studies New and in the Future* (Oxfordshire, Routledge 1992), at 295–337.

12 *See* footnote 11.

13 *See* footnote 10, 393.

14 Xaq Frohlich, "The Rise (and Fall) of the Food-Drug Line: Classification, Gatekeepers, and Spatial Mediation in Regulating U.S. Food and Health Markets" in Angela N. H. Creager & Jean-Paul Gaudillière (eds), *Risk on the Table: Food Production, Health, and the Environment* (New York, Berghahn Books 2021).

their identity shifts, and they can further cross boundaries. The tournaments of value from various communities thus define the social classification of objects.

The key to connecting the classification of a commodity with its value is knowledge. As objects flow through a community, knowledge regarding their production or consumption is distributed, and classification stands at the core of knowledge production. The concept from classification through knowledge to commodity provides a conceptual framework for further discussion of categories of foods and drugs and the borderland between them.

Classification systems are deeply embedded as infrastructure in clinical trials for pharmaceutical products.[15] The primary objective of such studies, the gold standard of which is the double-blind randomized controlled trial, is to prove the effectiveness of a drug. However, the effectiveness of a drug is highly sensitive to its classification. A simple example is that researchers can define the experimental and control groups by using any chosen interventional or observational criteria as categorical boundaries. This is assured to produce results, usually considered scientific fact, of either positive or negative findings based on the classifications. If a drug undergoing clinical trials is approved and enters the market, knowledge of its approval is circulated as if the classifications involved were naturally clear and rigid. However, the process of coproduction is often ignored, and the boundaries between categories of objects are never definitive.

From this broad perspective, the categories of foods and drugs can be regarded as being on a continuum, with safety and effectiveness being the distinguishing features of the food and drug ends of the spectrum, respectively. Regulators and manufacturers emphasize the safety of foods but stress the effectiveness of drugs; this delineates the boundary of the two categories. However, safety and effectiveness are not mutually exclusive. A pharmaceutical trial cannot be conducted without the safety of the drug first being proven. Moreover, ordinary foods can become health foods or functional foods if they are confirmed to have health effects. Therefore, the clear-cut boundary between foods and drugs is more akin to a traditional artifact, and safety and effectiveness alone are not sufficient for defining and justifying the current regulatory system.

To elaborate on how the circulation and exchange of an object shapes the knowledge and regulations rooted in the borderland between categories, I documented the social life of glucosamine products in Taiwan. Not every country or region regulates glucosamine products as drugs; for example, glucosamine products are considered drugs in Europe but foods in the United States. Following a scientific review by the TFDA, glucosamine products in Taiwan could be classified as foods or drugs depending on their ingredients. Therefore, both food and drug forms of glucosamine are currently available on the market. By retrieving documents from two databases, I traced the history of one particular glucosamine product, Viartril-S, the most common drug

15 Yeh-Han Wang, *Pharmaceutical Knowledge and Classification: The Development of Iressa and the Changing Diagnostic Practices of Lung Cancer* (Master's thesis, National Yang-Ming University 2018).

made with glucosamine sulfate in the world. First, to examine the production of knowledge on the medical effectiveness of glucosamine products, the PubMed database was searched for studies by using the keywords "glucosamine" and "osteoarthritis" under the category of "clinical trial." Second, to investigate the social life of Viartril-S in Taiwan, I searched Taiwan's largest online news database, that established by *United Daily News*, for newspaper articles containing the keywords of "glucosamine," "Wei-Gu-Li," (維骨力, the Chinese brand name of Viartril-S), and "arthritis." Third, I searched Google by using the keywords of "Dona" (the brand name of Viartril-S in the United States), "Viartril-S," and "glucosamine" for supplementary content.

III. The Birth of a Hybrid: Production of Scientific Knowledge on Glucosamine

Glucosamine is a natural substance. It is an amino sugar and component of cartilage, found in animal tissue and human joints. In both the food or pharmaceutical industries, glucosamine can be manufactured by extraction from chitin in crustacean shells. The history of glucosamine production can be traced to before the 1970s. Glucosamine was initially used as a veterinary drug administered by injection.[16] After the mechanism of its absorption through oral consumption was established, an oral form of glucosamine was developed by the University of Pavia. The initial formula consisted of glucosamine sulfate, the sulfate salt of glucosamine. An Italian pharmaceutical company, Rottapharm, patented the formula and began to produce glucosamine sulfate as a human drug under the brand name of Viartril-S.[17]

A debate on the effectiveness of Viartril-S and its generic equivalents persisted for years and played a key role in the social life of glucosamine sulfate. Two different scientific claims were declared and accepted in Europe and the United States: one recognized its medical benefits on managing osteoarthritis, while the other denied its effectiveness. The scientific evidence and food–drug boundary produced by the trials distinguished the regulation of glucosamine in these two regions.

Clinical trials published in the 1980s and 1990s explored the effectiveness of glucosamine sulfate in treating osteoarthritis. Most of the studies were only limited to European journals. According to a search of the PubMed database, the earliest of these investigations were two small clinical trials conducted by the Rotta Research Laboratorium that enrolled 30 and 20 patients with osteoarthritis, respectively. Both trials were published in the same journal, *Current*

16 "A History of Glucosamine: The Good, the Bad and the Ugly", *available at* www.dcpracticeinsights.com/mpacms/dc/pi/article.php?id=56005 (last accessed Jun. 23, 2020).

17 Taiwan official website of Viartril-S, *available at* www.viartril-s.com.tw/index.html (last accessed Jun. 23, 2020).

Medical Research and Opinion, in 1980.[18] Improvements in joint pain, tenderness, swelling, and restriction of movement following glucosamine consumption were reported. The safety of glucosamine sulfate was also demonstrated; no toxicity, adverse effects, or drug interactions were documented. Both of the studies concluded that glucosamine sulfate could be used to treat osteoarthritis. A series of additional trials were conducted in the early 1980s.[19] Although the effectiveness of glucosamine in treating arthritis remained under debate, the European Union (EU) regulated all types of glucosamine products as drugs. Because official regulatory documents are not available, the exact timing of the approval of Viartril-S in Europe cannot be determined. However, based on the time of the import of Viartril-S to Taiwan, its European drug permit must have been issued no later than the early 1980s. Although these trials were flawed from the viewpoint of current pharmaceutical regulation, the knowledge they produced created a boundary for classifying glucosamine as a drug.

By the 1990s, Viartril-S had gained popularity across Europe. In the United States, the regulation and circulation of this product were considerably different. Rottapharm introduced glucosamine sulfate to the market under the brand name "Dona" no later than the 1990s; no details about the product in the United States before the 1990s can be found. Glucosamine products are regulated as dietary supplements in the United States according to the provisions of the Dietary Supplement Health and Education Act of 1994.[20] Because glucosamine is produced by extraction from a food material, Dona and all other glucosamine-containing products are legally considered foods. Nevertheless, Rottapharm patented their glucosamine sulfate product in the early 1990s. To circumvent this patent, other pharmaceutical companies developed products using another form of glucosamine salt, glucosamine hydrochloride (HCL). Glucosamine HCL soon became another popular ingredient in glucosamine supplements.

Clinical trials conducted in the United States reached a different conclusion from those in Europe regarding the effectiveness of glucosamine. However,

18 G. Crolle & E. D'Este, "Glucosamine Sulphate for the Management of Arthrosis: A Controlled Clinical Investigation" (1980) (7) Curr Med Res Opin 104–109.

J. M. Pujalte et al., "Double-Blind Clinical Evaluation of Oral Glucosamine Sulphate in the Basic Treatment of Osteoarthrosis" (1980) (7) Curr Med Res Opin 110–114.

19 E. D'Ambrosio et al., "Glucosamine Sulphate: A Controlled Clinical Investigation in Arthrosis" (1981) (2) Pharmatherapeutica 504–508.

Vaz A. Lopes, "Double-Blind Clinical Evaluation of the Relative Efficacy of Ibuprofen and Glucosamine Sulphate in the Management of Osteoarthrosis of the Knee in Out-patients" (1982) (8) Curr Med Res Opin 145–149.

M. J. Tapadinhas et al., "Oral Glucosamine Sulphate in the Management of Arthrosis: Report on a Multi-Centre Open Investigation in Portugal" (1982) (3) Pharmatherapeutica 157–168.

P. Vajranetra, "Clinical Trial of Glucosamine Compounds for Osteoarthrosis of Knee Joints" (1984) (67) J Med Assoc Thai 409–418.

20 Dietary Supplement Health and Education Act of 1994, Public Law No. 103–417, 103rd Congress, October 25 (1994) https://ods.od.nih.gov/About/DSHEA_Wording.aspx#sec5

the glucosamine used in US studies is different. Specifically, they investigated glucosamine HCL, not glucosamine sulfate. The authors of a clinical trial published in *Osteoarthritis and Cartilage* in 2000 declared that their study was the first glucosamine clinical trial in the United States and that "the American literature is devoid of human clinical data while the data is copiously available from the European literature." However, the therapeutic they examined was not glucosamine sulfate (as studied in the European evidence they cited) but rather glucosamine HCL combined with other components also intended to promote cartilage repair.[21] Although their results revealed "effectiveness in the management of osteoarthritis of the knee," most other trials yielded different conclusions. A notable trial published in the *New England Journal of Medicine* in 2006, sponsored by the US National Institutes of Health, recruited 1,583 patients with osteoarthritis.[22] The researchers also examined glucosamine HCL instead of glucosamine sulfate.[23] Although they found that glucosamine HCL "may have some efficacy in patients with moderate-to-severe symptoms," their conclusion was more conservative: the overall results revealed no significant difference between glucosamine HCL and the placebo. Their findings support the regulatory status of glucosamine as a food in the United States. The results of this trial have been widely accepted and cited by medical professionals who deny the effectiveness of glucosamine, but few have mentioned the differences between the form of glucosamine investigated in the European and US trials. It depends on how you classify glucosamine (distinguish glucosamine HCL from sulfate form or lump them together) to regulate them as food or drugs.

Although clinical trials seem to conclude the debate on effectiveness, the testing material is problematic because of the same regulation dilemma. US studies have noted the differences between the glucosamine used in trials and the glucosamine available on the US market. Both the 2000 and 2006 US studies cited previously indicated that the categorization of glucosamine products in the United States as dietary supplements limited the real-world application of their findings. As one study stated, without "the stringent standards of the pharmaceutical manufacture," a "substantial variation between the content listed on the label and the actual content" was detected in glucosamine supplements on the market. Because the therapeutics used in trials were formulated according to pharmaceutical standards, their commercially available versions should not be expected to have equivalent effectiveness. One pharmaceutical company applied to sell glucosamine as a drug, but its application was rejected.[24]

21 The components combined with glucosamine HCL in the trials were the low molecular weight sodium chondroitin sulfate and manganese ascorbaste.

22 Glucosamine/Chondroitin Arthritis Intervention Trial (GAIT).

23 Glucosamine HCL 250 mg and sodium chondroitin sulfate 200 mg in a capsule used in the GAIT. Daniel O. Clegg et al., "Glucosamine, Chondroitin Sulfate, and the Two in Combination for Painful Knee Osteoarthritis" (2006) (354) N Engl J Med 795–808.

24 Yi-Chin Lin, "The Health Authority Redefines Blockbuster Drug "Wei-Gu-Li" Redefined as Health Food" (「維骨力」明星藥 認定健康食品), *United Daily News*, Nov. 17, 2004.

This explains why the trials conducted in the United States tended to ignore positive outcomes associated with glucosamine. The history of glucosamine in the United States reveals how classificatory regulations limit the production and flow of medical knowledge.

Europe and the United States' experiences with glucosamine provide different examples for understanding knowledge production, food–drug regulation, and their relationships. Although the European trials demonstrated the effectiveness of glucosamine sulfate, the design and conclusions of these trials have been criticized. Even after a series of clinical trials were conducted in the 1990s and 2000s, not all medical professionals were convinced. The US trials did not tarnish the perception of glucosamine sulfate in Europe because the examined therapeutic was different. Rottapharm argued that its patented crystalline form of glucosamine sulfate has better bioavailability and is better absorbed in humans than are other forms of glucosamine sulfate. A 2015 Cochrane review of 20 randomized controlled trials determined that glucosamine sulfate was demonstrated to be effective in 10 trials specifically testing crystalline glucosamine sulfate.[25] Therefore, from the viewpoint of Rottapharm, the distinction between glucosamine sulfate and HCL was not sufficiently clear. The optimal marketing strategy was to differentiate Viartril-S from other glucosamine products.

Clinical trials on glucosamine have involved the governance frameworks of various countries and regions in a process of categorical coproduction, partially driven by pharmaceutical companies and partially consequent to local regulations. On the one hand, the trials produced scientific knowledge under the existing framework of food–drug regulation. On the other hand, this knowledge created new boundaries between forms of glucosamine, spurring a persistent debate on the status of glucosamine and further obscuring its category The history of glucosamine sulfate in Taiwan further reflects this process. Its social life involves the international flow of knowledge production from Europe and the United States as well as local regulations and Taiwan's National Health Insurance (NHI) reimbursement scheme. The local experience also demonstrates how the Health Food Control Act failed to regulate such a hybrid in the food–drug borderland.

IV. Ineffective Drug or Effective Food? The Social Life of Viartril-S and Regulatory Politics in Taiwan

The regulation of glucosamine products has been more complex and problematic in Taiwan than in the United States or Europe. In Taiwan, Viartril-S is regulated as a drug but has finally become a conceptual food–drug hybrid. This product was originally introduced to the Taiwanese market as a drug.

25 S. Persiani et al., "Glucosamine Oral Bioavailability and Plasma Pharmacokinetics after Increasing Doses of Crystalline Glucosamine Sulfate in Man" (2005) (13) Osteoarthritis Cartilage 1041–1049.

According to the latest edition of the drug permit license for Viartril-S,[26] this product was approved as a prescription drug in its current form and dosage in 1999. During that time, however, Viartril-S was not as widely used as it is now. A 2006 report in *Business Today* stated that Viartril-S was initially not considered an effective drug and had relatively low revenue.[27] This changed when its coverage by the National Health Insurance Administration (NHIA) was approved. The distributor of Viartril-S, Great Union Company, promoted the drug to physicians by emphasizing the scientific evidence for its effectiveness. The company provided physicians and their families with free samples of Viartril-S, a marketing strategy that proved successful—Viartril-S became a bestseller.

Owing to the success of Viartril-S in the drug market, its Chinese brand name, Wei-Gu-Li, became adopted as a general term referring to all glucosamine-containing products in Taiwan, regardless of whether they were categorized as foods or drugs. The Chinese name is suitable for the marketing of this product because its meaning is "maintain your bones well." The distributor retained the brand name after it had acquired a general meaning. Thus, the distinction between Viartril-S and other products was further obscured, as was the boundary between foods and drugs. The public confusion on what Wei-Gu-Li exactly refers to led to safety and regulatory issues.

A modification of medical reimbursement policy worsened the situation. After the criteria for reimbursement were modified to reduce costs at the end of 1998, the NHIA reduced their payments for glucosamine by one-third in 2003. These challenges pushed Great Union Company to turn to the market of self-paid drugs, and their successful marketing further aroused the awareness and increased the demand of consumers. New concerns were aroused because glucosamine products were widely available in overseas markets and the import was not strictly regulated. For example, Viartril-S was marketed as a dietary supplement under the brand name "Dona" on the US market. People could easily purchase Dona and bring it back to Taiwan without a prescription.[28] At the same time, many glucosamine-containing products, mainly imported from other countries, were sold under the name "Wei-Gu-Li" although they were not Viartril-S. News reports of fake drugs and exaggerated and misleading advertisements occasionally appeared. The blurred boundary between Viartril-S and other glucosamine products, and between foods and drugs, potentially harmed consumers.

26 Research database of drugs, medical devices, and cosmetics approval, *available at* www.fda.gov.tw/mlms/H0001D.aspx?Type=Lic&LicId=02010641 (last accessed Jun. 23, 2020).

27 Che-Liang Lin, "Wei-Gu-Li, The Legend of Old Bones" (維骨力 老骨頭打造的傳奇), *Business Today*, Oct. 28, 2006, *available at* www.businesstoday.com.tw/article/category/80393/post/200609280043/ (last accessed Jun. 23, 2020).

28 Huei-Huei Chen, "Wei-Gu-Li: Available in Pharmacy, Coming Soon" (維骨力 藥局賣 快了), *United Daily News*, Jan. 30, 2005.

Because of the wide market availability of Viartril-S, arguments about its safety and effectiveness drew attention from an increasing number of people as well as from the TFDA. Some patients considered terminating their prescriptions because of the increased cost and doubts about effectiveness.[29] Nevertheless, many people were willing to pay for the drug for themselves or for older family members out of filial duty.[30] Although the drug's effectiveness was up for debate, most medical professionals respected patients' choices because of its established safety. However, messages from medical professionals were confusing. Several well-known physicians indicated that they did not oppose long-term or high-dosage use.[31] However, they also mentioned the risk of allergy, and several reported instances of adverse reactions, although such reactions had not been definitively linked to glucosamine.[32]

In view of the potential harm resulting from this confusion, the TFDA announced a new regulatory framework for glucosamine products in November 2002. Specifically, products containing glucosamine sulfate would be regulated as drugs, whereas those containing glucosamine HCL or the glucosamine free base (nonsalt form) would be regulated as foods.[33] The decision was supposedly made on the basis of the medical literature. The announcement appeared to draw a clear line separating glucosamine-containing products into food or drug categories according to their active ingredient. This classification scheme was unique and reinforced the status of glucosamine as a food–drug hybrid, leading to further confusion. This is because most people were not aware that glucosamine products could be classified on the basis of the active ingredient's chemical structure.

The food–drug boundary became further blurred in Taiwan when the effectiveness of glucosamine sulfate was challenged in the scientific literature. In consideration of its well-documented safety and food status in the United States and Japan, the Department of Health[34] published draft regulations to downgrade glucosamine sulfate from a "prescription drug" to an "instruction

29 Chin-Yi Huang, "Exclusion of Glucosamine from Reimbursement Impacts Drug Market" (葡萄糖胺不給付 藥品市場衝擊大), *Min-Sen Daily News,* Jan. 20, 2004.

30 Che-Liang Lin, "Wei-Gu-Li, The Legend of Old Bones" (維骨力 老骨頭打造的傳奇), *Business Today,* Oct. 28, 2006, *available at* www.businesstoday.com.tw/article/category/80393/post/200609280043/ (last accessed Jun. 23, 2020).

31 Yi-Chin Lin, "The Health Authority Redefines Blockbuster Drug 'Wei-Gu-Li' Redefined as Health Food" (「維骨力」明星藥 認定健康食品), *United Daily News*, Nov. 17, 2004.

Chin-hsiu Lin & Guei-Wen Hsueh, "The Dealer: Research Target in the U.S. Is Different from Wei-Gu-Li; Physicians: Do Not Jump to Conclusion Because of Small Sample Size" (廠商說法 美研究標的 與維骨力不同 醫師看法 樣本數太少 不宜驟下定論), *Min-Sen Daily News*, Feb. 24, 2006.

32 Guei-Wen Hsueh, "Glucosamine, Including Wei-Gu-Li, Will Not Increase Cartilage" (維骨力等葡萄糖胺無助增加軟骨), *Min-Sen Daily News*, Nov. 11, 2005.

33 "What Is the Difference Between Glucosamine?", *available at* https://blog.xuite.net/arlenea8q33/blog/304032488- (last accessed Jun. 24, 2020).

34 Now the "Ministry of Health and Welfare."

drug" in February 2004.[35] According to a news report, the authorities even considered classifying it as a food under the condition that the distributor agree to advertise the product without its health claims.[36] However, the potential market after reclassification did not appeal to the company. The representative of Rottapharm in Taiwan expressed their resistance to classifying Viartril-S as a food or instruction drug. My translation of a newspaper report published at the end of 2004 is as follows:

> Great Union Company, the distributor of Wei-Gu-Li, indicated that they would provide the Department of Health with proof from clinical trials to allow the product to remain in the category of prescription drug. The General Manager, Yen-Chang Wang, stated that Wei-Gu-Li, with the English brand name "Viartril-S," refers to the patent owned by its Italian manufacturer, rather than serving a general term for glucosamine sulfate. Research published in the Lancet proved that early usage of Viartril-S could delay joint degeneration.

By emphasizing the effectiveness of Viartril-S with reference to a study published in a well-known medical journal, the distributor attempted to clarify the difference between Viartril-S and other generic drugs or glucosamine products, insisting that Viartril-S should remain classified as a prescription drug. However, this did not change the policy. The change was formally implemented in January 2005,[37] after which glucosamine products with food and drug classifications were both available on the market but with different distribution protocols. Specifically, glucosamine food products could be sold everywhere, whereas glucosamine drugs were only available in pharmacies. However, this difference in product flows was so negligible that even media reports could be ambiguous and misleading. A news report confused the categories of instruction drugs and Health Food and claimed that "Viartril-S" was going to be reclassified as Health Food.[38] Relevant authorities also released conflicting messages: Although instruction drugs are generally not covered by the NHI program, they stated that glucosamine sulfate products, including Viartril-S and

35 Once reclassified as the instruction drug, the glucosamine sulfate can be freely sold and purchased without prescription in neighboring pharmacies. In terms of the regulation, the only trivial difference between another drug category, over-the-counter drug, is that consumers should take it under the instruction from pharmacists. However, this never limits access to the drug in the market. Being classified as either one actually makes no difference from the viewpoint of consumers or even the market.

36 Hsin-hsin Wei & Chin-Ru Shih, "Reclassified as Food, Blockbuster Drug for Osteoarthritis, Wei-Gu-Li, Will be Purchasable Everywhere (關節炎 明星藥 維骨力擬列食品 到處買得到)", *United Daily News,* Nov. 30, 2004.

37 Huei-Huei Chen, "Wei-Gu-Li: Available in Pharmacy, Coming Soon (維骨力 藥局賣 快了)", *United Daily News,* Jan. 30, 2005.

38 Yi-Chin Lin, "The Health Authority Redefines Blockbuster Drug 'Wei-Gu-Li' Redefined as Health Food (「維骨力」 明星藥 認定健康食品)", *United Daily News*, Nov. 17, 2004.

more than 30 generic drugs, would be covered. However, the reimbursement criteria were still criticized by some for being too "strict."[39] All of these messages complicated the public perception of glucosamine and made it difficult for both laypeople and healthcare professionals to clearly understand glucosamine products.

Although glucosamine HCL was widely recognized as a Health Food because of its close relationship with glucosamine-containing drugs, it was regulated as an ordinary food. Manufacturers of glucosamine food products cannot apply for them to be marketed as Health Foods because the symptoms they purport to relieve are not included in Track 1 criteria. No new categories of healthcare claims have been added to the criteria in 12 years. Furthermore, in early 2018, health authorities indicated that an animal model protocol for evaluating health claims concerning glucosamine HCL had been proposed and was under review.[40] The inflexibility of Health Food regulations has complicated the regulation of new health food products.

After encouraging the blurred distinction between Viartril-S and other glucosamine products, Great Union Company attempted to clarify the difference after entering the market of self-paid drugs. The story of Viartril-S in Taiwan is not only a marketing success story but also an example of an object situated in the borderland between categories established through interactions among knowledge production, categorical shifts, and regulatory contexts. For more than a decade, the distribution of glucosamine followed two divergent paths. First, patients with knee joint osteoarthritis could be prescribed glucosamine sulfate, either self-paid or reimbursed by the NHI, by physicians in hospitals or clinics. Second, both the dietary supplement glucosamine HCL and the instruction drug glucosamine sulfate were widely available in supermarkets and pharmacies. Therefore, although consumers were free to purchase whichever product they preferred without restriction, knowledge and discourses on glucosamine products were mixed. The distribution of glucosamine in Taiwan thus demonstrates the social life of a food–drug hybrid.

Although Great Union Company successfully introduced its product into the market of self-paid drugs and generated large profits, Viartril-S was recategorized as self-paid much later than expected. After its reclassification as an instruction drug in 2005, news reports stated that the NHI program would soon stop covering glucosamine sulfate prescriptions. However, in response to negative responses from the public and politicians, the NHIA continued to delay the date on which coverage would be withdrawn. In a news report in 2014, an unnamed physician wondered, "Does the NHIA dare to [not cover

39 Shih-Chieh Hsu, "Are the Reimbursement Criteria Too Strict for Wei-Gu-Li? (維骨力給付過硬?)", *United Daily News*, Aug. 4, 2005.

40 Protocols of effectiveness evaluation for joint health added on the list of health food scheduled to pass the review in the first half year, IQC.TW, Feb 6, 2018, *available at* https://iqc.tw/48082 (last accessed Jun. 23 2020).

glucosamine sulfate]?"[41] The report also estimated that the number of patients prescribed glucosamine sulfate was approximately 0.7 million and noted that only 10% of Great Union Company's revenue came from the NHI market. From 2010 to 2020, the NHIA has determined the coverage but not the classification of Viartril-S. Although Viartril-S has remained classified as a drug, its wide distribution is more comparable to that of a Health Food. In 2018, 13 years after its reclassification, Viartril-S was officially removed from NHI coverage.

V. Conclusion

By tracing the knowledge production and social life of Viartril-S in the United States, Europe, and Taiwan, this chapter proposes several concepts concerning food–drug regulation and the boundary between the two categories. Specifically, this boundary is defined by the interaction between scientific evidence and regulatory frameworks. An object that belongs to one category can change categories and redefine the boundary when it is exchanged on the market. Second, knowledge production from clinical trials may not help clarify the blurred categories of foods and drugs. Third, modern regulatory frameworks largely dependent on classification and knowledge generated from such infrastructure may have difficulty regulating products that fall between the food and drug categories. Governing authorities must balance safety and effectiveness in their regulatory decisions or choose to prioritize one over the other.

41 Chien-Fu & Chia-Chen We, "The National Health Insurance Considers Not Paying for Glucosamine-contained Agents This Year" (葡萄糖胺製劑 今年健保擬不給付), *United Daily News,* Mar. 14, 2014.

14 Classification as a Technology of Governance

Food or Drug in South Korea

Eunjeong Ma

I. Opening A Pandora's Box: *Baek Shu Oh* Disaster

In the early 1990s, the professional organization of Western medicine (or biomedicine)-trained pharmacists, the Korean Pharmaceutical Association, demanded the government integrate Korean medicine into Western biomedicine. As shown in the following, they contended that the existence of two medical systems complicated consumer choices, adding an additional financial burden both on the government and on consumers. A principal reason for the integration of Korean medicine under biomedicine was to do with the global trend that scientific medicine was universally accepted.

> When one is sick, there are two types of hospitals that one can visit. One is a (Western) hospital/clinic where the smell of antiseptics hangs in the air and modern medical instruments are installed; the other is a Korean Oriental hospital/clinic where the scent of herb extract is very strong and patients are taking acupuncture lying in the bed. This parallel image of two medical cultures was captured by the Korean Pharmaceutical Association as a problematic situation, in the sense that Korean consumers were spending on medical and pharmaceutical services way more than they should.
>
> (KPA 1995)[1]

About a decade later in 2015, a biotechnology company, Natural Endotech, was at the center of public attention because of phytoingredient-based products it had extracted from medicinal plants. Employing novel scientific methods, the firm extracted an herbal compound consisting of three commonly used medicinal plants, *Cynanchum wilfordii*, *Phlomis umbrosa*, and *Angelica gigas*. The compound was certified by the Korea Food and Drug Administration (KFDA) for use as a functional ingredient with health claims to alleviate

1 KPA (Korean Pharmaceutical Association), *Uiryo Ilwonhwa e gwanhan Jaryojip* [*A Collection on the Unification of Medicine*] (Seoul, The Korean Pharmaceutical Association (KPA) 1995).

DOI: 10.4324/9781003271918-18

menopausal symptoms. Considering the scarcity of commercial products for middle-aged women, the related products became a market hit in no time. However, the use of such products turned into a nightmare when the Korea Consumer Agency (KCA),[2] a governmental consumer protection organization, publicly denounced the authenticity of the products in circulation on the market, contending that authentic *Cynanchum wilfordii* (*baek shu oh*) plants were not used. Based on the random sample analysis, the agency alleged that most commercial products were adulterated with morphologically similar *i yeop u pi so* plants. The agency presented an opinion that the use of *i yeop u pi so* could pose a public health threat for two reasons. First, reliable scientific evidence was not available to prove that the consumption of the *i yeop u pi so* plant was safe to human beings. Second, research suggested that *i yeop u pi so* plants could cause adverse health effects such as hepatotoxicity, weight loss, and nervous breakdown.[3]

The agency's exposure horrified the public with the fear that they might have been consuming toxic products, and they demanded an immediate answer from responsible regulatory authorities about the safety of *baek shu oh* products. However, it took about two years for the Korea Ministry of Food and Drug Safety (MFDS) to conclude that the safety of the products is dependent on the process of how they are prepared. Authentic *baek shu oh* plants are safe to take only if they are extracted in hot water, whereas they are hazardous to consume if prepared in powder form. The Ministry also asserted that *i yeop u pi so* plants cannot be used as food or drug ingredients.[4]

The *baek shu oh* case provides an entry point for examining the technology of food governance in South Korea, which is comparable to a Pandora's box. Until that time, food and drug regulation had been left to the MFDS, and their authority and credibility had remained unscathed. The controversial case, however, opened the black box of governing mechanisms of regulatory agencies and consumer markets. I would argue that the explosive expansion of the health food market can be best understood as an asymmetric assemblage of post-colonial relations linking domestic and international regulatory authorities, consumer market agencies, techno-scientific research institutions, the academy, and medicinal plants. At one level, the South Korean government played a major role to lay the legal and financial foundations to set the stage for winning global markets in the realm of innovative drugs, whether

2 KCA (Korea Consumer Agency), *Most Baekshuoh products in Market Circulation are fakes* (Press release, Seoul, Korea Consumer Agency 2015), *available at* http://www.kca.go.kr/brd/m_32/view.do?seq=1791&multi_itm_seq=0. 2015.

3 KCA (Korea Consumer Agency), *Most Baekshuoh Products in Market Circulation Are Fakes,* April 22 (Press release, Seoul, Korea Consumer Agency 2015), *available at* https://www.kca.go.kr/kca/sub.do?menukey=5084&mode=view&no=1001668276

4 Ministry of Food and Drug Safety (MFDS), *Ministry of Food and Drug Safety, Disclosure of the Safety Test Result of Baekshuoh·Iyeopupiso*, August 22 (Press release, Seoul, Ministry of Food and Drug Safety 2017).

biosynthetic or phytochemical. The government funded academia, research institutions, and industry to collaborate to develop patentable ingredients. The industry assembled regulatory requirements to pass domestic and international regulatory thresholds. The *baek shu oh* case revealed the very precariousness of regulatory assemblages that the pharmaceutical industry haphazardly mobilized to get into the market

II. Introduction: Two Medical Systems and One Drug?

In 2021, consumers of healthcare services face the same destiny as their predecessors in the 1990s, if not a more complex one. There are two legally recognized medical systems in coexistence, Korean medicine and (Western) biomedicine. What the KPA depicted about consumer choices in the 1990s has changed little over time but rather been normalized as status quo.

This chapter examines the advent of manufactured herbal products whose therapeutic principles are based on Korean medicine. The mass production and marketization of herbal medicines and related products has accelerated in the past few decades. Like many other Asian medical systems, Korean medicine has been around for thousands of years, with variations and modifications over time accommodating and emulating Western medicine and differentiating from Chinese medicine and Japanese *Kampo*.[5] As scholarly works have noted,[6] Asian medical practices and principles are pluralistic and diverse and cannot be captured under the umbrella of Western medicine, biomedicine, or scientific medicine (however it is termed). Medical systems have developed in unique ways that are impossible to lump together even under grand traditions of Chinese medicine, Ayurveda medicine, and Unani medicine. Healing practices are as pluralistic as there are diverse histories and cultures within and across Asia.[7]

South Korea maintains a mutually exclusive, dual medical system. The two medical systems—Western medicine (WM) and Korean (Oriental) medicine (KM)—are independent, autonomous, and separate at the institutional and practice levels. Each of the two systems has distinct formal educational institutions,

5 C.R. Ko, N.P. Ku & S. Seol "A Comparative Study on the Traditional Medicine Policies between Korea and China: Focused on the Second Korean Medicine Development Plan and the 12· 5 Traditional Chinese Medicine Development Plan" (2014) 17(2) Journal of Korea Technology Innovation Society 421, 421–47; H. J. Lee, "Hanguk Hanuihak ui Jeonmunhwa Gwajeong e gwanhan Yeongu (A Study of the Professionalization of Korean Oriental Medicine)" (Ph. D. thesis. Dept. of Sociology. Daegu, Korea, Keimyung University 2001).

6 C. Leslie, *Asian Medical Systems: A Comparative Study* (Berkeley and Los Angeles, University of California Press 1976); C. Leslie & A. Young (eds), *Paths to Asian Medical Knowledge* (Berkeley and Los Angeles, University of California Press 1992).

7 J. S. Alter (ed.), *Asian Medicine and Globalization: Encounters with Asia* (Philadelphia, University of Pennsylvania Press 2005); J. Farquhar, *Knowing Practice: The Clinical Encounter of Chinese Medicine* (Boulder, Westview Press 1994); Y. Lin, J. M. Betz, J.S. Bindra & S.C. Bobzin (eds.), *Drug Discovery and Traditional Chinese Medicine: Science, Regulation, and Globalization* (Boston, Kluwer Academic Publishers 2001).

hospitals and clinics, and licensing requirements. Each also had its own nationwide association, with branches in each provincial city, and each publishes internal newsletters and specialized journals.[8] Korean medicine (*han ui hak* 韓醫學 in Korean) is also known as Korean Oriental medicine in English. In 2012, the nationwide professional organization of Korean medicine doctors decided to change its official name to the Association of Korean Medicine (AKOM), signifying that it represents the medicine of Korea.

This parallel medical system reflects a series of political and social transformations that took place in twentieth-century Korea: colonial experience, post-war politics, state-driven modernization projects, and democratization movements. Japanese colonial experience was a defining moment in the history of Korean medicine, during which the hierarchical relationship between the two medical practices, institutionally and epistemologically, took shape. Japanese colonial authority institutionalized WM in the public domain—education, the licensing system, public health policy, and hospitals—whereas KM became marginalized and pushed to the private sector.[9]

Han yak, medicinal herbs or herbal remedies, are based on Korean medicine and have long been used for therapeutic and preventive purposes in South Korea. As with the advent of technoscience and medical technologies and their entry into healing practices, the status and perception of *han yak* have changed accordingly, As evidence grounded on scientific ideas and methods is accepted as a norm in the circulation and governance of pharmaceuticals at the national and international levels, health products derived from natural plants, including

8 S. Lee et al., "Knowledge of, Attitudes Toward, and Experience of Complementary and Alternative Medicine in Western Medicine- and Oriental Medicine-Trained Physicians in Korea" (2002) 92(12) *American Journal of Public Health* 1994, 1994–2000; H. J. Lee, "Hanguk Hanuihak ui Jeonmunhwa Gwajeong e gwanhan Yeongu" (A Study of the Professionalization of Korean Oriental Medicine) (Ph.D. thesis. Dept. of Sociology. Daegu, Korea: Keimyung University, 2001); H. J. Lee, "The Globalization of East Asian Traditional Medicine and the Change of Medical Hegemony" (2013) 22 *Society and Theory* 377, 377–398; H. J. Lee, "A Study of the Development Model of Chinese Traditional Medicine - Centering on the Process of the Professionalization" (2003) 17(3) *Journal of Physiology & Pathology in Korean Medicine* 611, 611–616; Lee, H. J. and Kwon Y. K., "The Changes of Oriental Medicine and Medical Market in Korea." (2002) 16(1) *Korean Medical Journal of Oriental Physiology & Pathology* 52, 52–54.

9 H. J. Lee, 'Hanguk Hanuihak ui Jeonmunhwa Gwajeong e gwanhan Yeongu (A Study of the Professionalization of Korean Oriental Medicine)' (Ph.D. thesis. Dept. of Sociology. Daegu, Korea: Keimyung University, 2001); Park, Y. J., "Japan's Oriental Medicine Policy in Colonial Korea." (2008) 17(1) Korean Journal of Oriental Medicine 75, 75–86; Park, Y. J. "The Arguments for Scientific Reconstruction of Oriental Medicine in Korea, in 1945–50" (2011) 79 YŎKSA WA HYŎNSIL: Quarterly Review of Korean History 305, 305–326; Park, Y. J. "The Establishment of National License System for Oriental Medical Practitioner in Korea, 1945~51" (2011) 154 The Journal of Korean Studies (東方學志) 345, 345–376; Park, Y. J., "Acculturation of Herbal Medicines and Changes in Traditional Medicine in Liberated Korea" (2014) 71 Journal of Korean Modern and Contemporary History 188, 188–211. D. W. Shin, "The Formation of the Colonial Policy of Medical Care – Focused on the Policy of Korean Traditional Medicine" (2002) 30 Korean Culture 333, 370; D. W. Shin, "Traditional Medicine under Japanese Rule after 1930s" (2003) 12(2) Korean Journal of Medical History (醫史學) 110, 110–128.

functional foods, dietary supplements, and drugs, have been gradually brought under the purview of legal and regulatory frames.[10]

The Korean case has similarities with so-called "traditional medicine" in Asia, in that medical and pharmaceutical culture has developed in the fluctuating political environments.[11] And the shaping of the herbal pharmaceutical industry is a prime example to illustrate the complexity and heterogeneity of medical culture. It has emerged at the "confluence of 'traditional' medical knowledge, modern science, policy regulations, and the capitalist market".[12] Like many other Asian medicines, Korean medicine and drugs have turned into a lucrative, innovative industry that can be best understood as an asymmetric assemblage of post-colonial relations linking domestic and international

10 Kim, J. S., Lee S. W. and Kim Y. K., "A study about policy regime for the protection of the rights of Korean traditional medicine in the world market: Focusing on Chinese legislation cases " (2014) 14(1) *Journal of Law and Politics Research* 103, 103–139; Lee, T. H., "The Dispute on the Modernization of Korean Medicine after the Restoration of Independence – Based on the 1950s and from the 1990s to the Present" (2012) 16(3) *Journal of Society of Preventive Korean Medicine* 53, 53–73; Lee, T. K., Kim B. S., and Kim G. S., "The Oriental Medicine the Traditional Drink Study on the Herbal" (2013) 21(2) *Korean Journal of Oriental Medicine; Park,* Y. J., "The Arguments for Scientific Reconstruction of Oriental Medicine in Korea, in 1945–50" (2011) 79 *YŎKSA WA HYŎNSIL: Quarterly Review of Korean History* 305, 305–332; Park, Y. J., "The Establishment of National License System for Oriental Medical Practitioner in Korea, 1945–1951" (2011) 154 *The Journal of Korean Studies* (東方學志) 345, 345–376; Park, Y. J., "Acculturation of Herbal Medicines and Changes in Traditional Medicine in Liberated Korea" (2014) 71 *Journal of Korean Modern and Contemporary History* 188, 188–211; Shin, D. W., "The Formation of the Colonial Policy of Medical Care – Focused on the Policy of Korean Traditional Medicine" (2003) 12(2) *Korean Culture* 30 333, 330–370; Shin, D. W., "Traditional Medicine under Japanese Rule after 1930s." (2003) 12(2) *Korean Journal of Medical History* (醫史學) 110, 110–128; I. S. Yeo, "Traditional Medicine Seen from the Perspective of Western Medicine during the Late 19th and Early 20th Century in Korea" (2007) 16(2) *Korean Journal of Medical History* 161, 161–176.

11 Kim, J. S., Lee S. W. and Kim Y. K., "A study about policy regime for the protection of the rights of Korean traditional medicine in the world market: Focusing on Chinese legislation cases" (2014) 14(1) Journal of Law and Politics Research 103, 103–139; Lee, T. H., "The Dispute on the Modernization of Korean Medicine after the Restoration of Independence – Based on the 1950s and from the 1990s to the Present" (2012) 16(3) *Journal of Society of Preventive Korean Medicine* 53, 53–73; Lee, T. K., Kim B. S., and Kim G. S., "The Oriental Medicine the Traditional Drink Study on the Herbal" (2013) 21(2) *Korean Journal of Oriental Medicine*; Park, Y. J., "The Arguments for Scientific Reconstruction of Oriental Medicine in Korea, in 1945–50" (2011) 79 YŎKSA WA HYŎNSIL: Quarterly Review of Korean History 305, 305–332; Park, Y. J., "The Establishment of National License System for Oriental Medical Practitioner in Korea, 1945–1951" (2011) 154 *The Journal of Korean Studies* (東方學志) 345, 345–376; Park, Y. J., "Acculturation of Herbal Medicines and Changes in Traditional Medicine in Liberated Korea" (2014) 71 *Journal of Korean Modern and Contemporary History* 188, 188–211; Shin, D. W., "The Formation of the Colonial Policy of Medical Care - Focused on the Policy of Korean Traditional Medicine" (2003) 12(2) *Korean Culture* 30 333, 330–370; Shin, D. W., "Traditional Medicine under Japanese Rule after 1930s" (2003) 12(2) *Korean Journal of Medical History* (醫史學) 110, 110–128; I. S. Yeo, "Traditional Medicine Seen from the Perspective of Western Medicine during the Late 19th and Early 20th Century in Korea" (2007) 16(2) *Korean Journal of Medical History* 161, 161–176.

12 S. Kloos et al., "The transnational Sowa Rigpa industry in Asia: New perspectives on an emerging economy" (2020) 245 *Social Science & Medicine* 112617.

regulatory authorities, consumer market agencies, techno-scientific research institutions, the academy, and medicinal plants. The processes of the transformation of herbs and herbal remedies into contemporary or modern pharmaceuticals or health products are strongly tied to domestic and international political environments. The pharmaceuticalization of Korean medicines (herbal remedies), from the raw materials to production processes and to marketization, has been a state's business, in particular starting with the colonial government and accelerating with the postcolonial governments. The notion of "assemblage" is relied on and resonant with "pharmaceutical assemblage" that refers to "the heterogeneous, contingent elements that come together, through the process of pharmaceuticalization, in the form of the traditional pharmaceutical industry and contemporary health care".[13] The state, whether a colonial state or a nation state, has been at the center to initiate and drive to assemble, both with regulatory and legal networks and funding opportunities, heterogeneous and contingent elements to produce new entities that may be aligned and harmonized with international regulatory standards. There are two layers of asymmetric relations that I take note of regarding the herbal pharmaceutical industry in Korea. First, the state has played a dominant role, with a strong interest in enhancing its visibility and status in the global markets, aiming to emerge as a strong market player. The postcolonial governments' will to participate in and lead the global markets set a precarious or ambivalent stage towards Korean medicine and drugs. This leads to the second asymmetric relation implied here. Second, as "(scientific) evidence"-based medicine and pharmaceuticals are set as global regulatory standards, Korean medicine, whose understandings about the body and diseases are not in sync with western biomedicine, is in a position to speak and prove with scientific and biomedical idioms and symptoms. At one level, the Korea herbal pharmaceutical industry is a story of colonial–postcolonial relations, and they are interlocked with complex political and economic contingencies of the time, such as globalization, commercialization, and consumerism, to name a few. Hence, with particular attention to legally recognized herbal products, this chapter presents a transformation of herbal medicines over the past several decades in South Korea.

First, this chapter is situated in historical contingencies conditioned to shape the contemporary medical and pharmaceutical practices and policies. During and after Japanese colonial occupation (1910–1945), Western medicine was referenced as a scientific and advanced medical system to emulate within official sectors such as public health policies, medical education, hospitals, and medical and pharmacy laws.[14] Although Korean people had been consuming

13 S. Kloos, "The Pharmaceutical Assemblage: Rethinking Sowa Rigpa and the Herbal Pharmaceutical Industry in Asia" (2017) 58(6) *Current Anthropology* 693, 699.

14 GG.M. Lee, "A Study on the General Public Understanding and Utilization of Korean Traditional Medicine in Colonial Period" (2006) 15(2) *Korean Journal of Medical History* 222, 222–231; Y. J.

herbal medicines and associated therapeutic and nutritional services and products based on Korean medicine, the government stayed ambivalent towards Korean medicine, treating it as something to be modernized, abolished, or integrated into scientific medicine.[15]

During postcolonial nation-building periods, because of Korean people's heavy reliance on Korean medicine and the shortage of medical personnel and facilities, the government had to endorse Korean medicine in the laws. Practitioners of Korean medicine mobilized their manpower, whose styles of practice were diverse, and institutionalized the educational system to emulate its contender, western biomedicine.[16] In early 1990s, the South Korean government was under international pressure, in particular from the United States, to strengthen intellectual property rights in pharmaceutical products. The government began to align pharmacy policies and laws in accordance with global standards, and evidence-based medicine and pharmaceuticals served as policy guidelines to establish research and development plans of medicine and pharmaceuticals including Korean medicines.[17]

Second, this chapter is set in the context of localization of global trends, namely government-driven market formation. Changes at the global level affected the ways in which herbal medicines or natural resources were perceived from regulatory and governmental perspectives. The rise of Asian medicine in

---

Park, "Japan's Oriental Medicine Policy in Colonial Korea" (2008) 17(1) *Korean Journal of Oriental Medicine* 75, 75–86; D. W. Shin, "The Formation of the Colonial Policy of Medical Care – Focused on the Policy of Korean Traditional Medicine" (2003) 12(2) *Korean Culture* 30 333, 330–370; D. W Shin, "Traditional Medicine under Japanese Rule after 1930s" (2003) 12(2) *Korean Journal of Medical History* (醫史學) 110, 110–128.

15 D. W. Shin, "The Formation of the Colonial Policy of Medical Care – Focused on the Policy of Korean Traditional Medicine" (2003) 12(2) *Korean Culture* 30 333, 330–370; Shin, D. W., "Traditional Medicine under Japanese Rule after 1930s." (2003) 12(2) *Korean Journal of Medical History* (醫史學) 110, 110–128.

16 H. J. Lee, "Hanguk Hanuihak ui Jeonmunhwa Gwajeong e gwanhan Yeongu (A Study of the Professionalization of Korean Oriental Medicine)" (Ph. D. thesis. Dept. of Sociology. Daegu, Korea, Keimyung University 2001); Y. J. Park, "The Establishment of National License System for Oriental Medical Practitioner in Korea, 1945–51." (2011) 154 The Journal of Korean Studies (東方學志) 345, 345–76; Y. J. Park, "Acculturation of Herbal Medicines and Changes in Traditional Medicine in Liberated Korea." (2014) 71 Journal of Korean Modern and Contemporary History 188, 188–211; B. H. Cho, "Chimguyeongyeokeul Dulreossan Jeonmunjikganui Jipdangaldeung" [Jurisdictional Conflict between Professions: The Fall and the Rise of the Acupuncturist System in the Folk Sector] (2003), 14 *Bogeongwa Sahoegwahak [Public Health and Social Science]* 87, 87–126.

17 T. K. Lee, B. S. Kim & G. S. Kim, "The Oriental Medicine the Traditional Drink Study on the Herbal." (2013) 21(2) Korean Journal of Oriental Medicine 37, 37–48; K. Park, et al., "Establishing Good Safety and Effectiveness Evaluation System for Globalization of Herbal Medicines" (2017) 43(1) The Journal of the Korean Public Health Association 39, 39–51; M. J. Son, et al. "A Study of Korean Medical Knowledge System Which Korean Medical Doctors Want" (2012) 16(3) Journal of Society of Preventive Korean Medicine 89, 89–105; A. D. Sung, et al. "The Need for Evidence – Based Treatment and Standardization in Korean Medicine – Focusing on Consumer Opinions from the Ministry of Health and Welfare's Survey on Usage of Korean Medicine (2008, 2011, and 2014) –." (2016) 20(3) Journal of Preventive Medicine and Public Health 31, 31–43.

global markets has attracted the attention of regulatory bodies and the pharmaceutical industry at the domestic and transnational levels. The South Korean government has also supported the pharmaceutical industry to develop innovative herbal products in order to create "innovative yet traditional" drugs for the biomedical disorders of an international as well as Korean clientele. To put it bluntly, it was a government-driven reformulation regime in the drug industry.[18] The government began to allocate research and development (R&D) resources to the modernization and commercialization of medicinal plants, which inevitably relied on the knowledge of Korean medicine.[19] Starting in the 1990s, the South Korean government recognized market values of Korean medicine in the domestic and global markets and began to put heavy research and development money into the commercialization of KM.[20]

Third, this chapter is set in the periods when KM practitioners collectively and strategically fought for governmental attention and resources, which opened up widely political, epistemic, and ontological battle ground over *han yak* (herbal medicines) between supporters of scientific medicine and KM.[21] The former is represented by the government, the pharmaceutical industry, and pharmacists and physicians trained in the tradition of western biomedicine. The government's initiatives to commercialize traditional Korean medicines rekindled deep-seated, unsettling issues among interested professional organizations over how to legally categorize new medicinal compositions. The classification and categorization of purportedly novel products have posed regulatory challenges such that a simple food versus drug demarcation does not apply to products with health claims.

18 L. Pordié & J. P. Gaudillière, "The Reformulation Regime in Drug Industry: Revisiting Polyherbals and Property Rights in the Ayurvedic Industry" (2014) 8(1) East Asian Science, Technology and Society 57–79.

19 S. Eom, "A study on the Problems and Improvement Proposals on Legal Definitions in Respect of Herbal Medicinal Preparations, Crude Drug Preparations and New Drugs from Natural Products" (2014) 27(4) Journal of Oriental Medical Classics 181, 181–98; H. J. Lee, "The Globalization of East Asian Traditional Medicine and the Change of Medical Hegemony" (2013) 22 Society and Theory 377–98; H. J. Lee & Y. K. Kwon "The Changes of Oriental Medicine and Medical Market in Korea" (2002) 16(1) Korean Medical Journal of Oriental Physiology & Pathology 52, 52–4.

20 E. J. Ma, "The Medicine Cabinet: Korean Medicine under Dispute" (2010) 4(3) East Asian Science, Technology, and Society 367–82; E. J. Ma, "Join or Be Excluded from Biomedicine? JOINS® and Post-colonial Korea" (2015) 22(1) Anthropology & Medicine 64–74.

21 The distinction between scientific medicine (or biomedicine) and Korean medicine is neither absolute nor firm. With the distinction made, it does not mean that Korean medicine is not scientific, either.

III. Transformation of the Pharmaceutical Industry

Economic growth at the societal and national levels began to be reflected in the increased consumption of health products starting in the 1980s.[22] In the early 1990s, the characteristics of the Korean pharmaceutical industry were as follows: first, the industry by and large was focused on producing finished products as opposed to investing in researching and developing innovative entities. Second, the Korean pharmaceutical industry was composed of medium- and small-scaled companies, without giant, international pharmaceutical companies.[23] Viewing the lack of large pharmaceutical companies as having to do with the lack of knowledge-based, innovative drugs in the global markets, the government intended to induce comparatively competitive domestic pharmaceutical companies to invest in developing biosynthetic drugs. Consequently, the government set an urgent agenda for R&D projects to facilitate the generation of patented pharmaceuticals, whether biosynthetic drugs or botanical drugs: to transform the ecology of the pharmaceutical industry. Other than those pharmaceutical companies and research institutes that were devoted to synthetic biomedical drugs, this governmental initiative also provided a timely opportunity for those who were interested in translating the knowledge of natural resources into health and pharmaceutical products. The South Korean government recognized Korean medicines (*han yak* or herbal medicines) as a national treasure with high potential in global markets if and when they were transformed into patented pharmaceuticals.[24] Given that Korean medicines had been popularly used among Korean citizens over thousands of years and that their scientific evidence was not established, the government took the initiative to lead research and development in the domain of Korean medicine and drugs. With the recognition of the government, heavy investment in Korean medicine ensued in order to systematize, digitize, and commercialize herbs and Korean medicines or herbal medicines. From the outset, the goal was clearly to increase the market share in the global markets by reinventing natural resources to appeal to the scientifically minded international clientele.

South Korean governments sponsored the transformation of herbal medicines under the names of modernization, scientization, or globalization. In order to meet the global standards based on scientific evidence, the government looked at the utility of so-called reverse pharmacology. It refers to processes and methods to reformulate and simplify the compositions of Korean medicines in

22 C. J. Han & Y. H. Kim, "Study on Consumption of Health Functional Foods According to Climacteric Symptoms in Middle-Aged Women" (2014) 14(6) Journal of the East Asian Society of Dietary Life 768, 768–75; C. G. Son, "Progress of Functional Food Market in Korea and Strategy of Korean Medicine" (2014) 35(1) Journal of Korean Medicine 68, 68–74.

23 KHIDI (Korea Health Industry Development Institute). *2016 nyeon jeyak saneop bunseok bogoseo [The 2016 Annual Analysis of the Pharmaceutical Industry]* (Chungcheongbuk-do, KHIDI 2016).

24 K. Park, et al. "Establishing Good Safety and Effectiveness Evaluation System for Globalization of Herbal Medicines" (2017) 43(1) The Journal of the Korean Public Health Association 39, 39–51.

order to create new "traditional" drugs for the biomedical disorders of an international as well as Korean clientele. Reverse pharmacology is similar to reverse engineering, making use of traditional medical and pharmacological knowledge. Based on time-tested herbal formulas and clinical experiential knowledge, it identifies candidate plants and pharmacologically active components to develop new drugs. As compared with R&D processes in synthetic drugs, reverse pharmacology saves R&D costs, time, and resources.

IV. Innovative Pharmaceutical Industry and Innovative Nation

From the beginning, the government used an innovation model akin to a triple helix, conditioning that academia, public and private research institutes, and industry should collaborate with each other in order to create new knowledge and products. In this model, the government plays a role in formulating policies and laws and supporting research and development of innovative knowledge and technologies. Academia and research institutes make a strategic alliance with industry to develop and commercialize innovative products.[25] In the case of South Korea, universities, public and private research institutes, and pharmaceutical firms constituted helices, with the government coordinating both helices and interrelated governmental institutions to facilitate research and development of new products based on and derived from Korean medicines. It was a top-down innovation model in which the government took the lead and oversaw the cluster of participating parties. The South Korean government looked into a modified triple helix model, that is, government-industry-research institute-academia complex, as a practical solution to create the pharmaceutical industry. The role of the government was clearly defined from the beginning, in that the government was responsible for creating the legal and regulatory foundations to facilitate the cultivation of the industry in additional to financial support. Considering colonial and postcolonial legacies and that public health–related laws and regulations were instituted based on Western biomedicine, the government felt a need to reestablish legal foundations to cultivate a pharmaceutical industry fit both with local and global contexts. The intended goal was clearly set to establish a domestic pharmaceutical ecosystem to mass-produce natural drugs that were marketable to the domestic as well as international markets. The government's aspirations could be summarized as follows: first, research and development of natural resources should be prioritized with full support from the government; second, newly invented or innovated knowledge should be transferred to the industrial sector for commercialization. Considering the long medical and cultural history that Korean medicine had for the Korean population, the government believed that

25 R. Arnkil, A. Järvensivu, K. Pasi & T. Piirainen, *Exploring Quadruple Helix: Outlining User-Oriented Innovation Models*.(Tampere, University of Tampere 2010).

the South Korean pharmaceutical industry had a greater potential to win the global market.

On the one hand, the government's policy turn toward herbal medicines renewed business interests among social actors who were directly and indirectly involved in the value chains of herbal medicines, changing the geography of herbal medicines in complex ways. For instance, one clear indicator demonstrative of renewed commercial interest in herbal medicines was the rise of the cultivating fields to mass-produce herbs as opposed to hunting and gathering medicinal herbs in the wild, let alone adopting and implementing good manufacturing/laboratory practices in circulating herbs and related products.[26] Starting in the 1990s, a new social actor came to the surface in the business of herbs and herbal medicines, namely the herbal pharmaceutical industry. The herbal pharmaceutical industry refers to either a biotechnology company or a pharmaceutical company that utilizes and transforms herbs to produce commercial products. The emergence of the herbal pharmaceutical industry can be majorly attributed to governmental aspirations to arise as a competitive player in global markets.

The classification system of the pharmaceutical industry tells how the industry is imagined and understood by regulatory agencies. According to Korean Standard Industrial Classification (KSIC), the pharmaceutical industry is classified under three different categories: the manufacturing industry, wholesale and retail industry, and service industry. The herbal pharmaceutical industry is more specifically subsumed under the manufacturing industry without appearing in the other two categories. Part of the reason the herbal pharmaceutical industry boomed could be attributed to loosened regulatory measures to boost the industry. Less rigorous regulatory standards were applied to the processes of transforming natural resources into pharmaceuticals for the reason that natural resources had been empirically tested on human beings for thousands of years in Korea (referring to the medical tradition of Korean medicine and drugs). For instance, it was not mandatory to undergo animal tests for toxicity in laboratory, and in some cases, it was permitted to skip the first phase of clinical trials if sufficient evidence, whether clinical or historical records, proved the use of the medicinal plant efficacious.

While in the 1990s the newly created herbal pharmaceutical industry was more focused on the pharmaceuticalization of herbal medicines, in the 2000s, the government pushed the industry to innovate herbal medicines as global hits. For 14 years, from 2001 to 2014, the governments spent about 309.2 billion KRW on developing and commercializing natural products and about 2 trillion KRW on national health insurance to reimburse natural

26 H. H. Jeong, "Special Report: Baekshuoh, 5 Years Later" *Maeil Business News*, 2020, *available at* https://www.mk.co.kr/news/economy/view/2020/12/1303673.

drugs from 2003 to 2014.[27] Accordingly, the nominal growth of the industry was 2 trillion KRW between 2010 and 2013, of which 34% accounted for *han yak* products, including ginseng, herbs, manufactured herbal medicines. However, a more dramatic explosion of the market was observed in medical products and cosmetics based on or derived from Korean medicine and drugs.[28]

Despite the astronomical size of the public funds that had been spent on the pharmaceuticalization of medicinal plants, along with loosened regulatory measures, only eight pharmaceuticals were recognized as innovative natural drugs by 2015 by the Korea Food and Drug Administration, targeting non-specific chronic symptoms such as osteoarthritis and digestive troubles. Although they were approved as novel drugs, physicians of Korean medicine, who were excluded from prescribing and administering such drugs to their patients, contested the novelty of these eight natural drugs. According to Korean medical laws, jurisdictional boundaries over pharmaceuticals are delineated along medical licenses. Physicians of Korean medicine are not permitted to own prescription rights to novel drugs, even if they are made out of medicinal plants in accordance with principles of Korean medicine. Possibly more troublesome to the governmental agencies was the reality that such novel drugs were not able to enter the global markets, mainly because of the regulatory gap between the domestic and global markets.

In 2015, the National Assembly of Korea instructed the Board of Audit and Inspection of Korea to inspect a series of government-driven projects about the development of natural drugs. Through months-long investigation into the R&D projects, attention was paid to the following three issues, in particular: the effectiveness of the projects, that is, cost-benefit analysis; regulatory procedures to approve innovative natural drugs; and appropriateness of safety and quality management. The board decided to repeal a special bill about natural drugs, putting a closure on relentless doubts about the novelty of natural drugs since its birth. However, in 2018, similar rhetoric was cited again. The government aimed to develop ten global products comparable to *Artemisinin* and *Saponin* and to extend the market share from 2.2% in 2017 to 4.4% in 2022.[29] In late May 2018, the South Korean Ministry of Science and ICT announced that it would drive innovation growth in the domain of natural products and push interested industries, research institutes, academia, and governmental agencies to collaborate intimately. In order to facilitate the growth of the bio-economy (economic growth pertaining to and

27 The Board of Audit and Inspection of Korea (BAI), *Deposition Request of Auditory Result-R&D Implementation State of Natural Drugs* (Seoul, The Board of Audit and Inspection of Korea 2015).

28 S. Lee, "A Study on Medical Discourse of Oriental Medicine and Health Functional Foods – Focusing on the Consumption Discourse Analysis of Homegrown Agricultural Products –." (2015) 22(4) Journal of Agricultural Extension & Community Development 465, 465–79.

29 MSIP (Ministry of Science and ICT). *Cheonyeonmul Hyuksinseongjang Saengtaegye Joseong Bongyeok Chujinhanda [Boost the creation of the ecology of natural products innovation growth]* (Seoul, The Ministry of Science and ICT, 2018).

deriving from biotechnology) and natural products in the Korean peninsula, the government took the initiative again to develop higher value-added industry in natural products. For instance, in 2016, the government poured 140 billion KRW into research and development in natural products, which included the plan to utilize natural resources in North Korea because of the changing political environment between the North and South Korean governments.

V. Legal Entities as Governance Tools

The government's sponsorship meant that the political status of herbal medicines shifted from a cultural heritage to a subject of innovation. The government's efforts to transform Korean medicines opened up a political and epistemic space where professional boundaries and the ontology of drugs are renegotiated and redefined. At the discursive level, a recurring theme was that the two systems of knowledge were incommensurable, which by definition meant that medical and pharmaceutical principles and practices in Korean medicine could not be translated into those in biomedicine. For instance, in 2000, the government enacted laws pertaining to "laws to propel research and development of natural drugs" in order to nurture the innovative pharmaceutical industry capable of producing international blockbuster drugs. A legal definition of a natural drug[30] is "a medicinal product that is made of an entity with a chemical structure or composition not previously approved in a drug by the KFDA or a complex medicinal product that contains a new entity as an efficacious component not previously approved in a drug by the KFDA".[31] With the enactment of special laws to label the legal category of natural drugs as prescription drugs, the government also granted regulatory favoritism to the relevant industrial sectors to facilitate the development of natural drugs.

In 2003, the Korean government passed a law stipulating the safety, quality, and functionality of foods with health claims under the Health Functional Foods Act.[32] Health Functional Food is legally defined as a product intended to enhance and preserve human health with one or more functional ingredients or constituents. Health functional foods are very much akin to functional food or functional health products in international contexts, in that they are consumed to prevent nutrition-related diseases and increase physical and mental well-being. As a minimum measure to secure the safety and quality of foods with health benefits (in distinction both from pharmaceuticals and from nutritional/dietary supplements), the government required manufacturing companies, including pharmaceutical companies, to submit scientific and

30 A natural drug can be treated the same as a botanical drug in the US and a herbal medicinal product in EU. *See* S. H. Sung, "Cheon yeon mul ui yak pum [natural drugs]", *Webzine* 2012, *available at* http://www.ksmcb.or.kr/file/webzine/2012_10_03.pdf.

31 Korea Pharmaceutical Affairs Act, Act No. 14328, Art. 2(8) (2016).

32 www.law.go.kr/.

historical evidence for review, as most functional food ingredients are derived from natural products. Consumers tended to consume health products for purposes of boosting the immune system, which constitutes the largest functional foods market.[33] Thus, the government stepped in to assess, evaluate, and regulate foods with health claims, requiring them to go through a degree of review processes.

Naturalendotech co., Ltd (NeT) is a biotechnology company founded in 2001 with concentration on research and development and commercialization of natural ingredients. Looking into the domestic market structure, where health products targeted at middle-aged and older women were insufficiently developed, the company strategically focused on the development of health products for women. From the beginning, the company adopted the triple helix innovation model, although not intentionally, because a significant portion of R&D funds came through government research grants. As a small-sized biotechnology company, it strategized to get ahead of competing manufacturing or pharmaceutical companies by reutilizing natural resources and turning them into commercially marketable products via the means of techno-scientific innovations. By partnering with academia and research institutes, the company was successful in acquiring a series of patents for products that claimed to have significant effects on symptoms associated with women's diseases starting in 2003. The company sought both domestic and international patents almost simultaneously, targeting international clientele, too.

On the other hand, the changes in governmental actions opened a long-seated conflict, in particular over natural drugs, between the two professional organizations, Western biomedicine and Korean medicine. Under the current laws, Korean medicine doctors are not permitted to prescribe or administer prescription drugs, for the reason that such drugs are based on biomedical and scientific knowledge and methods. The underlying understanding was that Korean medicine and Korean medicines (*han yak*) were holistic without differentiating theoretical principles from diagnostic and therapeutic practices, nor telling the body from mind. This was translated into the understanding that Korean medicines did not differentiate prescription drugs from generics or over-the-counter drugs. Consequently, the legal and regulation action that natural drugs were labeled as prescription drugs incited a jurisdictional boundary

33 I. S. Jeong, M. K. Song & M. S. Lee, "Characteristics of Health Food Eating Among Middle Aged Women" (2005) 5(4) Korean Journal of Health Promotion 259, 259–66; S. Lee, "A Study on Medical Discourse of Oriental Medicine and Health Functional Foods – Focusing on the Consumption Discourse Analysis of Homegrown Agricultural Products –." (2015) 22(4) Journal of Agricultural Extension & Community Development 465, 465–79; H. A. Park, "Which Types of Dietary Supplements Are Used in Korea? Data from the 2015 Korea National Health and Nutrition Examination Survey" (2018) 10(3) Korean Journal of Health Promotion, 107, 107–12; C. G. Son, "Progress of Functional Food Market in Korea and Strategy of Korean Medicine" (2014) 35(1) Journal of Korean Medicine 68, 68–74.

war between Korean medicine doctors and the Western medical circle, including the pharmaceutical industry.

VI. Conclusion

This chapter has examined the emergence of a new type of herbal pharmaceutical industry and associated classificatory issues in South Korea. Emerging entities, whether biochemical, genetic modifications, or phytochemical, disrupt existing social order by challenging classificatory systems embedded in regulatory and cultural institutions.[34] It is also true that the classificatory system is (re)made to fit into the social and policy orders when a novel entity emerges due to advances in science and technology in a national context. A classificatory system is interlinked with cultural, historical, social, and political circumstances. The standards of classifying foods or drugs are significant in public domains, because they serve the purposes of securing and safeguarding the safety of foods or drugs. The official classification between food and drug has far-reaching consequences in many areas of public life, such as public policies, health food markets, and consumer perceptions.

In the South Korean national context, the creation of the legal categories "natural drugs" and "health functional food" has disrupted not only the market order of the pharmaceutical industry but in fact unfolded a complex postcolonial situation. The industry based on or exploitive of Korean medicine and drugs (*han ui yak*) has greatly expanded in the past few decades, partly because the South Korean governments have driven to commercialize natural products. As an emerging nation state in the global markets, the government has aimed to dominate postcolonial knowledge making and market creation as opposed to being occupied by multinational pharmaceutical companies that are characterized as neo-colonial powers in the global markets. The government's strong presence in pharmaceuticalization has offered opportunities for small and medium-sized companies to jump into the pharmaceutical industry as long as their business model is based on innovation.

34 G. C. Bowker & S. L. Star. *Sorting Things Out: Classification and Its Consequences*. (Cambridge, MA: The MIT Press 1999).

Index

Note: Page numbers in *italic* indicate a *figure* and page numbers in **bold** indicate a table on the corresponding page.